Computer methods
for architects

Computer methods
for architects

R A Reynolds, BSc, AMBCS

Butterworths
London Boston
Durban-Sydney-Toronto-Wellington

The Butterworth Group

United Kingdom	Butterworth & Co. (Publishers) Ltd London: 88 Kingsway, WC2B 6AB
Australia	Butterworths Pty Ltd Sydney: 586 Pacific Highway, Chatswood, NSW 2067 Also at Melbourne, Brisbane, Adelaide and Perth
Canada	Butterworth & Co. (Canada) Ltd Toronto: 2265 Midland Avenue, Scarborough, Ontario M1P 4S1
New Zealand	Butterworths of New Zealand Ltd Wellington: T & W Young Building, 77–85 Customhouse Quay, 1, CPO Box 472
South Africa	Butterworth & Co. (South Africa) (Pty) Ltd Durban: 152–154 Gale Street
USA	Butterworth (Publishers) Inc Boston: 10 Tower Office Park, Woburn, Mass. 01801

First published 1980

© Butterworth & Co. (Publishers) Ltd, 1980

British Library Cataloguing in Publication Data

Reynolds, R A
   Computer methods for architects.
   1. Architecture – Data processing
   I. Title
   721'.028'54   NA2728   80–40591

   ISBN 0–408–00476–2

Photoset by Scribe Design, Gillingham, Kent

Printed in England by Fakenham Press Ltd.,
Fakenham, Norfolk

Preface

After an early surge of enthusiasm in the 1960s, the use of computers by architects declined to a much lower level as the number of problems to be overcome became apparent. Since then, there have been many developments and it is now possible to make important gains from the use of these machines. In addition, the cost of computer power has dropped to a small fraction of its previous level. Thus I believe that the time has come for the architectural profession to take a fresh look at the possibilities of automation and for computers to take their place among the other office services.

This book is the result of ten years' experience of using computers in a medium-sized firm in private practice and is a practical guide, not a textbook. It shows where computers can help and how they can be applied. I also hope to point out the worst pitfalls, into most of which I have fallen myself at some time.

The text does not go into the details of such things as binary arithmetic and programming languages. Knowledge of these was essential in the pioneering days, and still is in advanced computer applications, where the machine is being pushed to its limits. But as far as the practising architect is concerned it can be compared with studying internal combustion theory before driving a car: it is interesting but unnecessary. An architect should understand the principles involved and thus be able to react intelligently, rather than try to write his own programs. In any case it takes just as long to learn to write good programs as it does to design good buildings.

I have attempted to avoid using jargon and technical terms where possible. Just as it is difficult to describe building without using terms like 'purlin', 'soffit' or 'dpc', so it is difficult to describe a new discipline without using its language. However, I have tried to explain the meaning of new terms. The effort of trying to understand the computer will be amply repaid for architects, who will come to find it one of the most powerful tools at their disposal.

Tony Reynolds

Contents

1 **Past and present** 1

2 **Using computers** 5
Benefits of using computers 5
Drawbacks of using computers 7
Job management 8
Information handling 10
Building design and analysis 11
Computer-aided draughting 12
Services engineering 13
Computers on a typical job 15

3 **Office organisation** 17
Time sharing and batch processing 17
Equipping for batch processing 18
Equipping for time sharing 20
Minicomputers 23
Equipping for minicomputers 26
Interactive graphics 27
Equipping for interactive graphics 28
Microcomputers and personal computing 32
Analogue computers 34
Installing equipment 35
Working methods with computers 35

4 **Choosing programs** 38
Program availability 38
Purpose-written programs 38
Package programs 38
Information sources 39
Limitations on program use 40
Documentation 41
Demonstrations and discussions 41
Buying a program 44

5 **Using databases** 45
Database principles 45
Catalogues and coding 49
Databases in architectural design 51
CARDS — a fixed-structure database-
management program 54
System 2000 — a variable-structure
database-management program 56

6 **Computer-aided draughting** 59
Advantages of computer-aided draughting 59
Program classification 63

Working methods with interactive graphics 65
Working methods with non-interactive
graphics 69
MEDALS — a 2-dimensional non-interactive
system 71
CARBS — 2½-dimensional, non-interactive
aspects of a versatile system 73
DAISY — a 2-dimensional interactive
system 74
ARK/2 — a 2-dimensional interactive
system 76
BDS — a 2½-dimensional interactive
system 77
RUCAPS — a 2½-dimensional interactive
system 78

7 **Visualisation** 80
Principles of visualisation 80
Data-collection methods 84
The CADC visualisation programs 86
AUTOPROD 90
The Leeds Polytechnic modelling system 90

8 **Job management** 92
The need for job-management systems 92
Principles of critical-path techniques 92
Outputs from job-management programs 96
Data preparation — a worked example 99

9 **Simulation techniques** 101
The uses of simulation 101
Principles of simulation 101
Data-collection techniques 105
GPSS — an advanced simulation
language 106
Simulation packages 110

10 **Environmental analysis** 112
The need for environmental analysis 112
Program structure 112
Lighting analysis 113
Thermal analysis 113
Sunlight analysis 114
Air-conditioning analysis 114
Acoustical analysis 115
ESP — an integrated environmental
analysis system 115

CEDAR 3 — evaluation at the sketch design
    stage   117
RIBA calculator programs   120

11   Miscellaneous applications   121
The scope for computer programs in
    architecture   121
Design generation   121
Design costing   124
Cut-and-fill calculation   125
Job costing   126
Word-processing machines   127

12   The future   129

13   Sources of information   135

14   Glossary   138

15   Bibliography   141

16   Index   147

All the diagrams in this book, except where otherwise acknowledged, were generated by the author on a Tektronix 4081 computer installation through the use of a variety of programs.

Acknowledgements

The partners of the firm of Cusdin, Burden and Howitt have encouraged and supported the application of computers to architectural problems since 1964, and the practice has been one of the leaders in this field ever since. I wish to thank the partners for their persistence and foresight in backing these developments over so many years.

I must also thank my immediate superior, Mr David Campion, who has been the main force in initiating and guiding computer developments in our office, and from whom I have learnt a great deal.

Finally, I wish to thank Miss Dona Stringer for her skill in deciphering my handwriting and in typing the manuscript.

1
Past and present

Computers have in the past acquired a bad name in the architectural profession and are often treated with automatic suspicion or hostility by the practising architect. They are also little used by the profession; a recent survey[151] found that only a small minority of offices use a computer and much of this use is for accounting rather than for solving architectural problems.

In contrast to this situation, the other members of the construction team often make extensive use of computers and are rapidly increasing that use. For example, the structural engineers have had the laborious calculations in their work taken over by quite cheap and simple computers, and can now give more attention to general principles and to the testing of alternative solutions. The services engineers use computers for such applications as the design of optimal pipe and duct networks and carrying out comprehensive checks on heating and lighting provision. They can therefore specify economic yet adequate solutions with much greater facility than before. Some quantity surveyors are making use of computer libraries of standard phrases from which the greater part of a bill of quantities can be generated merely by making selections from a list.

At the other end of the construction process, the larger contractors normally use computers to make sure that they have the optimum number of men and machines on site and to organise the ordering of materials at the correct time.

The architect's suspicion seems to be a reaction from the over-enthusiasm of earlier years. It used to be thought that computers were going to transform the profession as they were transforming other trades. Ten years ago engineering design, for example, was undergoing a complete restructuring, as calculations could be done both automatically and almost immediately. This meant that the design team became much smaller and was also working at a higher level, thinking in terms of principles rather than specifics, so the work became more interesting and required rather different skills. The resultant design would also normally be better than the manual equivalent. At the time there seemed no good reason why the same process should not also apply to architectural design. When this did not happen, and after a series of disappointments, the general feeling became that an architect's work is simply too complex and too intuitive to be significantly aided by the computer.

Computers were first introduced in the 1950s and initially they were used for scientific calculations and for straightforward large-scale business uses such as payroll production. It was not long, however, before their possibilities were being explored in every field, including architecture. In 1963 Ivan Sutherland at MIT announced the now-famous SKETCHPAD system[11]. This used a television-like device connected to a computer and allowed the user to draw on the screen with a special pen in lines of light. Arcs, circles and straight lines could be produced with little effort, and repeated drawing elements or symbols could be defined once and thereafter called up and positioned as many times as necessary.

Three years later, William Newman at Imperial College in London developed a similar system for specifically architectural applications[8]. Standard building elements such as walls, windows and floor slabs were stored in the computer, and the user was able to select from them and assemble a plan on the screen. When the plan was finalised, the computer was able to produce a list of room areas automatically; compile a schedule of the building elements used; calculate the heat loss from the structure; and assess the natural and artificial lighting levels. It was little wonder that everyone assumed that such techniques would shortly be found in every architect's office.

The same period saw the rise of a number of design theoreticians, Christopher Alexander[1,2], L. Bruce Archer[130] and J. Christopher Jones[5] being among the best known. In principle they attempted to find the basis of design from which systematic rules could be found to enable design to be more logical and less intuitive. The methods they developed often required the use of computers, for example to reduce to manageable form large tables of the interaction of each activity area with all other activity areas, or to apply complex mathematical optimisation techniques. These ideas attracted a great deal of attention at the time and again it was felt that such techniques would soon become universal and would remove much of the necessity for creative ability and accurate intuition on the part of the designer.

At that time also, the economy was in good shape; there was a building boom and architects were finding it difficult to keep up with their workload. Labour was expensive and hard to find. There was therefore both the incentive and the finance to develop solutions that would reduce the dependence on manual effort.

The architectural profession has always shown a readiness to try new ideas, although whether this is a laudable tendency towards open-mindedness or a less laudable love of novelty is open to question, and the late 1960s and early 1970s saw a boom in attempts to use the computer. In that period not a year went by without several conferences on computer-aided architectural design being held; a number of books were published, and many working parties were set up to investigate and report on different aspects of the use of the computer in the construction industry. Hundreds of programs were written and architects confidently awaited the revolutionising of their profession.

To a certain extent this did happen. The architectural department of the UK's West Sussex County Council was one instance; it developed an almost complete design system using computer aids applied to the industrialised building system SCOLA. The architects worked at a screen rather than on drawing boards and by 1968 they were able to follow the entire design process through. From feeding in the basic activity relationships they were able to define and position spaces, correct for the Building Regulations and optimise for acoustic performance, heating requirements and many other things and finally produce priced and comprehensive bills of quantities and production drawings on a computer-driven plotter[10].

Another instance of the new approach was given by the UK Government's Department of Health and Social Security. The Department has always tried to aid the architect in the design of medical buildings and to this end has published two series of booklets: the *Hospital Design Notes*[7] and *Hospital Building Notes*[6]. These give such things as lists of rooms with their recommended areas, and the activities they would contain. In 1969 the Department introduced a whole hospital-design concept named HARNESS[4,9]. HARNESS aimed to provide a large measure of standardisation while at the same time retaining flexibility. Although the use of the computer was not essential to the system it was considered to be an important aid to its viability. Programs were developed to evaluate the manual design of departments in terms of circulation efficiency, heat loss and gain, site usage and capital cost. Another set of programs automatically assembled the departments around a services spine in the optimum manner, subject to the constraints of the brief. There were also programs to produce production documentation, including production drawings.

There were many other attempts to introduce computers, both on a large and a small scale, but

within a few years it became obvious that there was not going to be a revolution. When architects attempted to use computers for themselves they found that it was a full-time task with few rewards. A lot of new techniques had to be learned and problems solved, most of them just to get to grips with the machine and circumvent the restrictions imposed by the relatively slow and small machines available at that time. There were not many programs available, and those that were available normally concentrated on problems that required a lot of calculations, such as beam design, daylight factors, and heat loss: problems that were on the border of the architect's interest. The central problems that occupied most of an architect's time were not tackled at all. Further, these programs usually required large amounts of data collection and preparation and gave results that were completely incommensurate with the time and effort put in.

The much-touted draughting systems that were to replace drawing boards with television screens turned out to cost hundreds of thousands of pounds. This virtually ruled out their use in any but government-supported organisations and even in such organisations problems were encountered. It was found that the draughting speed was little, if any, faster than manual draughting and that there were also a number of serious disadvantages. For example, large drawings had to be broken down into smaller and simpler sections before they could be input, the screens were often only 20 cm square and difficult to use, and the drawings were displayed in very thick and clumsy lines.

The building design programs turned out to produce very naïve designs. Normally they would operate by attempting to optimise a single factor, circulation cost being the most popular choice; they did not take account of the thousands of other factors that must be considered in producing a workable design, and in a short time they were only used in experimental applications. The economic climate at that time was changing rapidly for the worse. The construction workload fell dramatically and architects found themselves with insufficient work and plenty of people about to do what work there was.

Public opinion was turning against industrialised buildings. It was found that such buildings cost almost as much as conventional buildings, took just as long to put up and were disliked by the people who had to live in them. There were also a couple of structural failures. Very little more industrialised building was put up, and it is this type that is best suited to computer handling as it involves choices from a limited range of components, details of which can be given to the computer in advance; something that is much more difficult with conventional building methods.

Some of the ambitious computer projects quietly closed down. West Sussex County Council architects' department went back to manual methods in 1974, after it was decided that the reduced use of the SCOLA system did not justify the costs of using the computer. The Department of Health and Social Security abandoned the HARNESS system in 1975 after it was found that the buildings produced were too expensive in the new financial climate and after incurring development costs estimated[3] to exceed £3 million. Most architects who had tried to use computers gave up, deciding that the results did not justify the effort or the cost.

Thus today there is a good deal of resistance to computers in the profession, and this is a perfectly correct and hard-headed reaction to the facts. However, progress has been going on quietly all the time and I believe that computers can now be of real help to the architect; not by way of revolutionary solutions but in straightforward boosts to the ordinary working methods.

The first advance, as is well known, has been in the reduced cost and the increased power of the machinery. Modern techniques allow the equivalent of thousands or tens of thousands of separate components such as transistors or capacitors to be contained within an element no larger than a fingernail. With this has come a dramatic decrease in costs. A calculator that in 1968 cost £200 and was the size of a typewriter can now be bought for less than £5 and will fit easily into a pocket. The same principle applies to true computers. The 'minicomputer' of today costs perhaps £5000 in basic form and can be kept in a desk drawer; the equivalent ten years ago could have cost £100 000 and filled a large air-conditioned room. It has therefore become quite feasible for most practices to purchase a small machine to help in their day-to-day work. As might be expected, the new technology also brings significant gains in speed and reliability.

The manufacturers have also had time to develop the programs that control these machines. Every computer that now comes onto the market will understand a variety of the 'high-level' languages that make programming much easier. They will also have a number of standard programs that carry out commonly encountered tasks such as sorting lists into alphabetical order, updating previously input information, or making a copy of a set of data. There will also be an easily understood language for using these programs.

The basic improvements in cost and power have made it possible to write much more useful and more easily used programs. In 1968 the computer used by my firm could only accept programs of up to 250 instructions and sets of data up to about 6000 characters. Today, the programs run into thousands of instructions and the data files into millions of characters. Thus it is possible and economic not only to solve the problem, but to make things a lot easier for the user. The data, for instance, can be made acceptable in a number of forms other than a fixed and rigid layout. The program can prompt the user with more information and the output can be neatly paginated, generally in a form in which it is suitable for issue. All this means that the programs are much easier to use, an advantage as important to the working architect as the lower cost of their use.

With the growth in the number of computers, they have become much more accessible. Whereas in 1968 there was only one computer in Britain that could be accessed by telephone by the public, there are now over 200. It is now possible for any architect with a rented teleprinter to use a wide variety of programs very cheaply. A number of firms have also invested in computers of their own.

One of the results of the improvements in technology has been the vast improvement in the ability of the computer to handle drawings. Computers essentially must work in numerical terms; thus the first problems that computers were used for were strictly numerical applications such as the calculation of projectile trajectories, and many computers could not even accept or print out textual information. Soon, the demand from the business world caused the introduction of textual processing. Then efforts were made by Sutherland and others to express a graphical structure in terms of numbers. These efforts succeeded, but the extra load on the computer means that graphical applications require a great deal of computer power and therefore can be very slow and expensive.

Today several manufacturers are making computers expressly for graphical applications. These devices are relatively cheap, typically between £20 000 and £50 000, and are organised so that information can be accepted and output in terms of graphical elements such as lines and arcs. Because they are dedicated to a specific task, the cost of processing need not be a problem. A number of architectural firms are now using such machines.

The number and quality of the programs available has of course improved over the years, not only because of the improvements in technology that have allowed them to become larger and more complex, but also because the nature of the basic problems has become better understood and the most likely approaches have been well investigated.

For example, there is not much interest in room layout programs today; it is realised that problems that require the synthesis of many demands, mostly with subjective values, are best handled by the human brain. It is the 'harder' and more structured problems such as production documentation and cost analyses that now receive most effort.

Programs are tending to come more and more from full-time professionals, both within and without the architectural profession. This is in contrast to the early years when almost all programs were coming from the universities. Such programs tended to be exploratory and so were normally of little practical use, poorly documented and badly written. They also tended to attack the more glamorous and challenging problems such as design theory rather than straightforward and uninteresting things like scheduling.

There has been a growth in government funding which has helped the development of very large programs where high capital investment is essential. This funding is both direct and indirect. Direct funding can be through maintaining organisations to write and market computer programs; the Computer-Aided Design Centre is an example of such an organisation in Britain. Indirect funding can come about in that government building departments usually have large computer budgets and produce programs for their own work that may eventually be used more widely. The Property Services Agency in Britain and the Department of Housing and Urban Development in the USA are examples of this.

For a program to be accepted nowadays, it must fill a genuine need, be well written and documented and easy to use. This last requirement usually means that the program will be a long one and so slow and expensive to produce. For this reason, few serious programs are now written for particular problems in particular offices; instead there has grown up a sizeable market in off-the-peg computer programs and a number of bodies now exist to evaluate and to publicise them.

In general, it can be said that attitudes to computing today are much more professional. Expectations are not as high and there is recognition of the fact that computers do not offer adequate solutions to some types of problem. However, the greater experience and more disciplined approach in conjunction with better and cheaper machinery have firmly established the viability of computers in many applications.

2
Using computers

Benefits of using computers

Over the years, attempts have been made to use computers to aid virtually every task in the construction process. The programs currently available that are of interest to the architect cover a very wide range. They include programs that provide assistance at a very general level, such as those that give rough costings at the feasibility stage, and programs that help with very precise and well-defined activities, such as the production of working details.

Most of the advantages of computers derive from their being able to carry out long and repetitive calculations and comparisons very much faster than a human can. This greatly increased speed means that certain results can be produced that would take a prohibitively long time, perhaps even years, by manual methods. The architect can use these results to gain more insight into a design and thus produce a better and more economical building than he could otherwise do. Alternatively, the design period can be shortened in order to complete the building sooner, or the design team can be reduced, thus increasing efficiency and making staff savings.

As time goes on, buildings are getting bigger and much more complex. The architect is now often called upon to design buildings or groups of buildings to accommodate many hundreds or even thousands of people; even ten years ago this would have been exceptional. As well as being larger, these buildings have to provide an ever-widening range of services. Rises in user expectations have forced the architect to pay more attention to the provision of such things as better lighting, air-conditioning and thermal comfort. Tighter legislation requires the architect to conform to many rules on construction, energy saving, fire precautions and so on. Advances in technology provide new materials and techniques by the thousand every year, many of which can be of great use in construction; but unless designers are to spend all their time reading, they cannot hope even to be aware of the existence of most of them.

Despite this increase in size and complexity, clients are demanding much shorter construction times than previously. Whereas building time used to be measured in years, it must now be measured in months. The reasons for this speed are mainly financial: the greatly increased cost of labour and machinery and the very high level of investment in large buildings require fast construction, especially in periods of high inflation and reduced money supply. As architects are normally responsible for the overall administration of the construction, the pressure on them can be very great.

The increase in size and complexity has also meant that full documentation is essential to the construction process. In fact, the time needed for the documentation of the building the architect has designed, including working details, specifications, schedules, architect's instructions, bills of quantities, and tender documents, takes as long and consumes twice as many man-hours as the design itself. The current distribution of an architect's time, as reflected by the Royal Institute of British Architects (RIBA) scale of fees, is illustrated by *Figure 2.1*. All the indications are that paperwork can only increase and this will further encroach into the time needed for design.

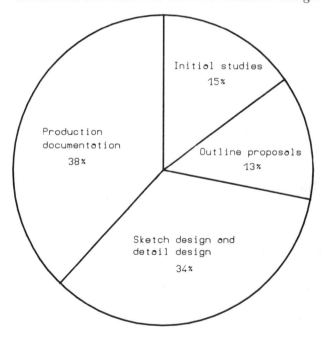

Figure 2.1 The distribution of an architect's work

Up to now, the reactions of the profession to these pressures have been to increase the size of the design team; to fragment the team further into self-contained categories to ease administration; and to apply increased standardisation and repetition to design. Unfortunately, these measures have drawbacks of their own, and are limited in their effectiveness. Increasing the size of the design team involves serious losses in the extra administration and coordination necessary. When the team becomes large, a great deal of time is lost in communication between the different groups and between individuals. The computer increases the productivity of individual members of the team and so keeps it small and cohesive, and therefore makes further gains by reducing the overheads of control and communication.

The fragmentation of the design team has been going on for a long time. Whereas an architect used to be totally responsible for the design in all its aspects, as well as the administration of the actual construction, the growing complexity of buildings has necessitated the use of many specialists in different aspects of design. In 1842, Pugin is recorded as having worked on 25 sizeable schemes aided by only one assistant[25]. By the 1920s a consultant engineer was normally used for larger projects and the quantity surveyor was formally established in Britain to prepare bills of quantities for costing and ordering.

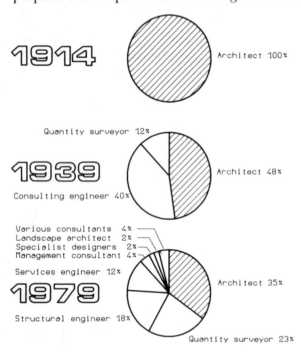

Figure 2.2 The participants in the design process

Today, a large project may use an architect, a structural engineer, a quantity surveyor, a services engineer, an environmental consultant, a landscape architect, an interior designer, a management consultant and even specialist designers who completely take over the design of highly serviced areas such as kitchens and laboratories. *Figure 2.2* illustrates this trend. Architects are becoming less and less concerned with design and more and more with the administration and coordination of all these different disciplines: a task for which they have not even been formally trained.

Computers offer the possibility of reversing this trend. This is because they can easily deal with the formulae and rules that most of the other disciplines use and can check large amounts of specialist information and previous solutions. This enables the architect to evaluate a particular aspect of a design without the need for detailed knowledge of the techniques used or the time in which to apply them manually. Costing, window design, provision of air-conditioning, heating plant location and sizing, pipe-work design, lift provision and many other specialist areas that have been farmed out to consultants can now be largely or entirely dealt with by the architect and a computer. With a knowledge of the general principles involved, an architect can test a hypothetical design and modify it in the light of the results until the best solution or the best compromise results. This reduction in fragmentation will not only save time because of the reduced overhead of administration and communication but will also typically result in a better design as the architect has more insight and more control over the solution.

The computer's ability to hold, scan and restructure large amounts of information is also very valuable in a number of ways: for example, at the detail design stage, in extracting potentially useful new materials or techniques from the multitude available. Flooring materials, say, can be scanned and suitable products of the right appearance, texture, strength and cost can be retrieved for closer consideration. This might replace days or weeks of research or provide an optimum result where otherwise the designer would specify a product that has been used before, just because of its familiarity.

At the production documentation stage, the computer can produce schedules and specifications and even bills of quantities much quicker than is possible manually. This documentation can also be used to provide information of use in later jobs. At present little feedback takes place because the time and manpower necessary to correlate and index the information are not available, and therefore reference to earlier jobs is difficult. However, once fed with information the computer can easily restructure it and integrate it with previous data to provide a database of working solutions that is readily available to other designers.

At present, feedback is usually through an architect's experience, but as buildings become more complex it is unlikely that any one architect can remember enough to work on experience alone. As a simple example, once the services to be provided in a laboratory are specified for one job (including electricity, gas, water, vacuum, fume cupboards, and special waste disposal) and scheduled by computer, they are easily accessible for reference on that job, and form the basis for subsequent solutions. They will not only comprise a suggestion and a checklist, but also, with possible minor modifications, can be copied automatically as part of the production documentation on the new job, thus saving typing and checking costs.

The greater emphasis on printed schedules, rather than on putting all information onto drawings, means that the quantity surveyor, tenderers, contractors and subcontractors who deal with lists and total quantities will be able to work faster and have less need to query the architect on ambiguities.

Drawbacks of using computers

Computers are not an unmixed blessing. They are unsuited, or less suited, to certain kinds of problem and they inevitably introduce difficulties of their own. The nature of the problem, or of the building or its scale, might preclude the efficient use of computers. They may impose extra and unfamiliar duties upon the architect, and they may disrupt the traditional way of working.

Obviously, a problem whose solution depends at least partly on subjective judgements is not normally suited to computer solution. For example, aesthetic valuations, or the considerations of human behaviour and relationships, cannot adequately be dealt with by computers. Because much of the power of computers lies in their ability repeatedly to apply the same process, the building itself must contain a reasonable amount of repetition. If this is the case, the information or process used in one situation can be used in many others, so producing an increase in efficiency.

A simple example of how repetition can greatly increase the efficiency of computer use can be given by a door schedule. If almost every door in a building is different, it will take a lot longer and cost a lot more to type in the details than it would do to produce a conventional schedule on squared paper. On the other hand, if, say, a range of ten doors has been specified for the building then it is usually quicker to produce a computer schedule than the manual equivalent, because it takes little time to input the details of the ten types and the computer can associate these with a compact list of door numbers and type references. Once the information has been put into the computer, neatly typed and paginated schedules will be available, as will a number of other facilities such as quick interrogation and retrieval.

A similar situation exists for most other computer aids. Thus a building that is completely unrationalised cannot be handled efficiently by computer. Surprisingly, it is also possible for a building to have too high a degree of repetition. An industrialised building system such as CLASP has a severely restricted range of components which can be fitted together in a flexible manner on a relatively coarse planning grid. One of the objects of such a system is

to simplify design by reducing the number of possibilities. It is often so successful in this aim that the scope for increased savings by mechanisation is far less. However, both one-off and system building have only a small share of the market nowadays, the one-off solutions because they are so expensive to design, and system buildings because they are felt to be inappropriate in most contexts.

Many architects are troubled by the fear that the use of computers may force a move towards more standardisation and repetition than would otherwise be necessary, and that this will be detrimental to the design. There is good reason to fear that this may indeed be the case, because the computer normally requires every item to be fully specified at the time it is introduced. Thus there is a strong temptation to use the nearest equivalent from a library of standards rather than go to the trouble of defining a special that will never be used again.

This may not be a bad thing if it discourages an unsystematic approach to the design problem. Also, it is true that the growth in size and complexity of buildings has forced the profession to make a lot of concessions to rationalisation already. Most buildings of any size are now planned on a modular grid and efforts are always being made, with varying degrees of success, to use standard ranges of components, standard working details and even standard designs for certain types of activity area such as hospital wards.

Some firms have been more successful in these endeavours than others. Many firms that feel themselves overwhelmed with paperwork and with administrative responsibilities are probably in that situation because they have not adopted, or have not been successful in adopting, a rationalisation policy. In such cases, there may be an impulse to bring in a computer to help with the paperwork. Such an attempt is doomed to failure. The computer can only help when the work to be done has been set out in some sort of structure and with a fair degree of standardisation; when this is done many of the paperwork problems will solve themselves without the aid of a machine. When it is not done the computer becomes an expensive hindrance to the existing manual methods.

Allied with the problems of repetition is the scale of the building. A small scale inherently cannot include much repetition and it is also much more easily comprehensible and controllable by a few experienced men. Therefore there are few communication problems and little possibility of extensive checks being necessary. In these circumstances, the computer can offer little help and in fact the extra overhead of using the machine may well actually slow the design process.

The type of building also determines the scope for computer aids. Some designs cannot easily be handled by computer because the program must inevitably make many assumptions about a building. At an elementary level, a program to check the amount of daylight coming in through a window will assume that the window is a rectangle. If it did not, a lot more data would be necessary and the program would have to be far more complicated merely to handle the very rare case of a non-rectangular window. This means that the architect who wants to specify a parallelogram-shaped window on a staircase, or a circular shape as in the traditional 'rose' window, will not be able to use the computer to check the natural lighting.

At a more important level, many computer-aided draughting programs assume that the walls in a building all run parallel to one of the edges of the paper. This would preclude the use of such a program on schemes like the Post Office Tower in London, which is cylindrical, or on a building that curves to fit the shape of a road or seafront. Equivalent assumptions exist in many other types of program and could conceivably force the architect to abandon good ideas merely because they are not ones that the computer can analyse.

In order to use computers successfully, the architect has to adjust his method of working, and in some cases this can impose extra burdens. One aspect of this is that the architect must work in a much more systematic way than formerly. This is because use of the computer to carry out a task normally involves a large overhead in time and money. This overhead comes from the administration required to organise the data, access the program, correct any errors found in the data, collate the output and so on. There is a multitude of small tasks to be performed when processing any amount of data; it is therefore much more efficient to process large amounts of data on relatively few occasions. This principle might cause the architect some trouble if he has been used to alternating between different aspects of a job. Manually, such alternation loses little time in the end and may even be a better way of working as it increases variety. When using computer aids, however, tasks should not be initiated until all the information is present and then they must be carried through to their conclusion.

The quality of life can also suffer. One of the most persistent computer myths is that computers will relieve the architect of the tedium of repetitive tasks. In fact, the opposite is true. The machine must have complete and accurate data before it can work and the collection and checking of this data is an extremely boring and repetitive task that will occupy a lot of time. Eventually, of course, time will be saved, but because data collection is a continuous and exacting task it will inevitably be more tedious.

This point was neatly put[17] by M.J. Cooley of the Associated Union of Engineering Workers: 'It has been frequently argued that computerised equipment could free man from the soul-destroying, routine, backbreaking tasks to engage in more creative work. Anybody who looks at a highly automated factory must surely question whether this is, in fact, so'.

The use of a computer in an interactive manner does tend to drive the man using it. Because the computer works and reacts so much faster than a man, it is almost always waiting for a response, and this paces the user at a higher rate than normal. The difficulties of sustaining this rate can cause a lot of stress.

Job management

One of the most valuable things that a computer can do for a large project is to control it more efficiently. Because of the scale of operations, each task has to be prepared for, introduced at the right time, and finished on schedule if large amounts of time and money are not to be lost. Also, a record must be maintained of the cash flow to ensure that the job is within budget. This is the sort of task that the computer is well suited to, as it requires the collation and accurate analysis of many separate reports. It is also the sort of task that most architects feel they have too much of.

The well-known critical-path technique is widely used for controlling projects. The job can be broken down into a number of separate tasks to be carried out in a certain order. A part of a typical diagram illustrating the organisation of activities is shown in *Figure 2.3*. By analysing the network in conjunction with the men and resources available, it is possible to predict within what period activities should start and finish and therefore which activities have least leeway and must be most carefully controlled. Potential bottlenecks can be pinpointed, accurate forecasts can be made of how many staff and what skills will be needed, and the ongoing cost of the project can be predicted. In theory, a critical-path network can be analysed manually, but in practice thousands of elementary calculations are necessary even in a simple network and so it is really not a practicable proposition.

An architectural practice can also check on the budgeting of the job as it affects the practice. Analysis of staff worksheets and expenses can tell the chief architect how much time and money has been spent on each job and hence whether any job is taking a disproportionate amount of resources. Balancing the office costs against a fee prediction can also be invaluable in forecasting the future financial position of the office. Again, it is possible to perform this analysis by hand, but it is a tedious and lengthy task that can be done more quickly, cheaply and accurately by machine.

PUMP INSTALLATION

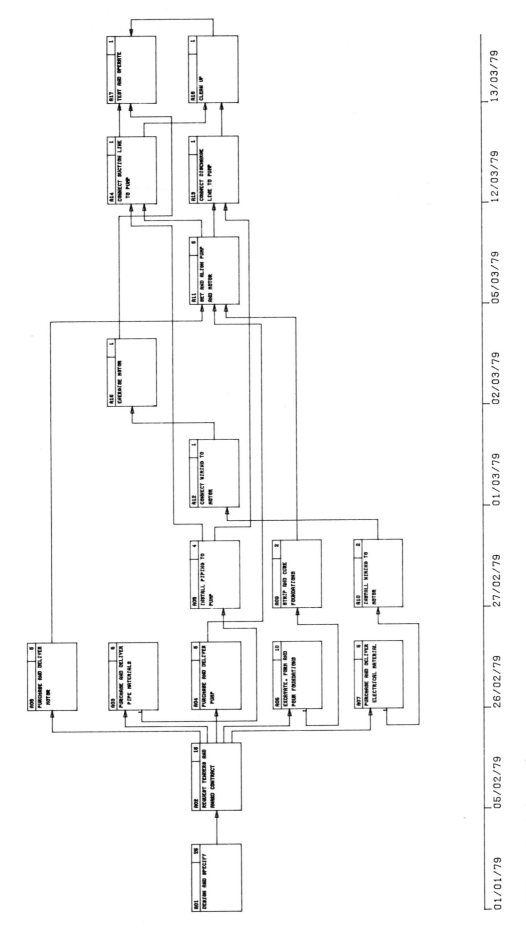

Figure 2.3 A project analysis network

Information handling

The computer's ability to store and manipulate large amounts of information in a short time is very valuable in many ways. The amount of information needed to document a building is now very great, and the amount that should be researched when designing the building is immense.

Most practices of any size now have a library that contains some textbooks and reference books but specialises in manufacturers' literature and up-to-date articles from a range of technical journals. This is a comparatively recent phenomenon; ten years ago only a few shelves of books would normally be available and a full-time librarian was not often thought necessary. In the future, it is clear that as more information is produced on every subject and as manufacturers continue to expand their ranges, the library will become an even more serious office overhead.

In principle, the computer can almost completely reverse this situation. Once a database has been constructed, the computer can easily scan it for certain characteristic data. Thus, in a materials database, the architect might ask for the brick section; then he might specify type, shape, colour and price range, and finally be presented with a list of the manufacturers producing that particular kind of brick. All this could be done by telephone via a teleprinter costing only a small sum to rent and taking up negligible space. Although a good idea in principle, the drawback in practice is that the database must be set up in the first place and thereafter kept up to date, and both of these operations are long and expensive for any volume of information. Keeping prices up to date is especially difficult in these inflationary times.

Many such projects have been tried and most have now been abandoned. Those that did succeed tend to have been set up some time ago when labour costs were considerably lower. To take a specific instance, in 1972 the firm of Barbour Index, which provides one of the best-known product-information services for the British construction industry, set up an experimental computer database inquiry system. Files were available on sanitary ware, such as baths and handbasins, and on bricks. The firm decided not to proceed with the project after the experimental period because it was not possible to guarantee enough use to justify the high cost of data collection.

An example of a more successful system might be that set up in 1965 by the South-Eastern Regional Hospital Board in Scotland. A database was created consisting of a complete and priced list of the equipment required in about 1200 different types of room found in medical buildings. At the sketch design stage an architect could input the number of rooms of each type in the design and receive an equipment checklist and cost analysis. This database was used by architects and hospital authorities on numerous occasions, but by the early 1970s it proved impracticable to keep the information up to date. The resulting gaps and inaccuracies caused a decline in user interest and the system then fell out of use.

At the time of writing, only a very few computer-held databases are available commercially to the architect, and none has achieved widespread acceptance.

Instead of trying to maintain a comprehensive list of every item that might conceivably be used, a more popular approach at present is to feed back information used on a real job. Thus when starting a job, reference will be made to the records of recent similar jobs to give a basis for the new scheme. Obviously, this cannot give a complete answer, but it has the advantages that no unnecessary costs are incurred and that the information is known to be up to date. Also, there tends to be a constant refining of the information. It becomes more consistent and more accurate as it passes through a number of jobs, something that cannot be said of comprehensive databases which tend to become less valid as concepts change.

A less well-known type of database is one that can hold standard text for specifications. At present, the architect often finds himself writing out identical paragraphs in specifications and architect's instructions for job after job, concerning matters like quality of workmanship and methods of procedure. A database containing a wide range of such paragraphs allows the architect to give a series of paragraph references which the computer can link together into a complete document with correct pagination and a guaranteed absence of typing errors. Obviously, arrangements are made for detail changes to the wording and for the introduction of non-standard paragraphs.

This has been a more successful application of database interrogation and there are a number of such programs, mainly for use by quantity surveyors. Here again, however, the costs of database construction can be high. In 1968 the RIBA set up a project to produce a National Building Specification, which is essentially a library of standard clauses for use on job specification. Development was halted in 1976, after over £180 000 had been spent, although the system remains in use in an advanced form[24].

Just as important as information retrieval is information manipulation, which tends to come into its own at a later stage in the construction process. A large amount of documentation will be produced for a sizeable building in the form of lists and schedules, and it is very difficult to do even elementary analysis of it. For example, just adding up the number of telephone outlets in a building could take days, and checking that each room that needs such an outlet actually has one can take even longer. When the production information is on a computer, however, tasks of this sort are greatly simplified. Adding up the total quantity of any item, or range of items, can be done in seconds, and the information can be broken down by department or in other ways if necessary. Similarly, it is possible to list all the rooms that do not have a certain type of item, without considering, say, corridors or bathrooms. In this way checks become extremely simple.

```
EAST CHEAM UNIVERSITY LIBRARY - FURNITURE AND EQUIPMENT
30 JULY 1979

ROOM    22124    GOVERNMENT PUBLICATIONS STACKS

(BIN11 )    2    BIN,WASTE PAPER
(BRD11 )    1    BOARD,NOTICE,PIN-UP,1000MM (W) 600MM (H)
(FIR11 )    4    FIRE-FIGHTING EQUIPMENT,CO2 EXTINGUISHER
(KIK11 )    3    KICKSTEP
(STA21 )   22    STACK,DOUBLE-SIDED,2300MM (H) WITH 200MM SHELVES+CANOPY

ROOM    22128    STACK ZONE, STATISTICS

(BIN11 )    2    BIN,WASTE PAPER
(BRD11 )    1    BOARD,NOTICE,PIN-UP,1000MM (W) 600MM (H)
(STA21 )   44    STACK,DOUBLE-SIDED,2300MM (H) WITH 200MM SHELVES+CANOPY

ROOM    22120    PERIODICALS STACKS

(BIN11 )    2    BIN,WASTE PAPER
(BRD11 )    1    BOARD,NOTICE,PIN-UP,1000MM (W) 600MM (H)
(KIK11 )    2    KICKSTEP
(STA27 )   28    STACK,DOUBLE-SIDED,2300MM (H) FOR PERIODICALS

ROOM    22120    READER ZONE

(CHA15 )  105    CHAIR,MEDIUM COMFORT
(REA32 )  105    READER PLACE,1000MM X 600MM

ROOM    2301    GENERAL COLLECTION

(BIN11 )    4    BIN,WASTE PAPER
(BRD11 )    1    BOARD,NOTICE,PIN-UP,1000MM (W) 600MM (H)
(CAS11 )    1    CASH BOX
(CHA15 )   76    CHAIR,MEDIUM COMFORT
(DES15 )    2    DESK,1200MM (W) 600MM (D) WITH DOUBLE PEDESTAL
(FIR11 )    1    FIRE-FIGHTING EQUIPMENT,CO2 EXTINGUISHER
(KIK11 )    1    KICKSTEP
(MCR11 )    1    MICROFILM READER
(STA21 )   11    STACK,DOUBLE-SIDED,2300MM (H) WITH 200MM SHELVES+CANOPY
(STN12 )    1    STAND,HATS AND COATS (PARADOX) SET OF 20
(TAB12 )    7    TABLE,1000MM (W) 600MM (D) WITH HEIGHT FOR STANDING WORK
(TRO11 )    2    TROLLEY,BOOKS (TO FIT IN LIFT)
(VDU11 )    1    VISUAL DISPLAY UNIT

ROOM    2304    OFFICE, ACQUISITIONS

(ASH11 )    1    ASH TRAY,DESK TYPE
```

Figure 2.4 A page from a computer-produced schedule

Editing of the information is also simple, but becomes most valuable when comprehensive changes are made. For example, the decision might be taken to put more electric sockets in all offices. This change would require lengthy checking and retyping of manual lists, but can be done by typing a single sentence when the information is stored on a computer. Rationalisation and cost-cutting exercises are also simplified when the computer can print out how many of each type of item are used and where they are positioned.

Figure 2.4 shows a page from a typical computer-produced schedule of equipment items.

Building design and analysis

At present, there are two principal ways of using the computer in design: in a generative way, to produce a room layout, for example; and in an analytical way, to check the viability of a proposed design. Although the generative approach is the one that has traditionally received all the attention, and indeed is still the subject of much research, it has been almost completely abandoned by practising architects because the results produced are inadequate. This is mainly because it is not possible to build into a computer program many of the most important factors that must be considered in a design. However, if the architect produces a design and the computer then checks such aspects of it as it is able to, it is possible to create a very powerful symbiosis of man and machine.

The difference between the generative and the analytical approaches can be illustrated by the simple example of window design. Calculation of the daylight factors from a given window is straightforward and the designer can easily ask the computer to check a solution to ensure that it meets the minimum standards. The design will already have taken into account such factors as the relative proportions of window to wall dimensions needed to give a pleasing impression both inside and outside, or the amount of ground and sky visible from different points. By modifying the design and rechecking, the user can get a good solution in two or three tries and at very little cost.

The equivalent solution with a generative program would be to produce a window design that met the daylight factors specification. There will be thousands of possibilities, even when using modular dimensions, and hundreds of these will meet the specification. Thus the alternatives are either to bury the designer in paper at great cost, or to choose a solution at random which may or may not meet the more subjective criteria.

The difference in the two approaches becomes even more marked when a more complicated design problem than window sizes is considered. A generative program for room layouts that only minimises circulation and ignores social customs, state of mind and body of the user, aesthetics, the activities taking place in the rooms, or the view from the windows is simply inadequate; just because a requirement cannot be fed into the computer does not mean that it does not exist. On the other hand, an analytical program can test a solution for circulation costs or other objective criteria after the architect has produced a design that takes into account the more intuitive factors. Thus the interaction between man and machine can take advantage of the abilities of each.

The simplest analytical technique is non-dynamic analysis, which consists essentially of evaluating formulae and checking the rules relating to fixed situations. Construction costs, energy use, lighting provision, solar gain and acoustic performance can be dealt with by this sort of analysis.

Dynamic analysis, or simulation, is a much more powerful technique than non-dynamic analysis. With this method, a model of an activity in progress can be run on the computer and by studying the consequences of the activity it can be seen if the design is suitable to contain it. For example, by modelling the arrival of people at a dining room and the time they take to be served and to eat, it is possible to check that the room has enough seats, or to predict how many staff will be needed. With this information, the designer can collect many of the vital facts that are needed to produce a design that is adequate but not wasteful.

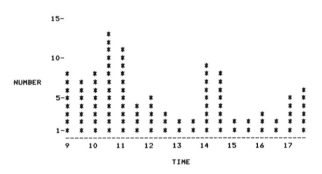

Figure 2.5 An output from a computer simulation

Figure 2.5 shows a typical output from a computer simulation predicting the fluctuations in the occupancy of a waiting room at half-hourly intervals. A designer could use this result to calculate the amount of space to be provided. In a similar fashion, the provision of lifts can be analysed; the flow of passengers and baggage through an air terminal investigated; or car parking requirements ascertained. None of the above examples is theoretical. Simulation techniques have been used to collect information on all these situations and many others. The amount of time needed to set up such models is not great and the computer costs are usually low.

Computer-aided draughting

The ability of computers to draw is undoubtedly their most exciting aspect for architects, and one that gripped their imagination for a long time before it became economically practicable. Clearly, it is this ability that gets right to the heart of an architect's work: the manipulation of spatial concepts. Since Ivan Sutherland's SKETCHPAD system, it has been hoped that spectacular results could be obtained by linking the architect and the computer by means of graphics rather than by textual and numeric communication.

There are several reasons why in fact virtually no progress has been made in using these devices in practice until very recently, but the principal one has been their lack of cost-effectiveness. Quite simply, graphics cost a lot of money even now, although only a tenth of the cost a decade ago. It is only in the last few years that the relative costs of labour and machinery have made this application economic.

Sutherland has written[23], rather derisively, that: 'Pen and ink or pencil and paper have no inherent structure. They only make dirty marks on paper.' This is true enough, but unfortunately the architect does not really need an inherent structure to a drawing. It is the drawing itself that contains the bulk of the information, and not what can be deduced from it. This is not the case in, say, aircraft design, where a drawing of a fuselage or a wing can be used as the basis for many complex calculations on airflow and structural strength; or in manufacturing, where the drawing of a component can be used to produce a tape that will control a machine to make that component. By these means, many important savings can be made that have few direct equivalents in architecture.

The principal way the architect can derive benefit from computer-assisted graphics is therefore in the improvement they give in draughting speed. Roughly speaking, to lease a realistically powerful interactive graphics device costs about the same as employing two draughtsmen; and as the machine needs someone to operate it, it follows that productivity must be increased by at least three times to be cost-effective. It is to the credit of all workers in this field that such performance is now possible.

There are many different ways by which the computer can speed up draughting. At the simplest level, standard drawing elements, such as staircases, doors, sinks, or columns, can be drawn once and then placed on the drawing as many times as necessary just by specifying the position and orientation. This can produce considerable savings provided the building is reasonably standardised.

The computer allows a drawing to be split into 'overlays' that can be drawn in any combination and at any scale. Thus the same structural plan can be used for all drawings of every scale that include that information. A building may typically have several such plans showing, for example, the structure alone, the equipment provision, a services plan and an overall site plan. By holding back certain of the overlays from each drawing, a lot of repetitive draughting can be eliminated.

The computer also makes alterations much easier. Thus if a floor plan is similar (although not identical) on two floors, one floor can be drawn, copied, and the copy modified. This is not normally practicable with manual draughting as the alterations will inevitably be messy; but it is a natural and easy procedure with computer drawings. A typical portion of a computer-produced floor plan is shown in *Figure 2.6*.

A drawback to draughting, at least to the interactive method that is the most productive, is that only one person can use the computer at a time. Thus even given a productivity of three or four to one, a single person cannot handle even a medium-sized building in the same time as a manual team of, say, six staff. The machine must therefore be used on

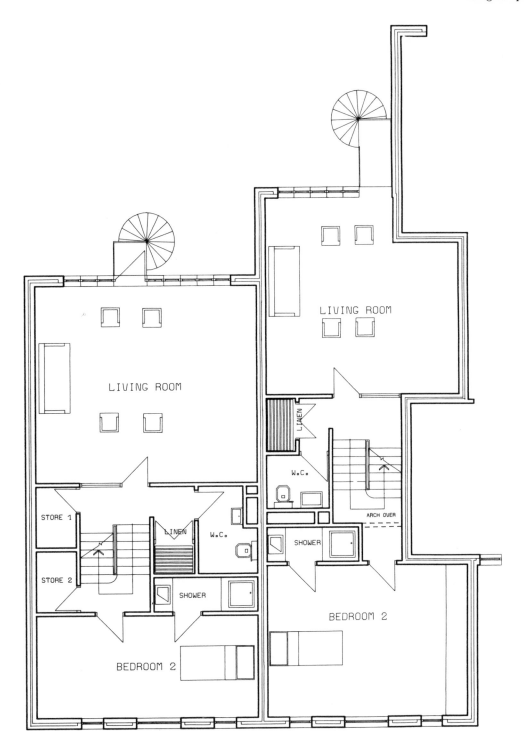

Figure 2.6 A computer-produced floor plan

certain parts or certain phases of the complete job. Despite the difficulties, a number of machines are currently being used successfully in architectural practices, and the next few years will certainly see a great increase in their numbers.

Another aspect of computer-aided drawing is the production of perspective views of buildings. Although these are not produced very often at present in most offices, because of the time they take to prepare, they can be of great help in design and in communication with the client. Once the building

has been described to the computer, views from any angle and at any distance can be produced in minutes for very low cost. *Figure 2.7* shows such a computer-produced perspective.

Services engineering

Services engineering is not at present of direct concern to architects, although fairly recently they were responsible for this aspect of design. However, many

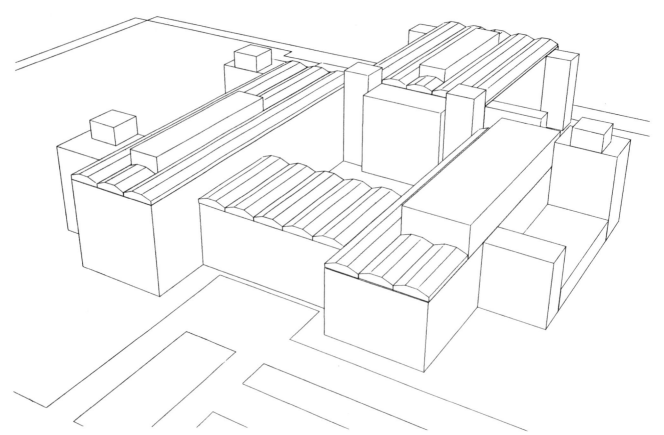

Figure 2.7 A computer-produced perspective (courtesy Design Office Consortium and the Computer-Aided Design Centre)

computer programs are now available to aid or evaluate virtually every aspect of services engineering. These programs typically can be run for very small sums. Thus even if the architect cannot eliminate the services consultant, he can at least check that the design meets the basic requirements. This will give tighter control over the design and will speed the entire design process, as fewer meetings with the consultant will be required to effect necessary changes.

There are a wide variety of such programs, reflecting the range of the services engineer's work. There are, for example, numerous programs to aid the design of pipe and duct networks. As a large building has many services such networks are a vital part of the design and should ideally be integrated with the other aspects at a very early stage. At present, the architect tends to make provision for the ducts and the services engineer has to try to modify the design later. The result is often an awkward and time-wasting compromise.

The design of drainage networks is another task that is subject to strict rules with few subjective criteria, and is therefore suited to computer solution. Although not of such importance to the building design, the ability to lay out and cost the drainage network for a housing estate in a matter of a few minutes can be invaluable, and can lead to important savings by modifying the housing layout at an early stage before so much work has been done that it becomes impracticable.

Environmental control is a vital consideration for the architect but is an area that demands many lengthy calculations. Here again, the computer is well suited to the task. The formulae to be evaluated are widely agreed and the computer can easily predict daylight factors, design artificial light layouts, check glare factors and predict solar gain. All these matters affect the design at a very basic level and should be checked by the architect at the sketch design stage before the shape of the building has hardened. *Figure 2.8* shows a typical output from such a program giving the daylight factor levels.

Most importantly, from an economic point of view, the computer can predict the size of the heating

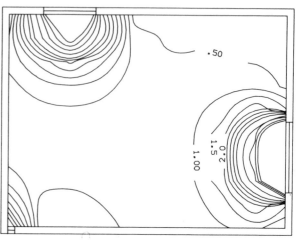

Figure 2.8 Computer-produced daylight factor contours (courtesy Design Office Consortium)

plant necessary. Heating is now a very expensive operation and the installation of heating plant is also expensive. The computer can take all the many factors involved — heat loss through the fabric, gains from the occupants or machinery, solar gain, thermal inertia of the structure and equipment — and quickly give the size of plant needed to maintain comfortable conditions in the worst case.

A variety of other programs connected with services engineering is available to perform such tasks as air-conditioning design, condensation checks, and noise transmission checks. The architect will find many of these useful, especially as they can perform checks that might not otherwise be done at all because of the shortage of time and money.

Computers on a typical job

To show how these techniques might be applied in practice, it is worthwhile to trace the progress of a typical job costing, say, £2 million through an office that has some familiarity with computers. We assume that the office has made no investment in machinery beyond the hire of a teleprinter to communicate with the computer of an organisation that sells processing time. A job of this size might reasonably require a team of four to run it for most of the time.

When the job is introduced, it must first be fitted into the office's work schedule. This can be done by using a critical-path analysis program. The user will have at his disposal various standard sets of data corresponding to the office's preferred method of working, which will typically follow one of the standard guides to procedure such as the RIBA plan of work or the Department of Health and Social Security's CAPRICODE workplan. This data can be modified according to the size and specific requirements of the job and a work programme produced in a couple of hours. Such preparation is well worthwhile as it helps to even out the workload and assists preparation for forthcoming activities.

Computer methods save perhaps three days over manual methods at the initial stages and, because the barcharts can be automatically recalculated and redrawn at the inevitable changes and hold-ups, may save up to two man-weeks over the entire job. The actual staff time spent on this job, together with all the other jobs in the office, will be monitored by means of computer analysis of the weekly time-sheets. Incidental expenses, both chargeable and non-chargeable to the client, will also be monitored by a similar analysis of expense accounts. Over the entire job, a man-week of administrative staff time will be saved.

When the brief is available, the archives are checked to find the most similar job that has been processed by the computer. As most offices tend to specialise in one or two types of building, a reasonable

match will normally be available after the computer has been used on a few jobs. The information in the archives will include room data sheets for each different room type, giving such information as the room area, its environmental requirements, special finishes and services, and a list of equipment contained. These sheets are a great help to the architect when preparing a general outline of requirements, and may save about two man-weeks in this period.

The room data sheets can be issued to the client for modification to his individual requirements, and to the specialist consultants to check them for correspondence to the latest standards. The sheets, with their modifications, can be used to prepare an initial database for the job and will help a lot in pricing and determining feasibility, which is the next step in developing the design. The savings here could be one man-week of the architect's time.

At the next stage of the project, the architect should determine the general approach to layout, design and construction to provide the client with outline proposals. The computer can help here by running simulation models of parts of the design, such as circulation patterns, lift use and the demands on various other facilities. The overall shape and orientation can be tested for excessive heat loss. Cut-and-fill optimisation can be performed to help determine the most economic siting. It is unlikely that much time will be saved by using these methods but they bring the intangible benefit of a better-understood design.

At the end of this stage the architect is ready to produce a scheme design. The room data sheets should be almost finalised and can be used by the designer as a checklist in preparing the sketch plans, or in delegating room layout work to a draughtsman or technician. The elimination of the need to refer to earlier jobs or to the library might save a few more days, and the possibility of making greater use of less highly trained staff can also be valuable. During this period a copy of the room data sheets should be made for the archives, to be used as the basis for future jobs. Strictly, this task is a feedback activity to be done at the end of the job. However, it will be found that it is more useful to have more general statements on the archived room data sheets than the very specific descriptions they will acquire at the detail design stage.

At the next stage the detail design is prepared. Computer analysis can be used here in a more specific manner, to check such factors as window sizes, artificial lighting provision, and acoustic performance. This will actually add a few man-days to the time taken, because otherwise the designer would probably have made an adequate estimate on the basis of experience. The advantage of using the computer is that it provides an experienced designer with more insight into what he is doing, and ensures that an inexperienced designer will produce a solution that is at least adequate.

As the exact sizes and types of component are decided, they should be noted on the room data sheets. This will add some days to the time needed to prepare the drawings, but by doing things in a systematic manner time will be saved in the later stages.

The next task is preparation of production information. Schedules of doors, windows and room finishes and lists of the fittings and other contract items can be extracted automatically from the information built up on the room data sheets. Savings of about four man-weeks can be hoped for in this period.

The job is now largely handed over to the quantity surveyor to prepare bills of quantities and tender documents. Obviously the improved production documentation will save him a great deal of time, perhaps as much as six man-weeks. However, as he works for a fixed scale fee this does not benefit the client, and it can be argued that the architect has been doing a consultant's work for him and has also been assuming the responsibility if there should be any mistakes in the documentation. In my view, the fact that this stage will be shortened helps the architect as it removes some of the pressure. Also, the increased responsibility is the inevitable concomitant of the architect's taking over more of the total design process, which is in itself desirable.

It is at this point that the job is sometimes found to be too expensive. Normally, this would mean that the architect would have to do more work to slim down the building, without being entitled to extra fees. The computer can help here by allowing the architect to find where the more lavish provision has been made, and by giving some indication of the effects of reducing it. Simulation studies could also be rerun to check for wastage in things like corridor sizes and lift provision. Rationalisation exercises can be easily carried out to reduce the ranges of components used. In all, a few man-weeks could be saved and the viability of the design will suffer the least harm.

At the tender action stage, the contractors and subcontractors will find their estimating easier and quicker as the information is more accessible than in the past. Here again, the advantages of using the computer are indirect and in the form of speeding up the job rather than in saving money.

In the subsequent stages the computer will be of little use to the architect, but the advantages of good documentation and a high degree of rationalisation will continue to be felt throughout the life of the job. Supervision will be simplified and the ordering and placing of components will be much easier with the

information in textual form as well as on the drawings.

Overall, therefore, the savings on the example given total perhaps ten man-weeks over the entire job, as summarised in *Figure 2.9*. Divided between four assistants, plus administrative staff overheads,

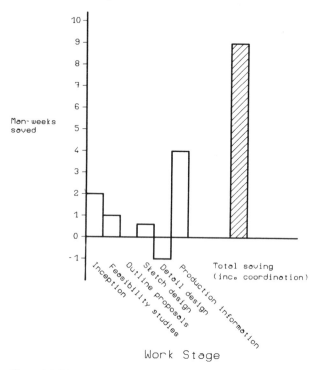

Figure 2.9 Typical time savings made by computer aids

the design time will be shortened by perhaps three weeks and the total construction time, allowing for the spin-off advantages to the consultants and contractors, by perhaps five weeks. As a typical computer section can handle eight to ten jobs a year, the total saving to the office will be significant, both in time and money.

The other advantage of computer methods will be a design that is normally better than could have been produced manually in a reasonable time. This benefit is difficult to evaluate as it enhances the architect's reputation; presumably in the long term it will lead to more commissions.

So even a job of average size can benefit from computer aids. On a larger job, the savings will be more than proportionately greater, as communication losses become significant with manual methods and coordination is more difficult. Greater investment in machinery can also bring increased benefits; using the computer to take over some of the draughting, for example, will usually make large savings in manpower.

3
Office organisation

Time-sharing and batch processing

The popular conception of computers is of fabulously expensive machines that need tending by large numbers of highly trained specialists. Unfortunately, this view is in essence perfectly correct. However, there are various ways to circumvent these difficulties, and an architectural practice that wishes to use computers has to decide which option best suits its needs.

The most popular option to date has been to hire a portion of a computer's time from a commercial bureau that specialises in this sort of thing. As an architect's problems are unlikely to occupy a large machine for more than a few minutes a week, processing can be done at a very reasonable cost. The hiring organisation shoulders the problems of high capital cost, servicing, and trained operators. There are other advantages: these include reliability, as many firms have more than one machine and can therefore maintain a service even if one should break down; free advice with programming or operational problems; and training courses, normally free or available for a nominal charge. A hired machine is also completely adaptable to the user's workload; he pays only for the time he needs to use.

Having access to what is usually a very large and very fast machine brings economic advantages of its own. An axiom of computing known as Grosch's Law states that the power of a computer increases as the square of its cost; thus using a larger machine for a short time is cheaper than using a small machine for a longer time. In fact, with the advent of minicomputers and microcomputers, which are very cheap machines indeed, this relationship is starting to break down, but such machines are unsuited to many classes of problem. Large size also implies that the computer is easy to use and normally has many standard programs available.

The most efficient way of using a computer is to present a problem as a single block of information: as a deck of punched cards, for example. The problem will take its turn in the queue for a portion of the machine's time and the results will be printed at the end of the run. This procedure is known as 'batch processing'.

For some problems, however, this is inappropriate. For example, if the user has to take decisions which depend on the results of earlier processing, the problem will have to be broken down into many small batch-processing jobs. In these circumstances, it is better for the user to be in contact with the computer while the processing is actually going on and to be able to intervene and direct the course of the calculation. The refinement of designs is a typical class of problem requiring this interactive approach. The user can present a design and the computer can comment on it in some way: in terms of cost or environmental performance, for example. The user can then alter the design in some respects and obtain revised comments. This feedback process continues until the user is satisfied with the result.

Contact with the computer is usually achieved by the use of a telephone link and a device known as a 'terminal' which can transmit and receive information. A computer accessed in this fashion will often have to deal with a number of users at once, but this is fairly easy to arrange. The computer works so much faster than a man can react that it can switch between users and ideally give each one the impression that he has the machine's complete attention. Typically, up to forty users can be accommodated in this arrangement, which is known as 'time sharing'.

The penalty paid for such an ingenious method of operation can be high. There is a sizeable overhead in computer time in switching from one user to another, so a user who requires a lot of interaction, as in a lengthy question-and-answer session, will pay anything from twice to ten times as much as the user who needs the same amount of computing done without human intervention. If a lot of users are connected to the computer at once, the response time to commands may lengthen, and it is extremely irritating to sit at a terminal waiting for the computer's reply.

A terminal can stand in an architect's office, and this gives the advantage of high accessibility. The computer can be contacted at almost any hour of the day or night in the time it takes to dial a number. As the terminal does not have to be connected to any particular computer, the user has a wide choice of machines across the country and even abroad and can shop around for the most economic rates and the

17

best programs. Batch processing is commonly carried out by the user actually visiting the computer centre with his problem in the form of punched cards or magnetic tape, but a terminal can also be used to initiate a batch processing job.

However, quick access can tempt the user into bad habits. Grosch's second law of computing states that time-sharing is like heroin: it is expensive, debilitating and the user has to become a pusher to support his habit. There is unfortunately a lot of truth in this; without self-discipline the user may become very careless about the way problems are presented and the number of runs repeated with slightly different data, because the computer will immediately point out mistakes, and alterations and resubmissions can be made in seconds. This approach is expensive and many firms have indeed gone into program marketing entirely to justify the sharply increased costs of development. With care and experience, costs should not be prohibitive: probably less than the salary of a junior assistant once things are going smoothly; and a lot of work can be done for the money.

There are many time-sharing and batch services to choose from, and not much to choose between most of them; they all have large machines, which tends to give easier and more economic usage, and none of them has a wide selection of programs specifically for architectural use. In general, the larger the company the better, as it will have more staff to help in specialist areas and will have a wider range of training courses and other facilities.

There is some advantage in choosing a bureau that has one of the more popular machines, as the user then has access to more programs. IBM is the obvious choice as they have over 60% of the world-wide market. In Britain, ICL machines are also very popular and both IBM and ICL have about 25% of the market. For architectural use, a bureau should have its own plotter; if it has to subcontract its graphical work this will inevitably slow down the production of drawings and diagrams and make these tasks more clumsy.

It is an advantage if the bureau is close to the user's office because with batch processing work little time will be lost in travelling, and with time-sharing work the risks of communication trouble will be less. If the bureau is more than a few miles away there may well be problems in sending information down the telephone line; and it gives a very bad impression if some words in a report are garbled, or if entire lines are missing.

It is not a good idea to have a contract with more than one bureau at once, although sometimes this is unavoidable, if both have certain very useful programs, for instance. Each bureau will have its own set of operating procedures which always take a long time to learn. If the operator has to switch constantly between systems he will almost certainly make many mistakes and the work will be considerably slowed.

A bureau with more than one machine has the advantage that the chance of an interruption in service is almost eliminated. Users can be switched to the remaining machine with no effect beyond a degradation in response time at a peak period. This can be of vital importance in meeting deadlines.

Equipping for batch processing

Of all the different methods of obtaining computer-processing time, batch processing is the one that requires the least capital investment from the user. The bureau provides all the equipment for the input of data and the output of results as well as the computer itself, so the user at most need only purchase some form of storage for the input and output media at his own office.

The input medium can be of various types. The heavy users who deal with tens of thousands of data records will usually use one of the magnetic storage media, such as magnetic tape, which form the most compact means of holding large amounts of information. Architectural firms will normally fall into the small- to medium-scale user category and at this level it is often more convenient to store data in physical form on punched cards or, more rarely, on paper tape. Physical storage media are easy to handle in limited numbers and are extremely cheap and rugged. However, they are much bulkier and much slower in moving information into the computer than their magnetic storage equivalents. Typically, physical storage can be input at a maximum of 1000 characters per second, while a magnetic tape can transfer information at up to 100 000 characters per second. Physical storage has become much less popular in recent years as programs and data files have grown, but it is still very widespread[33].

Punched cards are usually 80 columns wide, although not all of these columns need be used, for

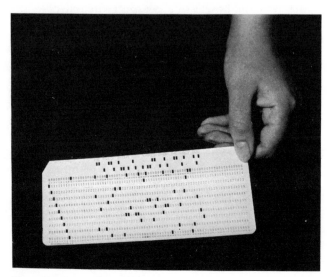

Figure 3.1 A punched card

example if blanks are left in the interests of readability. The punching machine will print out the text of the information present at the top of the card to facilitate human handling. A punched card is shown in *Figure 3.1*. Large numbers of punched cards can be prepared by commercial data-preparation services; there is a wide choice and most bureaux can also offer an in-house service. If there are only a few cards to be punched, or only a few to be corrected in a batch, it is more convenient for the user to prepare them himself. Manually operated card-punching machines (*Figure 3.2*) will normally be available in a bureau for the customers' use.

As they have to serve many customers on site, batch-processing bureaux use very high-speed input devices. An advanced punched-card reader can work at 20 cards/sec; *Figure 3.3* shows an example of one of these machines. The usual principle on which the faster card readers operate consists of shining a light

Figure 3.4 A line-printer (courtesy SIA Ltd)

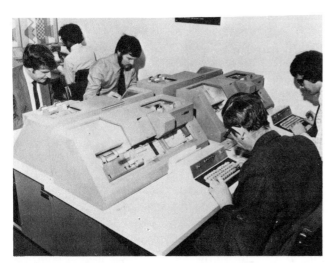

Figure 3.2 Card-punching machines (courtesy SIA Ltd)

Figure 3.3 A punched-card reader (courtesy SIA Ltd)

on each card and picking up the signals on an array of photo-electric cells where holes are present.

Bureaux must also provide high-speed output devices, most of which will produce results on paper. The machine normally used for this is called a 'line-printer' because it holds a complete character set for every column position on a line and sets up the entire line before printing it all at once. A line-printer typically works at 1500 lines per minute, but even at this speed many bureaux need several of them. *Figure 3.4* shows a typical line-printer.

High-speed printers normally print on pages of approximately A3 size (420 × 297 mm); there are a few machines that accept A4 (297 × 210 mm) but they have never become popular, which is surprising as the larger size is clumsy to handle. There is no standardised number of characters per line; various lengths from 120 to 160 characters are in use. The number of lines per page is similarly variable, but is usually between 50 and 60. The pages are joined to each other at top and bottom in a continuous chain. There are sprocket holes running down both sides to assist in feeding the paper through the printer. Results are awkward to handle in this form, so computer rooms are equipped with 'bursters' that tear the output into individual pages and trim off the sprocket holes. The pages can then be bound into a folder. If several copies are required, they can be obtained by using multi-part stationery with carbons. The output must then be passed through a machine known as a 'de-leaver' to separate out the copies and remove the carbons. Two- and three-part stationery is available for line-printers and gives reasonable reproduction.

During the course of calculations it will often be found that the computer's memory is insufficient to hold all the intermediate results. It is therefore necessary to have available some form of storage in which the machine can place data temporarily and retrieve it later. This process corresponds roughly to the use a human might make of a notebook to assist his own memory.

The simplest of such storage devices is a magnetic tape reader. It works on exactly the same principle as a domestic tape recorder and can hold a very large amount of information. The tape itself is 13 mm wide and typically 730 m long. It is the cheapest of all forms of storage; a tape can be purchased for a few pounds. The drawbacks of magnetic tape are that it is relatively slow and that it is not possible to skip backwards or forwards along the tape, so a long time may be spent in winding on and rewinding. *Figure 3.5* shows a bank of magnetic tape readers installed at a large bureau.

A more elaborate device is the magnetic disc. The storage principle is the same as that of tape: a special coating that will accept and hold a magnetic charge. The arrangement is radically different; the coating is put on both sides of a disc which is spun at high speeds. Reading and writing are done by heads on both sides that can move along the diameter of the disc; thus a combination of the movements of the disc and the heads will allow all of the magnetic surfaces to be accessed. The information can obviously be accessed in random order much more quickly than with tape, and this is often very useful.

Large-capacity disc units as used by bureaux will have a group of four or more individual discs sharing a common spindle with the reading and writing heads held on a single piece of equipment known as a 'comb'. This 'disc pack', as the arrangement is called, will hold a lot of information (at least five million numbers) and can be removed from the drive and stored for later use. The arrangement of the disc pack is shown diagrammatically in *Figure 3.6*.

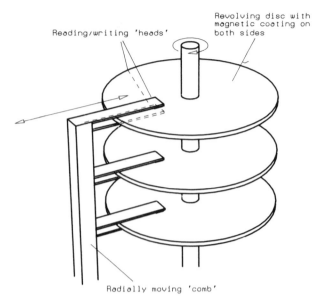

Figure 3.6 Disc-pack organisation

Equipping for time sharing

Virtually the only essential piece of equipment needed to use a time-sharing bureau is a terminal. The choice of terminals is very wide nowadays; there are many manufacturers of these machines and many different types available. The most popular choice is still a teleprinter, which is similar visually and in operation to a conventional typewriter.

The traditional terminal was almost always a 10 characters/sec teleprinter, which had the advantages of extreme cheapness, reliability and ease of use. For many applications it is still a very popular device. For larger-scale use, however, its low speed becomes a major handicap. Ten characters/sec may sound very fast, and is in fact about twice the speed of a good typist, but it means that a single A4 page of results takes about five minutes to print out, and this sort of delay is not really acceptable for any volume of printing. For this reason, faster terminals are becoming more popular, but higher speed brings its own problems, particularly in the increased mechanical demand. It is difficult to make typebars and other mechanical linkages work at such high rates, so the maximum speed for 'impact' printing is about thirty characters/sec, and even at this speed such terminals are inevitably very noisy, leading to operator fatigue and disturbance to other workers.

There are a number of alternatives to impact printing, one of the most popular being the use of heat-sensitive paper. This discolours when heated, so that a matrix of electrically heated needles can be used to form letters. Such devices can work comfortably at thirty characters/sec and are extremely quiet, usually emitting a low-pitched humming noise. They can therefore be used in open-plan offices. The disadvantage is that the print quality is

Figure 3.5 Magnetic-tape readers (courtesy SIA Ltd)

not as good as that given by impact printing and the paper itself tends to be flimsy and to discolour if exposed to daylight for a few weeks. Heat-sensitive paper is also a lot more expensive than ordinary stationery, but this should not be an important expense unless a great deal of printing is done.

There are various other types of electro-mechanical terminal that use such ingenious methods as magnetised ink droplets, and some of them can reach higher speeds than thirty characters/sec. However, there can be difficulties when using the public telephone network at these speeds and leasing a private line to a bureau is expensive. In any case, higher speeds than thirty characters/sec are not really suitable for interactive use, because the information comes out more quickly than most people can absorb it.

The standard line-width for most types of terminal is 80 characters. With standard stationery the terminal can be used to produce results on A4 pages, vertically. Conventional computer printers use a line width of about 140 characters and the standard stationery is of A3 size, horizontally. Therefore, if the high-speed printer at the computer bureau is to be used for some of the output (and this has advantages in cost and speed), there will be compatability problems. For this reason it is worthwhile considering a wide-carriage terminal that produces output similar to that of a high-speed printer. This sort of terminal is very useful for producing schedules and similar documents that are more easily laid out in columnar form.

Some terminals also have a lower-case option. This makes the documents produced much easier to read than the standard upper case throughout, and can greatly increase user acceptance. The difficulty is that most computer programs and programming languages are orientated around upper case for all text and have difficulty, if indeed it is possible at all, in transmitting or receiving lower-case characters.

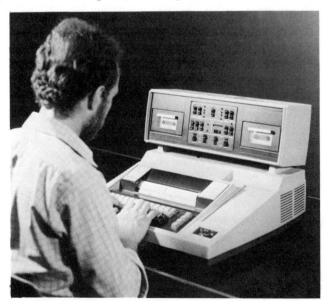

Figure 3.7 A teleprinter terminal

Figure 3.8 A visual display unit terminal (courtesy Hewlett-Packard Ltd)

An example of an advanced teleprinter terminal is shown in *Figure 3.7*. This is a Silent 700 model produced by Texas Instruments Incorporated. It uses heat-sensitive paper, and the version shown has magnetic cassettes for storing data and results. This type of terminal is, as its name suggests, a very quiet device.

An alternative to the various types of teleprinter is the visual display unit. This is a device similar to a television screen with a keyboard attached. Such devices are of course virtually silent and can work at almost any speed. Being almost completely electronic, rather than mechanical, they are also cheaper and more reliable than the conventional electro-mechanical terminals. *Figure 3.8* shows an advanced alphanumeric visual display unit terminal made by Hewlett-Packard Ltd. The unit shown has the useful extra feature of an integral printer, but most visual display units do not make any permanent record of the information transmitted and this can be a serious drawback. When the screen is full, with typically about 30 lines of information, the next line that is transmitted or received will force the top line off the screen; thus it is not possible to refer back to earlier results. In certain areas, aircraft bookings for example, this does not matter as the information is purely ephemeral and it is actually an advantage not to have lots of paper lying about. In general, architects are not in this position; they are trying to get results or documents for issue or for discussion. This can be achieved with a device known as a 'hard copy unit' that reproduces the information on the screen at that time. Unfortunately hard copy units are expensive, typically twice the cost of the terminal itself, and the print they produce is of poor quality. *Figure 3.9* shows a typical hard copy unit.

Some visual display units can also receive and send graphic information. These will cost rather more than simple textual displays but of course have a much wider capability as results can be presented partly or entirely in graphical form, provided the time-sharing service can support graphical applications.

Despite their apparent appeal, the use of graphical terminals with a time-sharing service is in fact now relatively rare. At one time there were numerous systems that used the combination to provide interactive draughting for a very low capital investment. Unfortunately, interactive graphics inherently require a lot of processing power and therefore the bills from the time-sharing service were very high: typically £30–£40 per hour. As a draughtsman can be hired for £2–£3 per hour it is impossible for such a system to be cost-effective. A further disadvantage is that graphical processing requires almost continual monitoring from the computer and this cannot be provided by a time-sharing machine that has other users to attend to. Thus there will be many forced

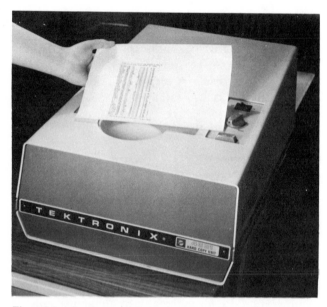

Figure 3.9 A hard copy unit

and irritating pauses in the work. It is now understood that interactive graphics requires a dedicated computer, and with the fall in the cost of machinery this has recently become economically feasible.

A terminal is connected to the telephone via a device known as a 'modem'. This converts the electrical signals that emit from and control the terminal into acoustic signals that can travel along the telephone line to the time-sharing computer. Normally the modem is a separate piece of equipment rented from the Post Office and typically fitted onto the base of the telephone (*Figure 3.10*). An option with some lightweight terminals is an acoustic modem which enables connection to be made using an ordinary telephone. This is not as reliable as a directly wired connection, but it means that the terminal is completely portable and can be carried into conference rooms or onto site. *Figure 3.11* shows a popular terminal of this type in use.

The final choice of terminal must depend on the sort of work that the user intends to carry out, but there is a very wide choice and almost all terminals are low-cost devices. Even a sophisticated model can be leased for the equivalent of about a quarter of the salary of a junior assistant.

When the user has finished with a program or with a certain set of data, it must be stored somewhere. The easiest solution is to leave it in the computer's storage system where it is ready for use at any future time. This is not usually practicable, however, because the number of files the user has will become unmanageably large and will cost a great deal to preserve with no corresponding benefits. Getting the data and programs into the computer in the first place is also rather expensive if they are typed in while the user is connected to the machine. It is much cheaper to type up the information while 'off-line', i.e. unconnected, and then transmit at the full speed of the terminal. There is therefore a need for some form of data storage at the user's end, and this can take a number of forms.

Figure 3.10 A telephone with integral modem

Figure 3.11 A portable terminal (courtesy SIA Ltd)

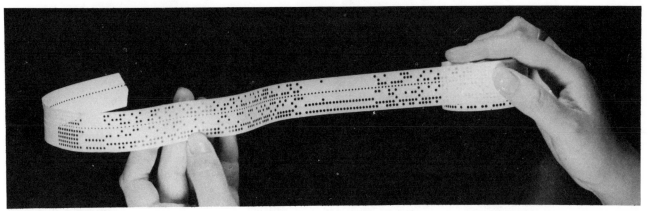

Figure 3.12 Punched paper tape

A few years ago, punched paper tape (*Figure 3.12*) was easily the most popular medium for this purpose and it is still widespread. Many teleprinters have a tape reader and a tape punch built in, so it is easy to prepare data and then transmit it, or take data transmitted from the computer and preserve it for future re-entry. This type of off-line storage is cheap and rugged, but it is difficult to correct at a later date, because altering even a single line involves reproducing all the tape before and after the change. Paper tape is also clumsy to use; in inexpert hands it can quickly get itself into knots and wrap itself around the furniture!

A fairly recent alternative to paper tape is magnetic tape cassettes. These are basically identical to domestic audio cassettes; they are the same physical size and shape, but the magnetic coating on the tape is of different formulation. A typical cassette is pictured in *Figure 3.13*. The cassettes themselves are expensive, but will store a great deal of information, typically 300 000 characters, and are re-usable. They are easy to use and convenient to store. It is possible to prepare data so that each line occupies a fixed size of block on the tape; thus editing lines in the middle of the tape does not involve complete duplication. Cassettes are completely silent in use, whereas any physical storage medium such as paper tape is almost invariably noisy. There is, however, the problem that data cannot be stored indefinitely on cassettes as the magnetic charge will tend to leak away. It is normally necessary to recopy all the data once a year to preserve it.

Figure 3.13 A data cassette

Some applications involve output that is not suited to the use of a terminal. A hundred-page schedule, for example, would take about four hours to print at 30 characters/sec; and graphical results cannot be received or displayed by most terminals. If this sort of output is often produced then it may be economic to install a high-speed printer or a plotter in the office. However, if special output is produced infrequently, then it is probably better to use the terminal to divert the output onto the equipment at the computer bureau. The results can then be collected, if the bureau is close to the office, or sent by private dispatching service or posted if less urgent.

The terminal and its ancillary equipment need to be installed in a convenient part of the office. If the terminal is of the impact-printing type an enclosed room will have to be provided, and often acoustic insulation will also be necessary, because otherwise the constant clatter will become intolerable to the other members of the staff. Such a room, sometimes jocularly known as the 'terminal chamber', is convenient from an organisational point of view but does in some ways tend to give an impression of isolation from the rest of the office, and this can hinder acceptance.

Minicomputers

Hiring computer time is the best solution for most practices wishing to use a machine for non-graphical applications, but if a great deal of work is done, there comes a point where it is more economic to buy a computer for the office's own use. Few architectural firms will need to consider a 'mainframe', i.e. a full-size computer, although a multi-disciplinary practice that has to run large structural analysis programs might justify one. The usual solution is to buy a 'minicomputer' which has limited processing power but which is cheap and rugged.

The term minicomputer is rather ill-defined these days, but broadly speaking it is applied to computers that have the same basic internal organisation as the large mainframe machines but in a simplified form which imposes restrictions in speed and facilities.

The restrictions will be felt in such things as memory size, which can only be a small fraction of that supported by a mainframe, and in the less flexible arithmetical capabilities. Minicomputers also tend to be physically small. The basic unit will normally fit comfortably on a desk top. A very popular model of minicomputer is shown in *Figure 3.14*; the computer itself is fitted into a rack below two disc storage units.

Figure 3.14 A minicomputer with peripherals (photograph copyright Digital Equipment Co Ltd)

Unfortunately, these machines bring problems of their own, some arising from the nature of minicomputers and some from the extra organisational tasks necessary. One of the first problems is that the low price of minicomputers is to some extent illusory. It is true that the basic central computing unit can cost as little as £5000, but by itself it cannot receive data or communicate results. A number of peripheral devices (printer, disc units, etc) are therefore necessary. These machines tend to be electro-mechanical in operation and, because of the high speed at which they normally work, have to be strong and manufactured to very close tolerances. The peripheral devices therefore tend to be expensive compared to the central computing unit which is purely electronic and so comparatively simple to manufacture.

The basic unit as supplied will have very little memory, perhaps for only about 8000 numbers; consequently it must be increased for most applications. There is also often an extra charge for the programs that control the computer. There are a variety of other accessories necessary that will bring the total cost to perhaps £20 000 for a usable machine.

Environmental control can also be costly. In theory, none is needed; the machine can stand in an ordinary office. In practice, this policy is not safe, especially in Britain where many offices lack air-conditioning or even adequate heating. The central processing unit will typically operate reliably between 0°C and 55°C, but the peripheral devices are often not so rugged. A magnetic storage system, for example, will be unreliable outside the temperature range 10°C–32°C and these extremes may well be exceeded in winter or in a hot summer. If a plotter is included in the set-up, a difference in humidity levels of as little as 10% from the standard can cause unacceptable distortion of the drawing. Even dust particles in the air can make certain of the high-speed mechanical devices fail catastrophically. Another consideration is that the power supply may need special stabilisation in some areas where the random use of heavy machinery can cause fluctuations in the voltage[28]. The sums of money in question are still not unreasonable for most practices, but are well above the amounts that appear to be involved when looking only at the price of the computer itself.

The major drawback of minicomputers arises from their nature. They are basically small, simple and comparatively slow devices originally designed for a narrow range of applications. Their earliest use was in laboratories monitoring experiments and analysing the results. Their users were scientists, well used to strictly logical thinking, and normally competent programmers. Later, they were used by engineers and others who wanted rapid calculating power at their fingertips. For such applications, involving many short programs that consist almost entirely of mathematical analysis, a number of small computers is a more efficient alternative to one large machine. Again, their users were technically minded and usually good programmers. As minicomputers became easier to use and acquired some basic programs and high-level languages, they expanded rapidly into many fields. Their essential philosophy remains unchanged, however, and this can cause them to be unsuitable in certain application areas.

The main limitation is the memory capacity; there is a maximum possible size to the memory which is usually quite low. A capacity of about 33 000 numbers is typical. This is not enough to deal easily with large quantities of information, and it also restricts the size of computer program to a maximum of perhaps 1000 instructions in a high-level language. Such a program is too short to give much flexibility or to make many concessions to the user. These restrictions make the program difficult to use in architectural applications which often involve a lot of data manipulated in a very free manner.

The simple design of minicomputers is also a problem. The basic operations that they can carry out are often much more restricted than in a full-size computer, and therefore more programming needs to be done to make up for the machine's deficiencies. Minicomputers are also normally only capable of holding numbers up to a maximum value of 32 768 (2^{15}) and, as supplied, often cannot deal directly with fractions. Thus if large numbers, or numbers that have fractional parts, have to be handled, extra programming has to be done, which uses up time and memory. Optional extra circuitry is usually available to handle fractions, but can be costly.

These and other design limitations tend to restrict the overall speed of a minicomputer to around one-tenth of that of a conventional computer. This can mean that work is delayed or that shift working is introduced in order to be able to handle all the processing.

The combination of small size and low speed means that it is often not practicable to write programs of any complexity in a high-level language. Instead, the programmer must use a language more orientated to the computer's mode of working than to a human's. A type of language called an 'assembly language' is normally chosen in these circumstances. Assembly languages are more compact inside the machine and therefore both take up less memory and execute faster, but they are extremely cryptic and difficult to use. A program in an assembly language will take several times as long to write as the equivalent program in a language more intelligible to human beings. Further, an assembly language is specific to one type of computer, and so cannot be run on a different model of computer without long and difficult conversion.

From a programmer's point of view the limitations of the machine make it much more difficult to get the machine to work as required, because a lot of effort has to go into trying to circumvent the limitations, rather than in trying to solve the problem. The standard programs that operate the machine will also normally be crude and limited, because of the need to conserve memory. Thus if the programmer wants to get the best out of the machine he must be familiar with the intimate details of these operating programs and be able to modify them to meet his requirements. The programmer must be very knowledgeable about all aspects of his computer in a way not seen since the early pioneering days of the 1950s. He must be highly trained and experienced and it is unlikely that he will be trained to appreciate an architect's problems as well.

One of the most serious drawbacks to owning a machine is that there are many organisational tasks to attend to that are not encountered when hiring time, because the bureau will carry them out. Even starting the machine up in the morning can involve a complicated 'bootstrapping' procedure to get the computer orientated. Someone has to be trained in this, and in such tasks as loading discs and copying data at the end of the day as a precaution against loss. The user is responsible for all these detailed points of operation and they can occupy a lot of time.

I have gone into the problems at some length to make the point that the purchase of a minicomputer is not an automatic choice and will not solve all an office's computing problems in one fell swoop. On the contrary, it will introduce all sorts of unfamiliar problems of its own. However, a large practice with a heavy workload would incur high bills in hiring time from a bureau and hence might be able to justify the capital expenditure of purchasing its own machine and paying the salaries of a couple of specialists to run it.

The inherent restrictions of minicomputers are not going to go away however many programmers are employed. It is therefore necessary to choose machinery that is capable of handling the sizeable problems encountered in construction work, or the purchase will be a white elephant. There are many manufacturers of minicomputers and the choice of machinery is bewilderingly wide. The field is much more open than that of mainframe computers, where IBM dominate the market. The largest manufacturer of minicomputers is the Digital Equipment Corporation, but there are literally dozens to choose from, mostly of American origin.

One of the most important problems, that of small memory size, can be dealt with by buying one of the machines that do not have this restriction. There are two basic solutions to the problem; the first is to purchase a minicomputer that has the same internal organisation as a mainframe computer and therefore has a memory capacity of millions of numbers. These obviously cost rather more, but can handle much more complex problems. The other way of getting more memory is to buy a machine with a 'virtual storage' facility. This is a method of using a magnetic storage device as an extension of the computer's memory, thus allowing a very large effective memory. The problem is that peripheral devices are hundreds or thousands of times slower than the central processing unit, and so great care has to be taken with program organisation if execution times are not to rise dramatically. As low speed is a restriction that cannot be circumvented, it is better to get a machine that is as fast as possible so as to be able to run, say, complex evaluations or produce long schedules in a reasonable time. A fast machine will be capable of about 1 700 000 additions per second, while a more usual speed for a minicomputer will be about 1 000 000 additions per second.

An architectural practice would be well advised not to rush into the purchase of a minicomputer, but to build up experience by using a batch or time-sharing service for a few years and to inspect other practices that have installed minicomputers before making its own decision.

Equipping for minicomputers

The most important type of ancillary equipment necessary to a minicomputer is some form of magnetic storage device, usually a disc system. A disc-pack unit as used at bureaux is usually too powerful and expensive for a minicomputer installation to justify, so the normal choice is one of the cheaper, but slower and of inferior capacity, variations on the disc storage principle.

One such variation is the 'cartridge disc'. This is a single disc about the size of a long-playing record permanently contained in a stout plastic case to protect it. When inserted into the disc drive the case opens to allow entrance of the read/write heads; thus the vulnerable magnetic surfaces are protected. This is a great advantage in minicomputer installations where the environment is often not clinically clean. A cartridge disc can typically hold 1½ million numbers. *Figure 3.15* shows a cartridge disc being inserted into its drive. Another variation is the 'floppy disc'. This is a disc made of a non-rigid material upon which the magnetic coating is deposited. The disc is only about the size of a 45 rev/min record and is kept permanently in a cardboard sleeve. Its capacity is even more limited than that of a cartridge disc, being about 200 000 numbers, and it is also slower. However, the individual discs are very cheap and convenient to use and store. They are also extremely rugged; I have known a floppy disc work after having been folded and pushed through a letter box! *Figure 3.16* shows a floppy disc being loaded into its drive.

All of these discs suffer from the fact that they are mechanical devices operating at very high speeds and therefore are, like a racing car, liable to breakdowns. At its perimeter, a disc is travelling at 40 m/s and the read/write heads are suspended just 0.003 mm above it. This gives very little margin for error; as the diameter of a human hair, for example,

Figure 3.15 Loading a cartridge disc

Figure 3.16 Loading a floppy disc

is 0.08 mm it is not uncommon for a catastrophic failure to take place in which the head makes physical contact with the disc and severely damages it. This 'head crash' is an extremely expensive business. The disc will be a write-off and the drive itself will need extensive repair. Worse, the information on that disc will be lost. In order, therefore, to guard against the loss of data representing perhaps months of work, it is necessary frequently to make a copy of the contents of a disc. This is normally done once or twice a day and of course does use up a lot of resources in human and computer time and in storage media. It is, however, essential procedure for any working installation.

Because of their complicated construction, disc units are not cheap. However, their high speed and convenience mean that they are to be found at almost all installations.

As well as the magnetic storage facilities, there must be some means by which the user can communicate directly with the computer, and vice versa. An ordinary teleprinter is often used for this purpose, as it is cheap and the low speed is not a handicap. The same comments apply as to teleprinters used as time-sharing terminals, which were described earlier.

In some installations the teleprinter will also be considered adequate for the output of results. Most architectural practices, however, will need to print quite large volumes of production documentation and similar results and in these circumstances a higher-speed printer is necessary. A line-printer as used with mainframe computers is usually too fast and expensive for a minicomputer, so a fast character-by-character printer is normally chosen. There are several different principles on which a character-by-character printer can be built, but on most types the print quality is better than that of a line-printer and it is practicable for them to have a larger character set, often including lower-case letters. A typical example will operate at 180 characters/sec.

Most minicomputers today have the option of a 'communications port' which allows them to be connected to a time-sharing service in the same way as a terminal. This can be useful in transferring data to or from media that the minicomputer does not support, such as punched cards.

Interactive graphics

The most advanced, but also the most complex and most expensive type of installation that an architectural firm is likely to choose is one for interactive graphics. As drawing forms such a large part of the architect's workload such an installation can also be the most productive of all.

The characteristic of interactive graphics is that the user can see the drawing appear on a screen as he gives the commands. It is also possible to create drawings in a non-interactive manner by typing a large set of commands and presenting them in a single block to a computer, which then produces output on a plotter without human intervention. This is much more economical of processing time and can be implemented using a bureau service or on a minicomputer. The advantages and drawbacks are compared with interactive graphics in Chapter 6.

The machines normally used for interactive graphics are minicomputers equipped with special facilities to input and output graphic elements. The items of equipment, such as the computer, screen, and coordinate input device can be bought separately but the interfacing of all these can be difficult and programs to drive them will have to be specially written. It is much more convenient to buy an integrated unit designed specifically for graphical applications and supplied with the appropriate programs. Several manufacturers are producing such devices; one of the most recent is shown in *Figure 3.17*. The workstation is a neat and compact unit that will fit easily into most office environments.

The problems associated with interactive graphics are very similar to those encountered with conventional minicomputers. The user again has to become concerned with the details of maintenance, environmental control, trained operators, and data storage. There are also problems that are exclusive to this form of working. The high cost of these machines means that in order to be cost-effective they must be

Figure 3.17 A stand-alone graphical workstation

used intensively. This can cause work-scheduling problems, because only one person can operate the machine at a time and therefore different jobs must be slotted in where possible and as necessary. Also, the computer work may have to be supplemented by manual draughting where necessary, and the coordination of these aspects can be difficult and may lead to confusion or duplication of effort.

The use of interactive draughting machines also implies some inflexibility. If too few are purchased a lot of the work will have to be done manually, but if too many are installed large sums will be lost if the workload should fall. If the workload should change significantly in either direction the computer work will not be able to respond quickly because it takes months both to terminate a lease and to obtain delivery of new equipment.

In theory, the computer can be used for other work besides draughting; but in practice this can be difficult to arrange. This is principally because the machine is being used inappropriately when only a fraction of its facilities are called upon. A minicomputer takes a relatively long time to perform extensive numerical calculations or to process large amounts of data and it is uneconomic to tie up the machine on this sort of work. However, the information contained on the drawings can be used as the basis for other results, such as automatic scheduling, environmental analysis, or costing, and it is obviously very desirable that this should be done.

The solution adopted by some systems is to tie the minicomputer into a time-sharing device. By this means the large machine can take over the heavy processing work, which it is well suited to. The difficulty is that, as two computers are involved, programming the system is more complicated.

The strain on both the user and on the office as a whole can be considerable. The productivity of the operator is raised by at least three or four times his performance on the drawing board, but this is at the cost of his being paced by the computer at a high rate. In our own office, we have found it inadvisable for a single person to work continuously with the computer for more than three or four hours a day. The upheaval in the office working methods is also serious. The computer's performance is not even over all aspects of the work. In some things, such as inputting arbitrary wall plans, it is little faster than a human draughtsman; in others, such as positioning repeated elements like doors or items of equipment, it can be ten times as fast. This inconsistency can throw out production schedules and make interfacing with manual work even more difficult.

Despite all the problems, interactive draughting is a very productive application of computers to architecture, and as the cost of machinery continues to fall will become even more so.

Equipping for interactive graphics

An interactive graphics workstation needs most of the equipment required for a conventional minicomputer installation, and the same problems apply. The main exception is that a high-speed printer, although useful, is not essential as the quantity of alphanumeric output will be relatively low.

The central item of extra equipment needed is a screen on which the drawing is displayed. There are several types, but the two most popular are the refresh screen and the storage screen. A refresh screen is controlled by what are effectively two computers. One monitors the user's actions and on the basis of these creates or modifies a list of instructions that define a drawing; the other, called the display processor, scans this list and keeps redrawing it on the screen. *Figure 3.18* illustrates this arrangement. In

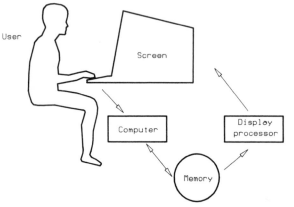

Figure 3.18 Refresh screen organisation

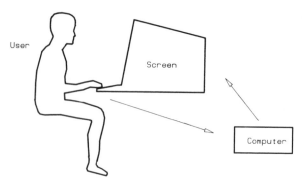

Figure 3.19 Storage screen organisation

contrast, a storage screen retains any information displayed on it indefinitely. Continuous redrawing is therefore not necessary and lines can be added as required to build up the drawing. There is consequently only a single computer between the user and the screen. *Figure 3.19* illustrates this.

Both types of screen have advantages and drawbacks. The storage screen, as might be expected, is cheaper than the refresh screen because only one computer is necessary rather than two. Also, it can hold a drawing of any complexity. A refresh screen can only hold a drawing of limited complexity for two reasons. First, the list of instructions is held in the computer's memory and this is limited. Second, the list of instructions must be redrawn at least 16 times/sec to avoid flicker, which is very irritating; the speed of the display processor imposes a typical limit of about 300 lines, and this is often not sufficient.

The big advantage of the refresh screen is that lines can be removed from the drawing or moved across the screen simply by altering the instruction list. With a storage screen, the whole screen must be erased and the drawing redisplayed with the correction made. This process can easily take a couple of minutes, and so can become a great handicap. Thus it is difficult to perform erasures with a storage screen and continuous movement is impracticable. When using the refresh screen, a user can reposition elements dynamically. A worktop, for instance, can be moved about until it is correctly positioned; this is not possible with a storage screen. The scale of a refreshed drawing can also be changed quickly, as it is just a matter of multiplying the length of each line in the instruction list. It is therefore possible to select and enlarge a single room or area to study it more closely or alter it more easily; with a storage screen a significant time lag is involved in doing this.

Thus there is a good deal to be said for both types of screen and neither is clearly superior. Many manufacturers make refresh screens, but the storage screen market is dominated by Tektronix Incorporated. This company has recently released a product that combines many of the features of both types of screen. Lines can be drawn and retained as on a storage screen, but it is also possible to draw lines that are visible but of such low intensity that they are not retained. Thus small portions of the drawing can be moved about, while the bulk of it forms a background. This does not give the full dynamic capabilities offered by refresh screens, and it is rather expensive, but it can be the best compromise for many applications.

Another sort of screen that is just beginning to become popular is the digital television screen or raster screen. This can use an ordinary domestic television set, which forms an image by writing dots of varying intensities or colours in a series of lines on the screen. Instead of the information for the image coming from a broadcast it is fed from a reserved portion of the computer's memory that has one location for each dot position on the screen. The user can alter the reserved memory and thus the image on the screen. This arrangement is illustrated in *Figure 3.20.*

This device provides a number of advantages. It is very cheap, because its principal component is a television set, possibly costing less than £100 because of the volume in which such sets are produced. It can also provide very good images indeed. A full range of half-tones and colours is possible and all sorts of hatching or stippling effects can easily be generated. Another important advantage is that screen size can be up to 660mm diagonally, while other types of screen usually have a maximum size of 533mm. The drawback is that the definition is poor. There will normally be 625 scan lines forming the image, while a refresh or storage screen will have 2048 or even 4096. Thus for architectural draughting, which normally involves finely detailed drawing and rarely requires half-tones or colours, this type of screen is less suitable.

Given a screen, the user needs devices by which he can communicate with the computer to instruct it to add to or modify the drawing. The most straight forward of these, and one that is normally provided, is a keyboard. This can be used to give commands, to call up specific pre-drawn elements, or to add text to a drawing. In addition, there are often special 'function keys'. These are not associated with any character, but rather with an entire operation. Thus one key might be labelled 'scale up' and when

pressed would enlarge the drawing to the next standard scale.

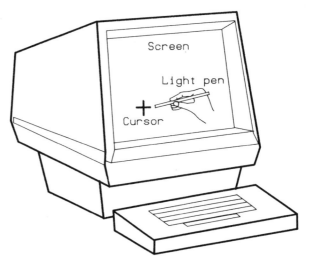

Figure 3.21 The use of a light pen

Most importantly, it is necessary to be able to indicate specific points on the screen. This might be done for a number of reasons. A straightforward example is erasing a line, when there must be some means of specifying the line concerned. Similarly, drawing a line requires the user to indicate the two end-points. At a more complex level, repositioning an object can be conveniently done by 'dragging' it across the screen. By continual adjustment of the position of an object it can easily be placed against a wall, say, or adjacent to another object. There are several other requirements that involve positional indication; they include recentring the drawing, and specifying the starting point of text.

The most famous device for indicating points on the screen is the light pen. This is a tube that signals the computer when it is placed over a line on the screen. It can only work with refresh screens. As the line under the pen is redrawn it will generate a signal; then by inspection of the point reached by the display processor in the instruction list, the screen position can be deduced. The use of a light pen is shown diagrammatically in *Figure 3.21.*

Despite the traditional popularity of the light pen, it has a number of serious drawbacks. The most important of these is that it cannot directly signal on the screen a position that is not on a line. To do this, the user must use the light pen to drag a pair of cross-hairs or other marking indicator across the screen. This is slow and clumsy, and puts a lot of extra strain on the computer, which is being signalled for a new pen position numerous times every second. Other problems with the light pen are that it is unreliable for faint lines or for lines near the edge of the screen. It is not particularly precise, and it is very poor ergonomically as the user has to hold the pen perpendicular to a vertical screen as he draws, which

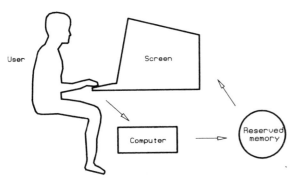

Figure 3.20 Raster screen organisation

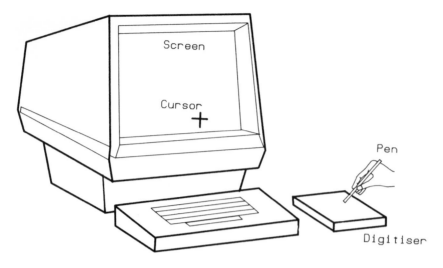

Figure 3.22 The use of a small digitiser

is very tiring. For these reasons, the light pen is being supplanted by other devices.

One such alternative is the digitiser, also called a pencil follower or tablet. This is a rectangular block, positions on which correspond to positions on the screen. A special pen is used which generates a signal when it is placed on the surface of the digitiser; its placing is conventionally reflected by a pair of cross-hairs displayed on the screen. The user can therefore indicate any desired position on the screen by feeding back the position of the cross-hairs into movements of the hand. This quickly becomes automatic and so provides a fast, efficient and ergonomically acceptable method of positional indication. The arrangement is shown diagrammatically in *Figure 3.22*. Another popular device is the joystick. As its name implies, it is a small lever that can be moved freely in two dimensions. Like the digitiser, it is used in feedback mode. The use of a joystick is shown diagrammatically in *Figure 3.23*.

A digitiser used solely to indicate points on a screen will usually be only a few centimetres square and rest under the right hand. However, it is possible to obtain digitisers up to A0 size. A device of this size has the advantage that a full-size drawing can be placed on it and traced over, thus inputting it into the computer. In this case the user tends to be working at the digitiser and only occasionally glancing at the screen to ensure that coordinates are being accepted. *Figure 3.24* shows a large digitiser in use. Another advantage of a large digitiser is that a section of it can be reserved for a 'menu' of special operations. For example, there could be a number of small squares, each marked with a different pre-drawn element. Placing the pen in one of the squares would call up the appropriate element. This use of the digitiser corresponds to the use of function keys, but far more options are possible than are provided by the usual dozen or so function keys.

Digitisers are especially useful for inputting arbitrary shapes such as contour lines. In this case it is usual for the computer to sample the position of the pen at fixed distance intervals or at fixed time intervals, so as not to collect too much data. A drawback of digitisers is that their large size makes them rather unwieldy; they take up as much space as a drawing board. They are also expensive; even a small digitiser will cost several thousand pounds, while a joystick is a fraction of that sum.

There are several other types of positional indicator, but the light pen, joystick and digitiser are the most common.

Figure 3.23 The use of a joystick

At some time copies of the drawing held inside the computer will have to be made on paper for issue. Copies of A4 size can be made by means of a hardcopy unit as already described in the section on time-sharing equipment. These units produce their output in a few seconds and are excellent for obtaining results for discussion or to give an impression of the situation. The output is, however, expensive and of unacceptable quality for most formal issues. The A4 size is also, of course, too small in many circumstances.

Full-size drawings require a plotter. Computer plotters are possibly the most primitive of all the common peripheral devices, probably reflecting the fact that most of their work consists of outputting results in the form of graphs and diagrams rather than quality work. Most plotters fall into one of two categories: flatbed and drum. Flatbed plotters work by moving a pen over a static sheet of paper, typically A0 in size. They can give very accurate results, and can accept any sort of paper, but they are rather expensive. A typical flatbed plotter is shown in *Figure 3.25*.

Figure 3.24 A large digitiser in use (courtesy SIA Ltd)

Figure 3.25 A flatbed plotter (courtesy Benson Electronics)

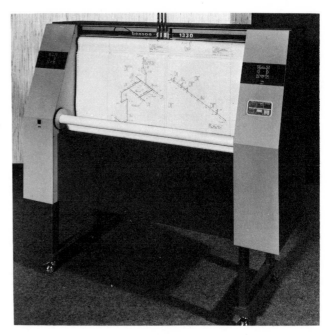

Figure 3.26 A drum plotter (courtesy Benson Electronics)

On a drum plotter (*Figure 3.26*), the paper runs over a drum that can rotate in either direction. A pen (or pens) is positioned above the drum and can move along the axis in either direction. Thus by combining the movements of the drum and the pen, lines can be produced at any angle. Drum plotters are relatively cheap and are usually sufficiently accurate for architectural practice.

Although in theory lines can be drawn in any direction, for mechanical reasons most plotters of both types are limited to movements in one of eight or occasionally sixteen directions. Lines which do not correspond to any of these directions are approximated by combinations of the standard directions in steps of typically 0.05mm in length. This usually gives a reasonable result, but lines which are very close but not quite concurrent with a standard direction often look very jagged.

Plotters usually provide a choice of three pens to use on a single drawing, and these can be selected by program. For architectural drawings, different thickness ink pens will normally be used as only these can give a drawing that will make a correct photocopy. However, different coloured ballpoint or felt-tipped pens are also available and these have the great advantage that they rarely dry up. Ink pens need careful cleaning and maintenance if they are not to dry up; the thinner nib sizes especially can cause a lot of trouble.

The faster plotters have a character set programmed into them, so that letters and numbers do not have to be made up of short individual lines. This does not have to be used if the user prefers a different style of lettering, but it is obviously much faster and more efficient to use the built-in set. The plotter's character set may, however, be restricted. For instance, it may not have lower-case letters and it will therefore be inefficient to use lower case even though it is available on the screen.

Plotting a large drawing is a slow business; it will normally take at least half an hour for a reasonably complex A0 sheet. This can be a serious problem with interactive draughting because most minicomputers can only do one thing at a time, so that when the computer is sending a drawing to the plotter, it cannot be used for any other purpose. One solution is to leave the computer to plot out the drawings overnight, but this is not very satisfactory because it is bad practice to leave a machine unattended. If a pen should dry up, for instance, an entire night's work may be wasted. Fortunately, the most modern minicomputers have extra circuitry that enables them to drive peripheral devices such as a plotter or a printer in the background while still giving their main attention to the user. This capability is known as 'spooling', which is an acronym for 'Simultaneous Peripheral Operation On Line'.

On a world-wide basis the plotter market is dominated by the American-based firm of Calcomp, but in Europe the firm of Benson Electronics Ltd is making 70%–80% of the sales at present.

An alternative to plotters is the electrostatic printer/plotters manufactured by several firms. These machines work by outputting dots at intervals of about 0.13mm across the width of the paper. By controlling the printing of the dots it is possible to produce alphanumeric results or drawings. Electrostatic plotters are very fast — a full-size drawing can typically be output in less than a minute — and they are also quieter and more reliable than conventional plotters. They are obtainable in various sizes; the biggest ones can accept paper 90 cm wide and so can produce A0-size drawings. The drawbacks are that the quality of line is not as good as that of a pen plotter and also that such units are very expensive. Coloured plots are of course unobtainable, but this will not usually be of much concern in architectural working. One interesting capability of electrostatic plotters is that they can provide half-tone illustrations like the one shown in *Figure 3.27*.

An ingenious alternative plotting method has been developed by the British firm of Laser-Scan. Their machine uses a laser beam and a moving mirror to trace lines onto microfilm. Very high quality, fast and accurate plots can be obtained at relatively low cost. However, the price of the machines themselves is high, and few purely architectural practices could justify the purchase of one.

Microcomputers and personal computing

With advancing technology it has become possible to construct more and more circuit elements on a single minute piece of silicon, which is a semiconducting material. Such constructions are known as 'integrated circuits' or, colloquially, 'chips'. The use of integrated circuits has led to computers becoming more powerful and capable of dealing with large problems and with many users, but perhaps paradoxically it has also led to the development of machines that are actually much less powerful than those formerly available.

A special type of integrated circuit is one that contains the entire calculating portion of a computer, in a necessarily rather simplified form. Such integrated circuits are called 'microprocessors' and form the basis of a range of computing devices. They are also being used in many other areas where cheap and relatively low-speed processing power has advantages over existing methods. Microprocessor-based computing machines are cheap and compact — the smaller ones fitting easily into a pocket — but their power and speed is limited. They are therefore suited to individual possession and use rather than the shared use that the cost and capabilities of mainframes or minicomputers make necessary and are consequently often referred to generically as 'personal computing' devices.

The simplest personal computing device is the pocket calculator. These became generally available in the early 1970s and have fixed programs built in that enable them to carry out the four basic arithmetical functions of addition, subtraction, multiplication and division. Many also have additional functions such as square root extraction or exponentiation.

The addition of another integrated circuit to provide a block of memory results in a device that is much more flexible, because the memory can be loaded with user-selected programs to control lengthy sequences of calculation as in a more conventional computer. A device with this facility is called a 'programmable calculator'. Programmable calculators are slow by computer standards, having about one-tenth the speed of a minicomputer and one-hundredth that of a mainframe computer, and have very little storage capacity; some models have a maximum capacity as low as 64 numbers. Despite their restrictions, their extreme convenience means that in many cases programs can be written that can with advantage replace rules of thumb, scratch-pad calculations or reference to tables.

Programs can be loaded directly by pressing keys on the calculator, but once loaded they can be stored on small magnetic cards and reinput as required. It is therefore possible for each user to build up a library of programs by writing them himself or by purchasing them from a commercial organisation.

The programs cannot be very large because of the limitations of memory size and microprocessor speed, but nevertheless many of the calculations required during the design of a building can be automated. For example, during the outline design stage, checks

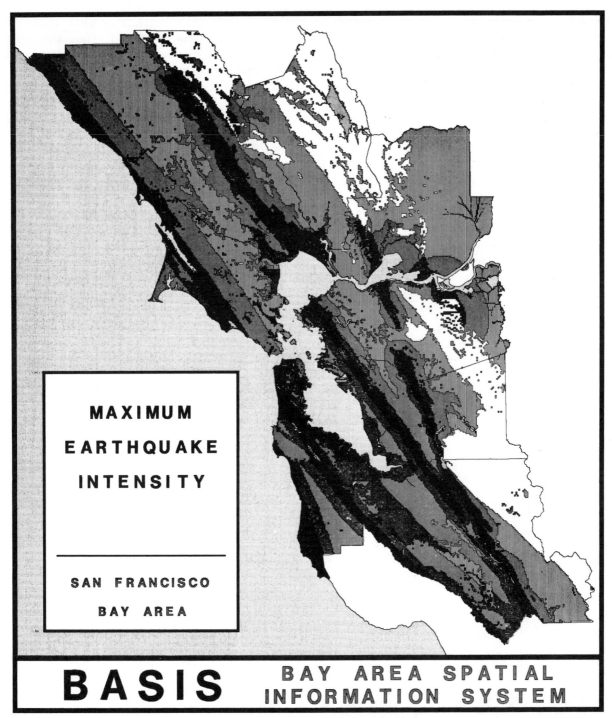

MAXIMUM

EARTHQUAKE

INTENSITY

SAN FRANCISCO

BAY AREA

BASIS   BAY AREA SPATIAL
INFORMATION SYSTEM

Figure 3.27 An output from an electrostatic plotter (courtesy Benson Electronics)

on column spacing and beam sizes will confirm that the structural basis is sound; heat loss and daylight factor calculations can be used to guide the shape and orientation of the building; and a variety of checks can be made on, for example, building regulation requirements, or the ratio of usable to circulatory space. At the detail design stage, programs can calculate the correct roof and drainage falls; the size of stair treads and risers; the U-values of the fabric; reverberation times; the glare from lighting fittings; or condensation risks. Running small programs like these can speed up design and produce a building

that is designed to closer tolerances and is therefore cheaper, and may make practicable comprehensive checks that might otherwise not be done at all.

To be portable, a programmable calculator must be severely limited in physical size and so cannot have peripheral devices such as a comfortably sized keyboard or sizeable storage devices. Printers are available for some programmable calculators, but they are proportionately very bulky and use paper that is only a few centimetres wide. *Figure 3.28* shows a popular programmable calculator mounted in a print cradle.

In order to provide facilities equivalent to those found on larger computers, more elaborate machines have been built around microprocessors called 'microcomputers'. These devices are relatively large — bigger than the average typewriter for instance — and are not intended to be portable. They can support a reasonable amount of memory, often as much as a minicomputer, and can drive peripherals such as teleprinters, cassette storage units, or visual display screens. High-level languages are usually available and this makes the machines much easier to program than programmable calculators. A popular microcomputer which has some graphics capability is shown in *Figure 3.29*.

Microcomputers were originally developed for the hobbyist, but are beginning to be used for simple business applications as a cheap alternative to a minicomputer. Microcomputers are faster than programmable calculators, but still have only half the speed of a minicomputer. As an illustration, an advanced microcomputer takes about five seconds to perform 1000 simple additions when programmed in a high-level language. The range of applications that can be handled is therefore limited in practice by the computational speed. When using a computer interactively, delays over, say, ten seconds start to become irritating to the user. Batch runs, where the machine is given the data and left for a few hours to solve the problem, are practicable, but of course repeated runs with modified data start to take up a lot of time.

Within their limitations, however, microcomputers can be very useful and can give basic computer power and experience to an office that could not otherwise justify a machine. Typical applications include detailed environmental analyses, cut-and-fill optimisation, scheduling equipment, critical path analysis, and office accounting. The nature of microcomputers makes them basically unsuited to tasks that require a lot of calculation or long searches of files on magnetic storage systems. Thus, for example, simulations will often take a prohibitively long time on a microcomputer because it is normally necessary to investigate thousands of separate activities. Database interrogation and updating is also often impracticable because it can easily take several minutes to find a single item in a reasonably sized file of information.

Several manufacturers now make microcomputers that are primarily intended for graphical applications. At present, however, they are comparable in price to a minicomputer, possibly because of the cost of the screen and other necessary peripherals. The processing-speed limitation means that large drawings cannot be manipulated without unacceptable delays, but microcomputers have been used to investigate the light and shade patterns on building elevations[10] and in the design of specialised but relatively small areas, such as kitchens and laboratories.

Figure 3.28 A programmable calculator and print cradle (courtesy RIBA Publications Ltd)

Figure 3.29 A popular microcomputer (courtesy Baroness International Public Relations)

Analogue computers

All the computers described so far have been of the type known as digital computers because they actually hold exact numbers, and this type is by far the most flexible and the most widespread. There are, however, several other principles on which to build computers, one of the best known of which is the analogue principle. An analogue computer uses different amounts of some physical quantity to represent numbers; thus a slide rule could be considered an analogue computer because length represents a quantity and cannot be measured exactly. An abacus is a type of digital computer because numbers are held directly and exactly as a row of beads. In practice, a large analogue computer will almost always use electrical voltage for its representative medium.

Analogue computers are faster than digital computers because the problem is solved as a whole rather than one step at a time. However, they can only be used for certain very restricted classes of problem, notably those involving differential equations. Digital computers are much more versatile and therefore suitable for a greater variety of applications.

Installing equipment

After the broad strategy of an office's approach to computing has been decided upon, decisions on the specific items of equipment to order have to be made. The method of financing this investment has also to be decided.

Getting information is not likely to be difficult these days; in fact the problem is that the choice is so wide as to be bewildering. The names of likely manufacturers can be obtained from the trade literature or from classified lists, and when contacted the manufacturers are invariably happy to send information about their products and to arrange demonstrations. The various exhibitions of computing machinery that take place throughout the year also provide opportunities to see what equipment is available. However, as there are, for example, hundreds of different models of terminal available, it is necessary to narrow the field to a handful of possibilities.

There exist organisations that can offer independent advice on equipment and on other matters, and some of these are listed in Chapter 13. Such organisations are normally aware of what other practices have installed and can usually arrange visits to see the machinery in use in a working environment. The study of working installations is probably the best basis on which to make a decision for a firm that lacks extensive experience. Although working methods can differ between offices, it can in general be said that the installations will have already encountered most of the problems and found ways around them. They may also be a source of the 'fill-in' programs that are often required to bridge gaps that the manufacturer has left.

It can be dangerous to leave the important decisions to the office's computing specialists. There is a common tendency for such people to be seduced by the glamour of high technology into advising the purchase of the latest and most highly advanced pieces of equipment; and such items are normally not very reliable. The famous slogan, 'if it works, it's obsolete' is not one that is acceptable outside academic organisations.

In fact, it is most unwise to pioneer anything, either in machinery or in programs. There are invariably many problems that only show up in actual use when the equipment is exposed to the wide range of applications found in the field. To get round these problems needs a lot of experience and determination; and unless an office has a great deal of confidence in its own abilities it is better to let someone else provide these qualities. Machinery that has been in use for some time will usually have settled down and the major teething troubles will have been identified and eliminated. It is important to make a reasonable investment in machinery right from the start. Attempts to cut the costs, intending to increase the budget later if things go well, are not advisable.

Starting off is difficult enough anyway, and if extra effort has to go into fighting inadequate machinery or in improvising to make up for missing facilities, development will take place very slowly.

The question of financing the equipment can be a difficult one. Outright purchase can be the best method if it is clear that the equipment will be kept for a long time, but the bigger installations may require a large chunk of a firm's budget. If the office has an unusually large job in hand at about that time, outright purchase may be a good way of absorbing excess cash that would otherwise be heavily taxed.

Leasing is an excellent option because of the rapidity with which equipment becomes obsolete and also because, as the office develops, it will wish to expand its computing capabilities. It also means, of course, that the outgoings per month are much less onerous. A problem is that leasing is expensive at present because of the prevalent high interest rates. A three-year lease costs about 40% of the purchase price every year, while a five-year lease costs about 30% of the purchase price each year. At these rates, leasing becomes less attractive, but the decision must be made on the basis of how much capital is available and on what plans a firm has for the future.

Working methods with computers

To operate the computer, a full-time specialist is a necessity. It is tempting to think of each architect coming to the computer with his data and running the programs appropriate to his problem, but this is not in fact practicable. There are literally dozens of detailed operations to be performed even to access the computer, and then perhaps hundreds to put in the data, correct it and run the program. Although these are trivial in themselves, it requires a lot of training and practice to become familiar with the procedures; even experienced operators will forget the exact forms if they have not used them for some time, and will have to consult the instruction manuals. Individual architects will have neither the time nor the inclination to become conversant with the details, but will require an intermediary.

Another problem is that architects are normally not particularly good typists, and so even simple questions can become slow and tedious when they are picked out at the terminal one letter at a time. It is more efficient if the architects state what they want to know and an operator is available to translate the query into the formalised language the computer will understand and type it in. A recent study by the University of Manchester Institute of Science and Technology showed that the use of a trained intermediary can cut computer costs to one-sixth of those incurred by casual users[51].

It is then necessary to decide who the operator is to be. It is a full-time job, and so it is not possible to assign one of the architects with an interest in that sort of thing, unless he or she is to give up designing. It is also not as simple as hiring a programmer, of whom there are many around these days, because there will then often arise what has been termed the 'whizz-kid barrier'. This occurs when a programmer is not really conversant with an architect's problems and the architect does not really understand the capabilities and limitations of the computer. In this situation the programmer tends to write or select programs he thinks may help, but which are often completely irrelevant. Thus there arises a barrier which is aggravated by the programmer's talking about the subject in terms that are quite incomprehensible to the average architect. What happens then is that both sides decide to leave each other alone; the architect continues with his manual procedures and the programmer goes away and writes a succession of experimental programs that he occasionally tests on small jobs. These programs are rarely of any use. Often the computer section will come to think in terms of rivalry with the architects instead of regarding themselves as providing a service.

This has happened to a number of practices; they support a computer section so as to feel that they are keeping up with the times, but these sections are perpetually in the process of research and development and do not impinge on the work of the office at all. Such departments have, for all practical purposes, degenerated into being exercises in public relations; they write magazine articles on their work and are able to impress visiting clients with their grasp of advanced technology. However, even seen as a public relations exercise they can hardly give the best results for the amount of money that must be invested in them.

One way to avoid the whizz-kid barrier is to have someone to act as a systems analyst. This is a sort of liaison man, who should have some familiarity with both architecture and computers and can therefore interpret between the groups. As this can be a part-time job, it could be handled by an architect with an interest in computers. Although this will improve communication, and a determined systems analyst can get good results from the computer group, it is a rather clumsy and unsatisfactory solution.

The best solution, and one widely adopted, is to get an architect trained in computer techniques to operate the machine. To do this he will largely have to give up designing and other purely architectural tasks and devote himself to this new discipline. Architects with the required skills and temperament are not as rare as might be supposed. Computer programming is a regular feature at many schools of architecture and some young architects come to specialise in this field much as others might in building technology or environmental control. The

great advantage of this solution is that there are no longer two sides; all parties speak the same language and regard themselves as part of the design team. As the computer operator is tackling the problems directly and with full understanding of the implications, he has the ability to make the programs both relevant and easy to use.

The staff selected to work with and to organise the use of computers should be given some working space that is near the machinery, but which is preferably not too isolated from the rest of the office. This can be difficult to arrange, because some items of equipment are noisy, but cooperation may well be hindered if the other members of the staff feel that the computer is in some way estranged from the rest of the office.

Space must also be found for data storage and for the results of computer runs. The results may occupy anything from a few centimetres of shelf space on a small job to several metres on a very large one; thus storage space may be quite considerable and a firm line should be taken about keeping outputs 'just in case' they are needed. In fact, if all intermediate outputs and updates are kept the mass of paper will greatly hinder checking. Shelf space is also needed for the many instruction manuals on using the computer and its programs, for periodicals, and for manufacturers' literature.

One of the principal problems of the computing staff will be to gain the trust and cooperation of the other workers. It is a common misapprehension that architects will flock to use the computer once it is available. In fact, the best that can be expected is wary interest. The worst is complete dismissal of the entire concept. The computer section must therefore go out and try to persuade the architects to use the machine. This involves publicising themselves and offering to take over some of the work on a project. A specific offer of doing some necessary task will rarely be refused, especially if it is one that most architects find uninteresting, such as scheduling, and it is one of the best ways of introducing architects to the possibilities of automation.

Talks, seminars and films are not so useful; difficulty is often found in relating the abstract ideas to the practical aids and they often only serve the purpose of boring or confusing the people they are meant to instruct. It is far better to show results than talk about them. Once designers can be shown that certain tasks can be done better by computers and with little adaptation on their part, they will normally be converted and actually ask for similar assistance on their next job. It is at this point that some of the less obvious aids, such as design evaluation or job management, can be offered to them and they will approach them in a more receptive mood. The attitude is important, as unless there is some determination to overcome the inevitable difficulties, the trial will be abandoned and will merely increase scepticism.

It is important that the computer keeps up with the design team. If, say, standard room-data sheets cannot be produced within a couple of days, the team will have done the job manually and the effort will be wasted. It is therefore necessary to produce everything as quickly as possible and, moreover, to keep it up to date. There is a temptation to save money by not updating documents until there are a large number of corrections to be made; this should be resisted because the computer documentation will be discredited if the user finds even one or two discrepancies and he will tend to look at the drawing instead, thus making the whole exercise pointless. Also, a large number of corrections will take longer to prepare and to check and so will cause unnecessary delays at some later time.

It is better not to start with a small job. Although it seems sensible to use such a job in order to find out the problems and pitfalls, in fact the problems encountered on a large job are radically different to those found on a small one, because if there is not a great deal of data it is often more efficient to perform certain stages by manual methods, whereas on a large job the same task may not even be practicable by hand. There is also the consideration that a large job will gain more from computer assistance and so the initial mistakes and false starts will not be so noticeable.

The architect must not be expected to indulge in any extended data-collection exercises. If he is asked to make a list of, say, all the doors in the building in a logical manner suitable for scheduling, he will prefer to go a little further and do the whole thing manually, thus increasing his control over the job for relatively little effort. If the data is more abstruse, such as the likely traffic between different areas in the building being designed, the job will probably not be done at all. It is therefore up to the computer section to organise data collection. This is almost inevitably a long and tedious task, but is essential if results are to be obtained.

It will be found that a couple of years will be needed to get the computer aids working smoothly and for the users to become familiar with the complications and possible short cuts. In that time it should be possible to get most of the office accepting the machine and making use of it on many of their jobs.

4
Choosing programs

Program availability

A computer is no better than the programs run on it, but it is not easy to obtain useful and reliable programs; in fact the pitfalls in this area make even the second-hand car market look unhazardous. After well over a decade of development this might seem a surprising statement. It might be expected that by now most of the basic programs would have been written and become well known as their use spread. The trouble is that the capabilities of computers have increased so much and so fast that they have outstripped program development. Computer manufacturers have poured hundreds of millions of pounds into designing and perfecting the machinery, but only a small fraction of that into program development. Virtually no effort has been put by the manufacturers into writing programs specifically for use by architects, as they have, say, for engineers or accountants. Presumably this is because architecture is not a rich profession and cannot afford to buy much machinery anyway.

Thus almost all programs used in the construction industry have been written by those directly concerned, and the sums involved are better measured in thousands rather than in millions of pounds. Also, the programs that were written, say, five years ago, now seem unacceptably crude and limited because computers are now capable of so much more than they were then; thus the same problems are being tackled again and again in more elaborate ways as the computers offer more capabilities that can be harnessed. Programming is still an art rather than a science and even with the extra aids afforded by high-level languages and standardised coding for commonly encountered problems, it can still take years to develop a good program.

For these reasons the range of programs available is not particularly wide, and many of them are obsolescent. Another and worse problem is that many programs are of little or no use, but it is only possible to ascertain this fact with a great deal of effort. The problem is common because it is relatively easy to write some sort of program, and once it is inside the machine it is only possible to tell how much work went into the program by its performance on a variety of tasks. Therefore the potential user may be deceived as to the usefulness of the program by means of glossy literature and carefully arranged documentation.

Having separated the wheat from the chaff, there is the additional problem that programs, even those written in high-level languages, are usually not easily transportable between different machines. Therefore, unless a version of the program required is available for the computer in use, a long and expensive conversion process must be undertaken.

Purpose-written programs

The obvious solution to these problems is for each user to write his own program. This seems a good idea, because the exact requirements can be specified and the programs written for any computer. Also, any problems that appear in use or any extra capabilities that may be required in the future can be handled quickly by the user's staff. Unfortunately, considerations of cost and lead time often rule out this course of action. A relatively simple program of 1000 instructions costs about £400 in computer time to write and takes about two man-months, given a good programmer. As the size of the program goes up, the costs and time increase out of proportion because of interactions within the program; thus a 4000-instruction program costs about £4000 in computer time and takes at least nine man-months to write. Above this level of complexity it will not usually be possible for one man to handle the project by himself, and there will therefore be additional losses due to communication between the programmers. Organisations exist that will write programs to order, but despite the gains of professionalism they are extremely expensive, charging typically £50 per day for a programmer plus computer costs. Therefore, for all but the simplest programs there must be a large cash investment and a lengthy lead time before the program can be put into use; for most offices this is not an economic or even a possible solution.

Package programs

Because of this, the current trend is strongly towards ready-made programs, usually called 'package' programs. The capital cost is relatively low as the development and documentation costs can be spread and, just as importantly, the maintenance costs are low and do not require the user to assign staff to this job. There is no lead time and usually a trial with a live job can be arranged to ensure that the program is relevant to the problems involved. There is also often the possibility of using the package on a royalty basis at a commercial bureau. Under this system the user will pay an extra percentage, typically 30%–40%, on the basic cost of the run. This will usually work out cheaper than an outright purchase, unless a great deal of data or very frequent runs are required.

The penalty paid for the use of package programs is that the user must adjust his manner of working to the standard method laid down by the designer of the programs and this may often conflict with the normal office procedure or may be so general, in order to be able to handle a wide range of cases, that it is inefficient or clumsy when dealing with a more restricted set of problems. A good package, however, will be usable in a natural sort of fashion which sometimes turns out to be better than the procedure the user has adopted up to that time. In any case, some changes in the manner of working have to be expected when changing from manual to computer methods.

Information sources

The first step in choosing programs is to find out what is available. The most convenient way to do this is to study one of the several guides to computers in the construction industry that are available. The most well-known of these at present are listed in the Bibliography[40,42]. Such guides normally give a brief description of the aims of each program, the machines on which it is available, and the name of the marketing organisation. They are usually organised so that programs performing the same tasks are listed together; thus the prospective user can see the choice in any application area. Additionally, browsing through these guides is a convenient way of finding out what scope computer aids might have within an office.

Some guides are available that only list programs dealing with a specific topic such as daylight analysis[106] or critical-path techniques[89]. They can, of course, go into much more detail and provide illustrations of typical data and outputs as well as much more information on the facilities available. They also often give the results of running sets of test data through the programs; this sort of comparison is obviously extremely useful to the prospective user. Unfortunately, preparing such guides is very expensive and they date quickly. Consequently, they are not available on a very wide range of applications.

Owing to the inevitable time-lag in collating and publishing such guides, by the time they are available they are generally a year or so out of date. In such a fast-moving field as computing, this can mean that very good recent programs will not be listed. A fruitful field for obtaining information on the existence and capabilities of the most important new programs is at conferences on computer-aided design. Papers are often presented on recently written programs describing the philosophy behind them and giving an evaluation of their utility in practice. These conferences are usually expensive to attend and it is possible to save money by only buying a copy of the published proceedings rather than attending in person, although of course personal attendance makes it possible to question the presenter of the paper directly on specific points.

Care must be taken before using these programs because many of them will have been written for research purposes to determine, for example, if a certain approach to a problem is feasible, or to test if a previously non-computer-aided task can be automated. Such programs, that probe the limit of technology, may not be suitable for use in an office environment.

An inherent restriction in both the above sources of information is that many programs that are useful to architects are of such a general nature that they will not be listed with programs specific to the construction industry. A good example is programs that can produce schedules; schedules are of use throughout the entire business field and can be very valuable to architects, but unless the program has special facilities to handle architectural information more readily than other types it will not be included in a list of architectural programs. Programs for simulation, survey analysis, and management control also come into this category. Therefore, in order to find programs to solve certain classes of problem, it is necessary to find other sources of information.

A useful source is one of the independent bodies concerned with computing matters, most of which maintain indexes of currently available programs. Some details of such organisations are given in Chapter 13. Commercial computer bureaux are also a fruitful field of enquiry as they usually offer a wide range of general application programs. If a few bureaux are contacted, basic documentation on a number of programs can be built up, and representatives are normally available to discuss specific programs in more detail.

A list of the programs of interest available can therefore be compiled from various sources. It will often be found on closer inquiry, however, that few of these programs are actually usable. The problem can be illustrated by the experiences of the UK's Design Office Consortium when they were evaluating programs to produce building perspectives[76]. Of the original thirty programs mentioned in the literature, only seven were available in the UK; the rest were obsolete programs with no support provided, programs of purely academic interest, or programs written in the USA with no agent in Britain. Of the seven, two were excluded as not really suitable and two because of insufficient support; thus in the end only one program in ten of those on current lists was actually usable.

Limitations on program use

Even this shortened list must often be shortened still further, because the user will not have a choice of any computer, but must use the one owned by the time-sharing bureau he has a contract with, or the one owned by his organisation. In theory, any program written in a high-level language can be freely moved between computers. There is a special category of program called 'compilers', several of which will exist in a typical computer; their function is to translate a program written in a standardised high-level language into the basic instructions that drive the computer. These basic instructions vary from machine to machine, and even within a manufacturer's range, and so transportable programs cannot use them. Unfortunately, in practice a program written for a compiler on one machine will not usually be accepted by a compiler on another.

There are a number of reasons for this, but one of the principal ones is that a program must communicate with the outside world if it is to be of any use; it must use data files, send output to various peripheral devices, and perhaps interact with the user at a teleprinter, and the characteristics of these matters are not subject to any standardisation. For example, something as simple as a different width on the printers belonging to different machines may entail long and involved rewriting of a program.

Another important reason is that, because of the influence of its basic instruction set, every computer has its particular strengths; to take advantage of these, and also presumably to have extra selling points, every manufacturer adds extra features to its version of a high-level language and may also drop certain features that are difficult to implement or inefficient on its machine. A programmer who has concern for efficiency and thus economy will tend to make use of the additional features, but it is exactly these features that make the program untransportable. With some languages this problem is worse than others. Fortran, for example, was last standardised in 1966 and did not include many features taken for granted today; therefore every compiler greatly extends the standards and every Fortran programmer is virtually forced to use these extensions since otherwise his programs are much clumsier and more limited. There is some consensus of opinion on the extensions, and most conform to an informal standard, but there are always many minor features that will need alteration when moving between compilers.

At the time of writing, a new standard for Fortran is proposed and in future the problems may become less acute.

There are similar problems with most other languages. Cobol, for example, often exists in its basic standardised state on small machines, but on larger machines often offers many more facilities, such as automatic file sorting or report generation. The original specification of Algol did not lay down any standards at all for reading in information or printing out results; this was done on grounds of efficiency but has meant in practice that it is difficult to transport programs in this language. A new standard for Algol does now exist which supplies this lack, but it is not yet widely implemented.

A high-level language has a limited vocabulary and so will impose constraints on the programmer, preventing him from making full use of the capabilities of the computer. A complex program may often need to go beyond these constraints; for example, in graphics applications where only a few and uncommon languages are capable of anything but the simplest operations. In such cases the programmer may need to write a portion of the program in the machine's assembly language: a language tied very closely to the computer's basic instructions and therefore capable of exploiting all its abilities, but one that requires complete rewriting of the program if it is to run on a different machine.

For all these reasons a program written for one machine will not run on another without conversion. Also, the less conversion a program needs, the more likely it is to be unsophisticated and inefficient. Conversion is always a slow and expensive process and if the person who wrote the program in the first place is not available it is usually cheaper to forget the whole idea of conversion and rewrite from the beginning. This is because a program is a difficult thing to understand; one must try to comprehend the sections of code as entities and from this deduce their purposes. If adequate documentation is available this is easier, but such documentation is not very often produced in detail because of the time it takes, and therefore the original designer is frequently the only person competent to make changes.

Some package programs are available for several machines, but they usually need sizeable teams of programmers to do this. One database-management program that is available in versions suitable for four computer ranges has a team of 200 to support it; this sort of effort is obviously beyond the scope of any architectural practice. The situation with minicomputers is even worse. Because of their limitations, programs for them are most often written in assembly language, and are therefore untransportable. Those that are written in high-level languages cannot normally be written in a general way, because inefficiency is such a problem on a small machine, and therefore conversion is made more difficult. One way to avoid conversion problems is to use different computer bureaux. There are so many of these that a machine of almost any type can usually be found. The difficulty is that changing machines leads to a great deal of confusion because of the different operating procedures, and this will be reflected in higher computing costs.

The amount of memory a computer has, or the types of peripheral devices it has connected to itself, can also hinder or prevent conversion. For example, programs to draw perspectives can normally only build up to a certain maximum complexity. This limit of complexity is set by the machine's memory capacity, and if this is too low the results may be unacceptable. Or, say, a scheduling program may only be able to handle a maximum number of items, which might involve having to break the job down into floors or departments in order to handle it.

Clearly, a program cannot be transported to another machine if some essential type of peripheral device is not available. However, the vendor may state that with some changes in procedure it will run without this device; but it may well be that without it the program is far more clumsy in use, possibly so much more as to destroy its cost-effectiveness.

Documentation

We have seen that the user must not only discover a suitable program, but also check that he has access to a machine on which it can be run. Having done this, the next step is to communicate with the vendors to ascertain more details.

The response to such queries can vary from a single photocopied sheet of typing to a glossy full-colour brochure full of pictures of smiling users and pretty machine operators; but in general, documentation falls naturally into two kinds. The first is a short glossy leaflet, usually from four to eight pages long and printed in one or two colours. This will describe the program in the sort of lyrical prose perfected by estate agents and will give a general idea of the problems that the program is capable of solving. The leaflet is free and is normally intended to make a quick impression on potential users in a wide range of trades; it cannot therefore go into the details of the amount of data required, or the types of output available, and cannot adequately describe the program from a particular user's point of view.

To comprehend the program more fully, the second kind of documentation is required: the user's manual. This is usually only issued on request and can be expensive. However, it is necessary to obtain such a manual to gain more insight into the value of a program for a particular application. The user's manual has to be written for someone familiar with the operation of the computer. It is therefore not usually comprehensible to an inexperienced person

and, even if understood, the implications of certain features may be overlooked.

The manual describes the specific actions of the program; it is therefore possible to pick up, sometimes by implication, a lot of information on the program's scope and validity. An example of the sort of vital point that may be omitted from the short summary is the number of assumptions made by the program. A serious fault of many programs, especially those that perform evaluations, is to make too many assumptions. Often there will be a file of 'basic information' which gives precise specifications for, say, the amount of glazing in a building, the cost of land and labour in different parts of the country, or the maximum gradient of roads to be built. It is possible to alter this file, but the required statistics may be difficult to collect, completely dwarfing the time that the program aims to save. However, accepting the basic information may give a solution inappropriate to the type of building in question.

If literature is not available on a program, or is brief and scrappy, the issuing organisation is probably not really committed to marketing programs, but is doing so after having written the program for some other reason. This reason is often the solution of an in-house problem, and so the program is not necessarily useless. However, care should be taken that it is not so tied in with a particular way of working as to make it unusable by anybody else, and a proper user's manual must be prepared before the program is purchased or it may prove impossible for anybody but the person that wrote it actually to use it. Documentation is always a long, tedious and expensive process, and so programmers are often unwilling to produce it, but it is absolutely essential not to have to rely on memory or precedent.

Unfortunately, it is not true to say that very good documentation must mean a good program. It may be expensive to produce documentation, but it is even more expensive to write a long program. Thus it is relatively easy to prepare a glossy description that makes an obsolescent or merely inadequate program look superficially good. Such bluffs are quite common, and can be difficult to detect until one actually tries to use the program.

Demonstrations and discussions

Assuming that the potential user's interest in the program still survives, he will normally want to see a demonstration mounted and talk over the details with the vendors.

Pre-arranged demonstrations can obviously be organised to bring out the best points and gloss over the worst; and in fact they usually are so arranged. One almost inevitable failing is that the basic data will come already prepared and in small quantities.

Hence it is not possible to evaluate directly how tedious or difficult the data is to prepare, and this must be deduced from careful study of the input. Also, the final costs of the demonstration will be unrealistically low, whereas a run with a full-size set of data might be prohibitively expensive.

Whatever its size, the situation that the data reflects will be the most favourable one for the program, although this is not always obvious at first sight. For example, a draughting program will often avoid curved lines that are not arcs or circles, because they are difficult to input; a perspective program will avoid all curved surfaces, because they have to be broken down into many inefficient and usually unattractive flat surfaces; and a scheduling program will avoid special cases, because they are clumsy to handle. If the vendor agrees, the best way to circumvent this is actually to send on, in advance, a portion of a real job in the office to be put through the program. The amount of data needed to represent it and the results and costs obtained should give a reasonably accurate picture of the validity of the program.

Some demonstrations are pre-recorded onto cassettes, and are played back a bit at a time with the demonstrator explaining the significance of each portion. This sort of demonstration is not really acceptable; it is too easy to cut out or edit the mistakes and awkward or lengthy pauses and leave an entirely false impression. The demonstrator has plenty of opportunity to practice the session and ought not to need additional advantages. Naturally, a film can give an even more misleading impression of the ease of use of a program, although a good film can use diagrams and close-ups to give a better idea of the scope and capabilities of the program than could be communicated at an almost entirely verbal demonstration.

One failing of some vendors of computer programs is to 'sell ahead': that is, to claim that certain improvements are being made to the program that will make it much more powerful or more useful for a particular application. Such claims are probably genuine, but should be ignored. It takes a long time to write, test and document a modification properly, and by then some other program may be on the market. Typical elapsed times between the decision to make a modification and its appearance in the commercial version are 1½–2 years. As the whole field is one of continuous and rapid development the next program will always be a better one, so a decision should always be made on the basis of what is actually available at the time.

Pre-recorded demonstrations and films both have the ability to fake program capabilities that do not exist, in order to sell ahead some facility; this is fairly common, and attention should be paid to the phrasing of the commentary in order to detect it.

However, most of the more reputable sellers of computer programs do not allow their salesmen to sell ahead.

A demonstration should give some idea of how much effort has to go into the input. Programs with tedious, repetitive or abstruse input procedures should be avoided as the program will then have difficulty in being accepted. For example, a user should not be expected to input coordinates to define a building shape. On any scale this sort of activity is extremely tedious and can be avoided by the use of devices such as digitisers. Cryptic input will take a long time to learn and will involve extra training of staff; conversely, input in a more 'natural' form, closer to plain English, usually means that the input is much more longwinded. The best method depends on the sort of users the program will have.

The form in which results are output is also important. In general, output should be terse and well presented. Pages should have numbers and titles to the columns. There should not be too much output; if an analysis of car parking covers a hundred sheets of paper, the user is not going to wade through it in order to comprehend the problem but will prefer to make a decision on the basis of experience. The judicious use of graphics, in the form of bar charts and graphs, can greatly simplify output, but possibly at the expense of increased administration due to the different ways that text and graphics are handled on most computer systems. A disproportionate amount of effort has to go into making input easy and output presentable, and so these are usually the characteristics of a good program.

There is some question as to whether the operation of a program should be interactive, i.e. taking data and giving answers in a question-and-answer session, or batch, where the data is presented and the results obtained in a single submission that does not involve the user. It is true to say that anything that can be done in batch can be done interactively, but not vice versa. Also, interaction can help to cut down the amount of output, as the user can be guided into the solution he requires, rather than having to choose the most appropriate from a range of results. However, interaction is expensive; the runs cost several times the amount for the batch equivalents and there is also a charge for remaining connected to the computer, even when not working. Interaction is therefore an unnecessary luxury unless it gives real benefits; often it is not essential and can make the difference between a program that is cost-effective and one that is not.

The support and maintenance given are a very important point to establish. The layman is often surprised to find that a programmer takes much longer to find and correct the errors in his program than he does to write it in the first place, but this process of 'debugging' is always necessary for even the best and most careful programmers. Some errors can remain in a program for years without being detected, until a particular unusual set of circumstances trigger the fault and produce nonsensical results. It is this sort of thing that is responsible for electricity bills for millions of pounds and similar well-publicised incidents. One therefore never knows when trouble may occur, and the vendor must be able to provide men experienced in the particular program in case of faults arising.

For the same reason, it is important to avoid being one of the first users of a program. No testing period on the vendor's machine, however prolonged, can simulate the variety of situations encountered in practice. Also, the practical use of a program will show up deficiencies and features that are unnecessarily clumsy, and over a period of time these can be corrected. The vendor should therefore be asked how long his program has been in use and how many users of it there are.

An apparently satisfactory answer should be checked out. I have seen programs and even compilers, one of the most basic aids of all, contain so many errors that they were unusable even after years of existence. This can happen when a program is written by a manufacturer of computers but does not find favour with the users, who turn to some alternative. Such a program is often still kept in the official literature on the grounds that it can do no harm to advertise it.

It is also worthwhile to check out one or more of the claimed users. Again, I have found that organisations that have bought a program sometimes find they cannot use it. It is then often turned over to the purchaser's computer section who fiddle with it to try and make it useful. Therefore when checking a claimed user it is important to make contact with the person who actually has to use the results, rather than the head of the computer section who will often regard the program as an ingenious toy or an interesting challenge.

Even after all this it is quite possible that a true picture of the program's worth will not be gained. An organisation that has spare capacity may ask some of its workers to use a computer program in their work more or less as an experiment; for obvious reasons government departments are more prone to do this in slack times than private companies. The persons involved will often be chosen because they have a strong interest or belief in the power of computers and hence are willing to put up with tedious or clumsy processes; they are also prone to deceiving themselves as to how much use the program really is. For these reasons it is useful to try to find out what value of work is being processed by the computer, and if it is a ridiculously small sum compared with the cost of the machines and the staff involved, to look very askance at the program.

It is useful to get some idea of the amount of effort that went into producing the program. A large investment by the vendor at least indicates a willingness to take trouble and to get things right. The size of the program, in terms of the number of instructions, gives a good guide. Any program of less than 1000 lines of a high-level language is probably trivial; it simply does not have the space in which to make input easy for the user, solve a reasonably complex problem and provide properly laid out results. A program of at least 4000 lines is almost certainly a professional job; as the effort of programming increases disproportionately with the size of the program, it indicates that a lot of time has been spent in programming.

Similarly, the number of man-years that went into writing the program is a guide to its quality. In some ways this is not such a good indication as the length; there is a difference between having one or two very good programmers and a larger number of averagely able and therefore cheaper men. This latter solution is sometimes called the 'Mongolian horde' approach, in which one tries to overwhelm the problem by sheer weight of numbers. It must be said, however, that both approaches produce roughly equal results in the end.

The language that a program has been written in is some guide to its effectiveness. An assembly-language program will be cheap to run, but as it is more difficult to write, errors are more likely to be present and certain to be more difficult to find and correct than in a program in a high-level language. Therefore it is important in this case to be certain of good support from the vendor. A program that contains many thousands of lines in assembly language is almost certain to be a professional product, as the investment in writing it is so high. Nowadays, however, even professional programs are often in a high-level language so that they can be converted to a range of machines. Small sections of a program in assembly language while the rest is in a high-level language are often a sign of professionalism: a practical realisation that efficiency can require compromises with philosophy.

The older languages such as Fortran and Cobol will normally run reasonably cheaply, because they make many concessions to the manner in which a computer works. More recent and sophisticated languages such as PL/1, APL or Algol 68 make life easier for the programmer by operating in a manner more natural to human thought processes, but because of this they tend to be much more expensive to run than the older languages. This is especially true when using small computers.

Certain types of problem are better suited to certain languages. For example, database retrieval and manipulation require a lot of computer resources and can be very slow and cost a great deal if the database is large or complex. For this sort of application, therefore, the efficiency of the language is the prime consideration, and at least some of the program should be written in assembly language. At the other extreme, complex decision-making programs may not need much computer time but will require the use of an advanced high-level language in their creation.

In theory, there are certain languages that are intended for particular application areas and which will be most efficient when applied to problems in that field. The name Fortran, for example, is derived from 'Formula translation', revealing its scientific origin, and the name Cobol from 'Common Business Orientated Language'. In practice, however, the distinction has become so blurred over the years as to have largely disappeared; even scientists want properly laid out results, and even businessmen need statistical analyses. The more modern computer languages tend to have neutral names. PL/1, for example, is derived from 'Programming Language 1' and APL simply from 'A Programming Language'. Another language that may be encountered is Basic, which is an acronym of 'Beginners All-purpose Symbolic Instruction Code'[37]. This is a popular language as it is easy to learn and to write. It is not, however, a language in which long programs can be written as it cannot be broken down into self-contained and therefore easily managed pieces.

The vendors of a program may be reluctant to talk about such technical matters, and will almost always refuse to divulge any specific details of the program's working. This attitude is unfortunate but understandable; the copyright laws of most countries, including Britain, have no application to computer programs, and so the only way a company can protect its investment is to keep the details secret. In fact, readiness to part with a program in its human-readable form probably means that little effort went into it[38,39,41].

It is wise to be particularly careful before buying a program emanating from a university or technical college. Such programs can be extremely good, because computer time is usually free and almost unrestricted, and extensive research facilities, plus a bias towards a logical approach, can ensure an adequate basic structure. Also, since they do not have to justify themselves commercially, the programs can

be very good value for money. However, programming is taught as a subsidiary subject in many disciplines nowadays, including architecture, and it is common for students to write simple programs as an exercise or to help with some part of their work. A program of this nature is obviously unlikely to be of any use in the working office, because of the programmer's inexperience in both computing and architecture and because it must be written as virtually a spare-time occupation. I have had experience of such programs being seriously marketed, complete with enthusiastic documentation.

Even with a good program, it is important to check that maintenance and support is available all the year round. University holidays occupy five months of the year, but it is as essential to have support in case of trouble when running a program as it is when running a car.

Buying a program

When the decision is finally made to use a program, the details of the contract should be checked. A typical large program may cost something like £4000 for a five-year term; the program will have a date-sensing mechanism incorporated to ensure that it will not function after this period. There will also be an annual maintenance charge of about 7% of the purchase price and this charge is often compulsory. A maintenance contract usually guarantees that an experienced programmer will be available to sort out any problems with the program and gives the right to any modifications produced during that time. Training courses will be available for the staff as will the necessary user's manuals. A limited number of courses and manuals may be available free on signing the contract; it is worth checking this as these items are often very expensive.

None of this expenditure can really be classed as petty cash, so it is up to the user to make sure that he really will save money by buying the program. If at all possible, it is safer to use a program available at a commercial bureau on a royalty basis and so pay an extra percentage on each run rather than a large lump sum.

I must apologise if this chapter appears to have given more warnings than Cassandra ever did, but the difficulties of obtaining even adequate programs would engender cynicism in the most forbearing.

5
Using databases

Database principles

Over the years, many programs have been written to deal with the handling of information on such specific subjects as product data retrieval, equipment scheduling, and specification editing. It is now recognised that all such programs are different aspects of database technology and that a single set of techniques can be used to handle almost any type of information. A database is essentially a mass of information organised so as to permit easy extraction of data items. Computers do not have to be involved; an ordinary filing system is a database, as is a dictionary, although the latter cannot be updated.

To get a clearer idea of the concept of organisation we can consider a list of clients such as would typically be used for secretarial purposes. The list might be divided into four columns, giving for each entry the client's name, address and telephone number and the name of a contact individual. This list can be thought of as a database having the structure illustrated diagrammatically in *Figure 5.1*. From a single 'root node' there is a branch to a node for each client, from which in turn there are branches to the actual items of data. This list is a rigid structure in that there are exactly four items of data for each entry, and so it lends itself to being laid out in columnar form. Many of the databases an architect will use also have this form; thus a room-finishes database might have entries under columns for the room

number, floor finish, wall finish and ceiling finish. Similarly, a database holding information on doors would have locations for the door height, width, handing, etc.

In general, however, a database may have an arbitrary number of branches from any node. Consider, for instance, a letter file; the letters will be grouped into the building projects they deal with, and there may be from one to hundreds of letters for each job. The projects may also be grouped into client sections so that the information associated with large clients having several jobs active at once can be easily accessed. This more complicated organisation is illustrated in *Figure 5.2*. Examples of databases that have such a variable structure include those for equipment, where any room may be empty or may contain dozens of items; and those for product data, where for any category, such as paint, there is a range of manufacturers and varieties.

The more complicated structure is more difficult to handle than a rigid structure, but is more flexible and compact for certain categories of information. Database-management programs exist to create a structure and to attach data to it, to update information, to interrogate it, and to produce schedules and totals to summarise the data or certain areas of it. These programs are normally general enough to operate on any structure and they are applicable to a wide range of information categories, including most of those with which an architect is concerned.

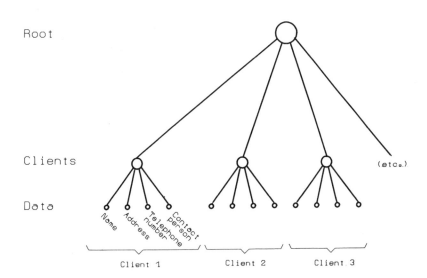

Figure 5.1 The organisation of a fixed-structure database

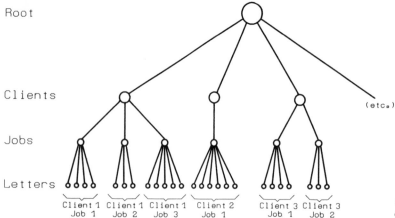

Root

Clients

Jobs

Letters

(etc.)

Client 1   Client 1   Client 1   Client 2   Client 3   Client 3
Job 1   Job 2   Job 3   Job 1   Job 1   Job 2

Figure 5.2 The organisation of a variable-structure database

Holding the data in computer-readable form rather than as printed lists can be advantageous in many cases. One advantage is that the initial creation of the database can be faster than the equivalent manual operations. This is principally because the computer can copy information used in one situation into any identical ones. Thus, for instance, if a standard list of equipment can be produced for an office, it need only be typed in once and can then be associated with perhaps dozens of rooms. The occasional exceptions to the standard can be edited individually. In some cases it may be possible to use an archived job as the basis for a new one to save even more effort. Information from the old database can be copied into the new one when the rooms have the same function. Provided the two jobs are similar types of building, a large part of the basic information for a project can thus be generated automatically.

Once the database has been created, it will need to be changed in some details as the job progresses. Here again, the computer can offer advantages provided that there is some sort of system to the alterations because the machine can use its basic ability to carry out the same sequence of operations again and again on different information. If, for example, the floor finish in all circulation areas is to be changed from vinyl tiles to carpeting, this can be done in a single instruction to the database-management program. Similarly, if a door or window type is to be changed throughout the building, extra filing cabinets put in offices, or any other consistent change made, it can be done much more easily with the help of a computer.

Conversely, the less consistent changes are, the less efficient it is to record them on computer databases. If there are only a few exceptions to the rule, little extra effort is involved. If, say, all offices except those of the managing director and his deputy are to have a cheaper type of carpeting, then the user has only to specify that these two rooms are to be excluded from the update; this does not involve much work, although the computer has to do a lot more processing to check every room number in the database to see if it is one of the exceptions.

If a particular standard change has to be made on a random selection of rooms, the user has to make more effort although probably not as much as with a manual schedule. For example, if all windows facing south were to be fitted with a different type of blind, the room numbers would have to be typed in individually as the orientation of a room is not a datum that is usually recorded in a database. This would involve a lot of checking and typing of room numbers, but would still be quicker than rubbing out old information and writing in the new description at many points in a typical manual schedule.

If, however, both the entries and the changes to be made are random, then it is inevitably a longer process to go through the formalities of using the computer program than it is to perform manual corrections. The use of the computer will also, of course, incur processing charges which can be high if a large database is to be scanned or a large number of corrections are to be made. In any design it is inevitable that at some time the client will go through the architect's proposal and require many detailed changes throughout the building. Making these changes will not be cost-effective when using a computer, but they will normally represent only a fraction of the total process of refinement of the design.

One problem with manual schedules is that once a change has been made it is difficult to find its source if it is queried later on. The client or a consultant may write a letter, or the architect may take a decision requiring a change to the design. Subsequently the source of the amendment may be queried or the previous entry may need to be known in order to evaluate the cost implications. This might require searching the letter or memorandum files, which could be a lengthy process. Many database-manipulation programs provide a facility known as an 'audit trail' that allows the convenient recording of changes. When this facility is used, the date of every change to the database is noted, together with the old item of information. At any later time, therefore, the day on which an amendment was carried out can be found and the search of the letter files is made much easier.

Also, all the changes made between particular dates can be listed and this can form the basis of a bill of amendments or allow the cost implications to be conveniently calculated.

Another important advantage of a computer database over manual methods is the ease with which it can be interrogated. Taking the example of an equipment schedule, this will probably be held with manual methods as a typed list organised in order of room numbers. So questions with the room number as a starting point, such as 'Is there a telephone in room 1234?', can be easily answered, but other questions, such as 'Which rooms have telephones?', may take a long time to answer as there is no index to this sort of information. The computer, of course, can scan a database very quickly, even given very complicated questions. It can also set up indexes on any basis so that if a lot of enquiries are to be made about telephones, say, a complete scan need only be done once and future enquiries will be even quicker and cheaper.

There are many occasions in the lifetime of a design when enquiries must be made. At the early stages consistency over the whole project can be achieved by cross-checking rooms. Later, odd checks might be made for various reasons, such as checking the lighting throughout the building, counting the total numbers of a certain item, finding the location of certain items, listing the data on some specialised type of room such as a darkroom, or printing a list of rooms with less than ten square metres of floor space per occupant. All these perfectly straightforward and common tasks, that would normally take hours of checking even on typed schedules, let alone on drawings, can be accomplished in minutes.

The final important advantage of computer methods is the more flexible and usually better-quality production documents that can be obtained. The copying of a single set of information into many locations and the automatic repeating of changes at many different points mean that the number of errors is likely to be lower than with typed schedules. The printing will always be clear and legible, which handwriting often is not, and will remain clear no matter how many revisions and corrections are applied to the database. Automatic titles, page numbers, running totals and cross-reference lists are also very easy to arrange.

The actual layout of the printed information can be varied as required and this can often give outputs that are much more readable than the manual equivalents. At the simplest level, certain categories of information can be omitted if irrelevant. Thus, for example, in a room briefing schedule it is possible to print only the columns dealing with environmental performance (temperature limits, relative humidity levels, lighting levels, etc) and this could be very valuable to a consultant checking the adequacy and consistency of the standards or to an engineer in

routeing services efficiently. A variety of subset schedules can be printed, each containing only the information of interest to a particular recipient.

As well as varying the content, it is also possible to re-order the output. Thus, for instance, a schedule might be output and totalled by departments for the client but in room-number order for the contractor. An important form of re-ordering is to produce an 'inverted' output in which the basic organisation of the data is reversed. For example, a typical schedule of equipment might consist of a page for each room, on each of which would be a list of the equipment found in that room. In its inverted form, the schedule might consist of one page for each different item of equipment in the project, on each of which would be a list of the rooms that contain that particular item. It is in this form that most subcontractors prefer to regard the information, as they work from a batch of fittings to the positions in which they are fitted, whereas the architect is given a location and has to specify the appropriate items. The architect has rather less use for inverted schedules, but they can be useful in the later stages of the design when checking, costing or rationalising. *Figure 5.3* shows a page from an inverted equipment schedule which corresponds to the equivalent schedule illustrated in *Figure 2.4*.

```
EAST CHEAM UNIVERSITY LIBRARY - FURNITURE AND EQUIPMENT
30 JULY 1979

ITEM   DES11        DESK,TYPIST WITH SIDE TABLE

( 2104B)      1     INTER-LIBRARY LOANS

ITEM   DES13        DESK,1000MM (W) 750MM (D) WITH SINGLE PEDESTAL

( 2114 )      3     CLERICAL SERVICES
( 2309B)      1     CATALOGUE BIBLIOGRAPHY REFERENCE

ITEM   DES14        DESK,1400MM (W) 750MM (D) WITH DOUBLE PEDESTAL

( 2101B)      2     CIRCULATION
( 2102 )      1     OFFICE
( 2103 )      1     OFFICE,SUPERINTENDANT
( 2104B)      2     INTER-LIBRARY LOANS
( 2114 )      3     CLERICAL SERVICES
( 2202 )      2     BINDERY PREPARATION
( 2203A)      6     GOVERNMENT PUBLICATIONS
( 2203B)     13     CATALOGUING
( 2203C)      6     ACQUISITIONS
( 2209 )      1     OFFICE, CATALOGUING
( 2210 )      1     OFFICE, GOV. PUBS.
( 3109 )      3     SPECIAL PROJECTS
( 3112 )      3     SPECIAL PROJECTS
( 3120 )      2     OFFICE
( 3121 )      1     OFFICE, SECRETARY
( 4106 )      1     OFFICE, KEEPER

ITEM   DES15        DESK,1200MM (W) 600MM (D) WITH DOUBLE PEDESTAL

( 2101B)      4     CIRCULATION
( 2104A)      2     ENQUIRIES
( 2203C)      2     ACQUISITIONS
( 2301 )      2     GENERAL COLLECTION
( 3103 )      1     OFFICE, ADMINISTRATION OFFICER
( 3301 )      4     READER/STACK ZONE
( 3305 )      2     STUDY ROOM
( 3306 )      2     STUDY ROOM
( 3307 )      2     STUDY ROOM
( 3308 )      2     STUDY ROOM

ITEM   DIS13        DISPENSER, SOAP

( 1111 )      5     LAVATORY, MALE
( 1115 )      3     LAVATORY, FEMALE
( 2117 )      1     LAVATORY, MALE
```

Figure 5.3 A page from an inverted schedule

It is characteristic of database-management programs that they are concerned with large quantities of information, and that most of the costs involved are due to reading and printing this information. Therefore, most of the problems associated with database techniques arise from the need to organise the data to make it suitable for computer processing. This is in contrast to scientific or statistical computer applications where the amount of data is usually small, perhaps a few hundred readings, and thus there are few organisational problems in its preparation. The output is also often short, perhaps merely a short list of numbers or a simple graph. The costs and problems with such applications are mainly concerned with the large number of calculations that must be performed.

One basic problem is to decide how much information a single database will contain. It might seem reasonable to have a database for each job, holding all the production information for that project. This would have the great advantage of keeping all the data in a single file in an hierarchical manner. In fact, this is not usually done. The principal reason for this is that such a database would be very large, perhaps millions of characters, and would therefore cost several pounds a day to store on a magnetic disc at commercial rates. The database structure would inevitably be complicated, extending to perhaps five or six levels, and this would cost much more to search and to update than if the data were divided into self-contained sections.

It is also not really appropriate to have all the data accessible all the time. At the start of a job, basic data such as room area and illumination levels are being decided and manipulated; at a later stage this sort of information is frozen and seldom referred to, but detailed information on doors and windows is being built up. Later still, door and window specifications are finalised but the equipment in the rooms must be rationalised and checked against the manufacturers' catalogues, and the room finishes must be chosen.

Thus it is more efficient in several ways to have a number of simple databases rather than a single large one. The drawback of breaking down the total job information into several parts is that some changes will have to be reflected in more than one database. A change in a room name, for instance, will affect all databases; but if reasonable care is taken in dividing up the information this problem should not be very serious.

One of the most important problems of database management is the security of the data — its vulnerability to being corrupted or destroyed. Manual methods are fairly secure, the greatest danger being that someone will discard a drawing or a vital piece of paper by mistake; but the damage of data in computer storage systems is a regular occurrence and must be guarded against. Damage can occur in several ways:

by simple error, as when a file is released or overwritten by mistake; by program fault, when the user's program or the computer supervisory program overwrites the file; by a mechanical fault, when the storage system physically damages the magnetic coating that holds the data; or by deterioration of the data, as when the signal on a magnetic tape fades with time or the tape itself becomes brittle.

The use of databases must therefore include provision for their security. This can most effectively be done by making extra copies of the data, usually every evening after the day's work. Making a copy of a database file takes a couple of minutes and involves relatively little expense; therefore at the cost of a slightly more complex operating procedure no more than a single day's work can be lost. Commercial bureaux take this precaution for their customers as a matter of course and store the copies in fireproof safes for perhaps a week or two. Thus if a mistake is overlooked at the time, recovery can still often be made.

In general, storage on magnetic disc is the most unsafe because it is subject both to program and mechanical failure. It is closely followed by punched cards which can be torn by the reading machinery, or dropped and shuffled. Magnetic tape is a relatively safe storage medium, being in general only subject to gradual deterioration. Given correct temperature- and humidity-controlled conditions, however, it is normally safe for at least a year.

A problem that has recently received a lot of publicity is the privacy of computer data. As computer files can be copied so easily, it is feared that unauthorised persons could readily obtain information they should not have, and as such files can be searched for specific information quickly and cheaply, violation of privacy could take place on a large scale. This has not previously been a difficulty because copying the contents of a conventional filing cabinet is slow and expensive and most of the information inside is not cross-indexed and so is not readily accessible.

While privacy is a serious problem, it is not in general relevant to an architect's databases because the information he collects is not particularly sensitive. It would be unusual, for example, for an architect to care who reads his door schedules; his problem is much more likely to be to find someone prepared to check them. However, occasionally information will be sensitive. If some building is being done for a defence establishment, for example, the names of the rooms could give away the function and status of the building and this might be undesirable.

Luckily, computer systems have to deal regularly with sensitive data such as that handled by banks or insurance companies and so normally have extensive security precautions. Database-management programs in particular can usually deny access to users who do not know the correct password and even allow some users access to certain sections of the data while denying access to other sections. At a more physical level, many computer rooms have automatic doors that require an identification card or knowledge of a code number before they will open. Privacy is a large subject in itself, but the average architect that uses a commercial bureau can usually leave the precautions to the bureau authorities with confidence[56].

The form of the output from a database-management program brings corresponding handling and user acceptance characteristics. The most popular form of output, because of its cheapness and convenience, is printed pages from a line-printer. If several copies are required, they can be obtained by using multi-part stationery with carbons, or by using the services of a copying bureau with facilities for accepting the continuous stationery produced by a line-printer. Machines are available that can copy line-printer output at a convenient A4 size so that the original output can then be discarded or archived.

Some offices may find large quantities of paper too clumsy to handle at all, at least on their bigger projects. In these cases it may be preferable to present the output on micromedia. One form of micromedium is microfilm, in which the pages are set out along the length of a strip of film as shown in *Figure 5.4*. Alternatively, the pages may be arranged in a rectangular array on the film, in which case it is known as a microfiche. An example of a microfiche is shown in *Figure 5.5*.

Figure 5.4 A reel of microfilm

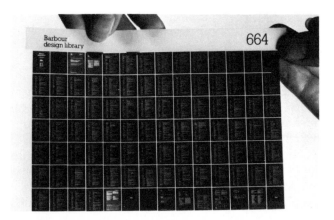

Figure 5.5 A microfiche

Figure 5.6 A microfiche viewer

Micromedia can be produced off-line directly from a magnetic tape containing the results. It is a very cheap and compact form of output, but of course has the great drawback of requiring special equipment to read it. A viewer must be purchased for the office, although simple models are surprisingly cheap. A typical low-cost microfiche viewer is pictured in *Figure 5.6*. If copies from the micromedia are subsequently required on paper, they will be expensive to produce. It is a lot cheaper to produce output on a line-printer from the original magnetic tape and copy that. Micromedia do present advantages when sending results abroad, for archival storage, for extremely large schedules, and for schedules which are often updated.

Catalogues and coding

There is some controversy over the best way to represent items of data in a computer database. The obvious method is to hold each item as a full line of text, such as 'sink, stainless steel, 1800mm (w) 600mm (d), left-hand drainer'. However, this is clumsy in use and will add to the cost of storing and accessing the database. A common answer is to use some sort of coding system to represent the data items, with a glossary or catalogue available to give the full equivalents[48,49].

Codes are not only much briefer and more precise,

but will also standardise the syntax of the information. Thus, for instance, they avoid the problem of someone writing 'underbench cupboard' and someone else writing 'cupboard, underbench'. When sorted in alphabetical order these descriptions will be at opposite ends of the list and it may be some time before it is realised that they are the same item. Coding also eliminates spelling mistakes, and this can be important when dealing with complex or unfamiliar terminology, as in hospital design.

The principal disadvantage is that a code is not immediately intelligible but must be looked up in a table of equivalents. This can be tedious and irritating if done often, and most architects dislike the use of codes for this reason. Also, because they lack the redundancy of a plain description, it is much more difficult to detect mistakes. For instance, spelling 'cupboard' as 'cupbaord' is unlikely to give a reader much trouble, but if its code is C1234 and it is written as C1324 the error might be overlooked completely if C1324 is a valid code for some other item. Therefore, extra checks are necessary at all stages if these errors are to be eliminated.

Codes can be made self-checking to some extent by introducing redundancy. Commercially, this is done by adding a 'check digit' to the code. The check digit, which may also be a letter, is derived by a suitable mathematical process from the other characters in the code, and if this process is properly chosen it will detect over 90% of possible errors. Despite their effectiveness, check digits are rarely used in the construction industry, perhaps because they are unfamiliar and need a computer to evaluate and validate them.

A more common way of introducing redundancy is to use mnemonic codes. For example, all cupboard codes might start with 'CUP', sinks with 'SIN' and so on. With a little practice, therefore, it is obvious at a glance what type of item is being referred to, and because most three-letter groups are unused, errors such as coding a cupboard with 'COP' or CPU' will usually be obvious. Unfortunately, completely mnemonic codes are very clumsy in use if the item has a large number of characteristics. A cupboard, for instance, may vary in its carcass size, the number of shelves, the handing of its door and in its finish. A completely mnemonic code would have to give each of these separately, as in 'CUP/C1/S3/LH/P' standing for 'cupboard, size 1, 3 shelves, left-hand door, painted'. Although reasonably clear, such a code is obviously impractically long. Many coding systems are therefore a mixture of mnemonic and non-mnemonic parts where, say, the code 'CUP55' stands for cupboard type 55, the details of which are referenced elsewhere.

The fact that items of data can be coded at all implies that there is a restricted list of alternatives to choose from. This in turn leads naturally to the possibility that there can be for some, if not all,

subjects a standard office catalogue to choose from when designing. If this sort of rationalisation can be achieved, it will make design and specification much more efficient, with both manual and computer techniques. It is very attractive to postulate the gradual building up of a catalogue, over a number of jobs, which will come to form an almost complete set of alternatives. However, my own experiences in attempting just this for several different classes of data over a number of years indicate that it is only possible in certain areas. The problem appears to be that although most of the items are common to many jobs, the odd few percent are entirely composed of one-offs that are only used on a single project.

One area in which it proved impossible to produce a standard catalogue was room names. It was found that, quite reasonably, the designers wanted the room name to reflect its function. Thus quite quickly hundreds of different names were acquired for offices, such as 'Domestic supervisor's office', 'Porter's office', 'Assistant secretary's office' and even personal names such as 'A. Smith's office'. Although these rooms were often identical in practice, their names showed such an uncontrollably wide variation that attempts to catalogue or code them were extremely inefficient. At the other extreme, it was found that the variations in possible room finishes tended to be very small. Descriptions such as 'emulsion paint', 'glazed wall tiles' and 'acoustic ceiling tiles' were used many times and repeated from job to job. It was therefore easy to construct a compact coded catalogue to choose from and to which additions were relatively infrequent.

Between these extremes, catalogues can be created for some subjects that consist of a hard core of items used on almost every job. Additional entries unique to a certain project have to be added as required. Obviously, the relative proportions of permanent to transient entries determine the cost-effectiveness of maintaining the catalogue. Joinery fittings are an example of such a subject. In my own office we have found that a catalogue of 2000 entries is sufficient to encompass about two-thirds of the joinery items in most buildings; the remaining one-third have to be detailed afresh on each job.

A problem with a catalogue larger than about a hundred entries is that considerable time can be spent in searching through it to find the most appropriate standard item or to find the code of an item. The entries will normally be sorted in alphabetical order with the most significant word first; thus a 'lockable steel cupboard' will be written as 'cupboard, steel, lockable'. This method breaks down when a description contains more than one word that could be regarded as significant. For instance, it is not obvious whether an acoustic hood for a public telephone should be looked up under 'acoustic', 'hood' or 'telephone'. To cut out abortive references, such items should be catalogued under all headings.

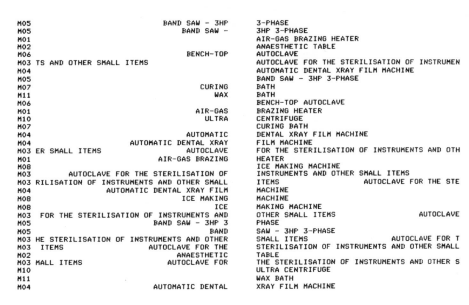

```
M05                              BAND SAW - 3HP    3-PHASE
M05                              BAND SAW -        3HP 3-PHASE
M01                                                AIR-GAS BRAZING HEATER
M02                                                ANAESTHETIC TABLE
M06                              BENCH-TOP         AUTOCLAVE
M03  TS AND OTHER SMALL ITEMS                      AUTOCLAVE FOR THE STERILISATION OF INSTRUMEN
M04                                                AUTOMATIC DENTAL XRAY FILM MACHINE
M05                                                BAND SAW - 3HP 3-PHASE
M07                              CURING            BATH
M11                              WAX               BATH
M06                                                BENCH-TOP AUTOCLAVE
M01                              AIR-GAS           BRAZING HEATER
M10                              ULTRA             CENTRIFUGE
M07                                                CURING BATH
M04                              AUTOMATIC         DENTAL XRAY FILM MACHINE
M04                    AUTOMATIC DENTAL XRAY       FILM MACHINE
M03  ER SMALL ITEMS                 AUTOCLAVE      FOR THE STERILISATION OF INSTRUMENTS AND OTH
M01                           AIR-GAS BRAZING      HEATER
M08                                                ICE MAKING MACHINE
M03         AUTOCLAVE FOR THE STERILISATION OF     INSTRUMENTS AND OTHER SMALL ITEMS
M03  RILISATION OF INSTRUMENTS AND OTHER SMALL     ITEMS                  AUTOCLAVE FOR THE STE
M04              AUTOMATIC DENTAL XRAY FILM         MACHINE
M08                              ICE MAKING        MACHINE
M08                                   ICE          MAKING MACHINE
M03   FOR THE STERILISATION OF INSTRUMENTS AND     OTHER SMALL ITEMS               AUTOCLAVE
M05                           BAND SAW - 3HP 3     PHASE
M05                                    BAND        SAW - 3HP 3-PHASE
M03  HE STERILISATION OF INSTRUMENTS AND OTHER     SMALL ITEMS                 AUTOCLAVE FOR T
M03  ITEMS                 AUTOCLAVE FOR THE        STERILISATION OF INSTRUMENTS AND OTHER SMALL
M02                              ANAESTHETIC        TABLE
M03  MALL ITEMS                 AUTOCLAVE FOR       THE STERILISATION OF INSTRUMENTS AND OTHER S
M10                                                ULTRA CENTRIFUGE
M11                                                WAX BATH
M04                              AUTOMATIC DENTAL   XRAY FILM MACHINE
```

Figure 5.7 A KWIC index

A popular method of laying out a catalogue, that deals automatically with the above requirement, is the use of a 'Key Word In Context' or KWIC index. In this type of presentation, each description is expressed in a natural manner, rather than with the most significant word leading, but is repeated and shifted on the line so that each word in turn is centred, omitting conjunctions and articles. The centred words are sorted into order, so that it is then easy to scan down the list and pick out a description on the basis of any of its key words. Computer programs are commonly available to generate KWIC indexes and a typical output is shown in *Figure 5.7*.

If it is found convenient to maintain a catalogue, it is possible to associate attributes with each entry in addition to its code. Such attributes might be the manufacturer's name, a reference to a detail drawing or formal specification, or the acoustic and thermal properties. If these attributes are available it is possible to perform many extra tasks automatically. However, the problem of gathering and of keeping all this extra information up to date often makes it uneconomic to go to these lengths.

One attractive attribute to add to a catalogue is the cost of the item, which of course aids the automatic pricing of that aspect of the job. However, there are serious difficulties. It is often impossible to get firm prices for a given item; different tenderers will frequently quote very different prices for similar products, sometimes by factors of three or four to one, even though the job totals may not vary much. There is the additional complication that quantity discounts are calculated on different bases by the various suppliers. It is cumbersome and inflexible to try to build these calculations into a computer program. Another important difficulty at present is that as all prices get out of date so quickly, it takes a great deal of effort to keep the catalogue up to date.

Databases in architectural design

There are a wide variety of databases that can be of use to the architect. Some are concerned with administration, such as those containing personnel details or the time spent on different projects; some may apply to any job, such as those that contain product data or technical information; and some may be specific to a particular job and hold production information relating only to that job. This last category are normally the most complex in their structure and also undergo the most changes during their lifetimes.

One of the first databases that can be created during the design of a building is that for room-briefing information. At an early stage in the design the architect is supplied with, or generates for himself, basic information on every room or activity area in the building. Initially, this information might consist of only the most basic facts such as the use, floor area and occupancy of the rooms, but later it can be refined to include environmental data, the services supplied, the finishes and so on. This data can be used at the feasibility and outline proposal stages of the design, to agree standards with the client and specialist consultants, and later as a check-list when designing the rooms in detail[46].

A convenient way to collect the data is for the architect to produce a set of skeleton data sheets, each containing the basic information on one room. These sheets can be circulated to all the members of the design team, each adding to them or modifying earlier information according to his area of specialisation and point of view. In this way, most of the information that the designer needs can be gathered quickly and with consistency. A typical sheet with handwritten additions is shown in *Figure 5.8*.

```
LOAMSHIRE GENERAL HOSPITAL              ROOM BRIEFING DATA


ROOM NAME                       ANAESTHETIC ROOM
ROOM NUMBER                     5013

01.ROOM USE                     - for the induction of Anaesthesia and Hypothermia
02.SIZE (SQ.M.)                 - 38.5
03.OCCUPANTS                    - 4
04.PERIODS OF USE               - 24 Hours.
05.FUNCTIONAL RELATIONSHIPS     Adjacent operating theatres.
06.SPECIAL CHARACTERISTICS
07.TEMPERATURE                  - 24-27°C  50% RH (adjustable)
08.VENTILATION                  - Supply and exhaust with high efficiency filters, 100% FA +ve pressure, NC 30 (Max)
09.ILLUMINATION                 - 100 lux (general) + special lighting
10.LIGHTING                     - 2 wall mounted anaesthetic lamps
11.DOORS                        - To admit bed. Single swing doors with 90° check, vision panels
12.WINDOWS                      - —
13.SPECIAL FINISHES             - Anti-static floor. A very high standard of clinical cleanliness.
14.SANITARY FITTINGS            - S/S sink
15.WATER SERVICES               - H+C
16.SPECIAL WASTES               - —
17.PIPED SERVICES               - Oxygen, Nitrous Oxide, Suction.
18.ELECTRICAL SUPPLIES          - For anaesthetic lamps & twin socket outlets, For clock.
19.SPECIAL ELECTRICS            - -
20.TELEPHONES                   - -
21.CALL SYSTEMS                 - -
22.CLOCKS                       - Synch. with sweep second hand.
23.FITTINGS                     - -
24.EQUIPMENT                    - -
25.MISCELLANEOUS                - -


PROJECT DESIGN BRIEFING INFORMATION
NOTE - DO NOT BE SPECIFIC AT INITIAL BRIEFING STAGE UNLESS
        IT IS IMPORTANT TO BE SO FOR FUNCTIONAL REASONS
```

Figure 5.8 A room-briefing schedule with handwritten amendments

These sheets form a valuable design aid in themselves but, as already noted, entering the new information into a computer database gives the advantages of better communication, easier amendment, interrogation facilities and the possibility of feedback into a later job of the same type. A typical sheet from a computer-held room-briefing database at an advanced stage in the job is shown in *Figure 5.9*. It is of a variable-structure form with several entries under certain headings such as service outlets.

As the job progresses, much of the information on the data sheets will be designed into the building and will no longer be of direct concern to the architect.

The room area is an obvious example of an item of data that is irrelevant once the outline scheme has been prepared. The number of service outlets such as telephone, electricity and gas are of little concern to the architect once they have been sketched in. The services engineer will be producing his own drawings to show routeings through ducts and trunking, and will consider the outlets to be only the final aspect of all this. Several other matters will similarly cease to be relevant.

Meanwhile, certain other items will have to be considered in more detail. Doors and windows, for instance, will have to be specified more precisely,

```
LOAMSHIRE GENERAL HOSPITAL            ROOM BRIEFING DATA            DATE 03/09/78


ROOM NAME                       ANAESTHETIC ROOM
ROOM NUMBER                     5013

01.ROOM USE                     INDUCTION OF ANAESTHESIA AND HYPOTHERMIA
02.SIZE (SQ.M.)                 38.5
03.OCCUPANTS                    4
04.PERIODS OF USE               24 HOURS
05.FUNCTIONAL RELATIONSHIPS     ADJACENT OPERATING THEATRES
06.SPECIAL CHARACTERISTICS      -
07.TEMPERATURE                  24-27 DEGREES C
                                50% RH (ADJUSTABLE)
08.VENTILATION                  SUPPLY AND EXHAUST WITH HIGH EFF.FILTERS,100% FA POSITIVE PRESSURE,NC 30 (MAX)
09.ILLUMINATION                 100 LUX (GENERAL)
                                SPECIAL LIGHTING
10.LIGHTING                     WALL MOUNTED ANAESTHETIC LAMP, 2 NO.
11.DOORS                        SINGLE SWING,VISION PANELS,90 DEG.CHECK,TO TAKE BED
12.WINDOWS                      -
13.SPECIAL FINISHES             ANTI-STATIC FLOOR
                                A VERY HIGH STANDARD OF CLINICAL CLEANLINESS
14.SANITARY FITTINGS            STAINLESS STEEL SINK
15.WATER SERVICES               HOT WATER
                                COLD WATER
16.SPECIAL WASTES               -
17.PIPED SERVICES               OXYGEN
                                NITROUS OXIDE
                                SUCTION
18.ELECTRICAL SUPPLIES          TWIN SOCKETS
                                TO ANAESTHETIC LAMPS
                                TO CLOCK
19.SPECIAL ELECTRICS            -
20.TELEPHONES                   -
21.CALL SYSTEMS                 -
22.CLOCKS                       SYNCHRONOUS,WITH SWEEP SECONDS HAND
23.FITTINGS                     -
24.EQUIPMENT                    -
25.MISCELLANEOUS                -
```

Figure 5.9 A complete room-briefing schedule

```
LOAMSHIRE GENERAL HOSPITAL                      ROOM FINISHES                    DATE:  30/04/79

*************************************************************************************************************
ROOM ROOM NAME              FLOOR               SKIRTING           WALL            WALL FINISH     CEILING           CEILING FINISH
*************************************************************************************************************
2201 STAIR (MAIN)           PVC WELDED SHEET    HARDWOOD           PLASTER         EMULSION PAINT  PLASTER           EMULSION PAINT
2202 ENTRANCE HALL          CARPET              -                  FACING BRICK    SELF FINISH     TIMBER SLATTED    SEALED
2203 DUCT                   CONCRETE            -                  FACING BRICK    SELF FINISH     CONCRETE          SELF FINISH
2204 RECEPTION              CARPET              PVC 100MM PLAIN    PLASTER         EMULSION PAINT  PERFORATED METAL  SELF FINISH
2205 RECEPTION COUNTER      CARPET              PVC 100MM PLAIN    PLASTER         EMULSION PAINT  PERFORATED METAL  SELF FINISH
2206 OFFICE - RECORDS       CARPET              PVC 100MM PLAIN    PLASTER         EMULSION PAINT  PLASTER           EMULSION PAINT
2207 OFFICE - NURSING STAFF CARPET              PVC 100MM PLAIN    PLASTER         EMULSION PAINT  PLASTER           EMULSION PAINT
2208 WAITING AREA           CARPET              PVC 100MM PLAIN    PLASTER         EMULSION PAINT  PERFORATED METAL  SELF FINISH
2209 TREATMENT ROOM         PVC WELDED SHEET    PVC 100MM COVED    PLASTER         OIL PAINT       PLASTER           OIL PAINT
2210 DISPOSAL ROOM          PVC WELDED SHEET    PVC 100MM COVED    PLASTER         OIL PAINT       PLASTER           OIL PAINT
2211 CUPBOARD - ELECTRICAL  CEMENT              -                  FACING BRICK    EMULSION PAINT  CONCRETE          EMULSION PAINT
2212 DUCT                   CONCRETE            -                  FACING BRICK    SELF FINISH     CHEQUER PLATE     MATT PAINT
2213 TROLLEY PARKING        VINYL TILES         PVC 100MM COVED    PLASTER/TILES   OIL PAINT       ACOUSTIC PLASTER  EMULSION PAINT
2214 PANTRY                 VINYL TILES         PVC 100MM COVED    PLASTER/TILES   OIL PAINT       PLASTER           OIL PAINT
2215 WASH AREA              VINYL TILES         PVC 100MM COVED    PLASTER/TILES   OIL PAINT       ACOUSTIC PLASTER  EMULSION PAINT
2216 TELEPHONE              CARPET              PVC 100MM PLAIN    PLASTER         EMULSION PAINT  PERFORATED METAL  SELF FINISH
2217 SERVERY                VINYL TILES         PVC 100MM COVED    PLASTER/TILES   OIL PAINT       ACOUSTIC PLASTER  EMULSION PAINT
2218 DINING ROOM            PVC WELDED SHEET    PVC 100MM COVED    PLASTER         EMULSION PAINT  PERFORATED METAL  SELF FINISH
2219 CLOAKROOM - PATIENTS   PVC WELDED SHEET    PVC 100MM COVED    PLASTER         EMULSION PAINT  PERFORATED METAL  SELF FINISH
2220 CLEANERS ROOM          PVC WELDED SHEET    PVC 100MM COVED    PLASTER         OIL PAINT       PLASTER           OIL PAINT
2221 CORRIDOR               CARPET              PVC 100MM PLAIN    PLASTER         EMULSION PAINT  PERFORATED METAL  SELF FINISH
2222 CUPBOARD - ELECTRICAL  CEMENT              -                  FACING BRICK    EMULSION PAINT  CONCRETE          EMULSION PAINT
2223 LOBBY                  PVC WELDED SHEET    PVC 100MM COVED    PLASTER         EMULSION PAINT  PERFORATED METAL  SELF FINISH
2224 STAIR (SECONDARY)      PVC WELDED SHEET    HARDWOOD           PLASTER         EMULSION PAINT  PLASTER           EMULSION PAINT
2225 STORE - OCC.THERAPY    PVC WELDED SHEET    PVC 100MM COVED    PLASTER         EMULSION PAINT  PLASTER           EMULSION PAINT
2226 STORE - OCC.THERAPY    PVC WELDED SHEET    PVC 100MM COVED    PLASTER         EMULSION PAINT  PLASTER           EMULSION PAINT
2227 HOSE REEL RECESS       ETERNIT             -                  PLASTER         EMULSION PAINT  PLASTER           EMULSION PAINT
2228 THERAPY AREA - GROUP   PVC WELDED SHEET    PVC 100MM COVED    PLASTER         EMULSION PAINT  PERFORATED METAL  SELF FINISH
2229 OFFICE - THERAPIST     CARPET              PVC 100MM PLAIN    PLASTER         EMULSION PAINT  PLASTER           EMULSION PAINT
2230 OFFICE - GENERAL       CARPET              PVC 100MM PLAIN    PLASTER         EMULSION PAINT  PLASTER           EMULSION PAINT
2231 THERAPY AREA -CRAFTS   PVC WELDED SHEET    PVC 100MM COVED    PLASTER         EMULSION PAINT  PERFORATED METAL  SELF FINISH
2232 STAIR (ESCAPE)         PAINTED METAL       -                  -               -               -                 -
2233 THERAPY ROOM - CLERICAL PVC WELDED SHEET   PVC 100MM COVED    PLASTER         EMULSION PAINT  PERFORATED METAL  SELF FINISH
2234 LOBBY                  WOODBLOCK           PVC 100MM COVED    PLASTER         EMULSION PAINT  PERFORATED METAL  SELF FINISH
2235 THERAPY ROOM - WORKSHOP WOODBLOCK          HARDWOOD           FACING BRICK    EMULSION PAINT  PERFORATED METAL  SELF FINISH
2236 OFFICE - TECHNICIAN    WOODBLOCK           HARDWOOD           PLASTER         EMULSION PAINT  PERFORATED METAL  SELF FINISH
2237 STORE                  WOODBLOCK           HARDWOOD           PLASTER         EMULSION PAINT  PLASTER           EMULSION PAINT
2238 STORE - TIMBER         GRANTOP             -                  FACING BRICK    EMULSION PAINT  CONCRETE          EMULSION PAINT
2239 THERAPY - REHAB.KITCHEN VINYL TILES        PVC 100MM COVED    PLASTER/TILES   OIL PAINT       PLASTER           OIL PAINT
2240 LAVATORY - FEM.PATIENTS VINYL TILES        PVC 100MM COVED    PLASTER         OIL PAINT       PLASTER           OIL PAINT
```

Figure 5.10 An output of fixed-structure information

whereas at the sketch design stage it was enough merely to indicate their presence. Similarly, the contract fittings must be expanded from a short and general list into a complete specification down to the manufacturers' models where appropriate. The room finishes may not have been noted at all in the room-briefing sheets, as detailed interior design is often left to a late stage; however, they must eventually be specified and scheduled.

This change in the emphasis on various items of information usually requires extra databases to be set up to cover the new subjects. Thus separate databases might be generated for doors, windows, furnishing, joinery fittings, sanitary fittings, or room finishes, depending on the designer's requirements. It is often possible to use some of the briefing database as a basis for the new databases, especially if it has been structured with this in mind from the outset.

The structure of the new databases will vary according to the type of information held. Door, window and finishes databases will typically have a simple fixed structure with single entries under a number of headings. The page from a typical room-finishes database in *Figure 5.10* illustrates this. Contract fittings or equipment databases will have a more complex structure with multiple entries in most rooms. Other databases may be set up to cater to the specific needs of a particular project.

The databases derived from a room-briefing database often relate directly to the working drawings, but outputs from them can usefully supplement the drawings because the information is then more accessible and less ambiguous. For example, a cupboard under a worktop might be overlooked on a drawing but not on a printed list.

Architects normally have to produce specifications to accompany drawings giving instructions regarding workmanship, the materials to be used, and methods of procedure. Specifications tend to be similar from job to job and so it is possible to create a database of reasonable size holding sections of text which can be extracted and combined to build up the finished document[47,57].

A specification database can take various forms, but a typical arrangement would be to group the text sections into such subjects as foundations, walling, and roofing. The text itself can be of various lengths; entire paragraphs can be held but excessive use of these will either lead to a very large database or to one allowing insufficient choice. At the other extreme, short clauses can be stored. Thus for instance a choice might be offered between 'the client shall be informed' and 'the architect shall be informed'. Combining clauses allows a wide range of sentences to be constructed from a compact database; however, it requires the user to do a lot more work as a typical paragraph will contain ten or twenty clauses. Practical systems use a mixture of text lengths according to the situation.

The production of specifications differs from other uses of database-management programs in that much more sophisticated facilities must be provided for editing the output. This is because the database cannot possibly hold all the text present on a realistic specification as specific manufacturers' names must be inserted, dimensions given, and non-standard paragraphs added to deal with unusual aspects of the job. In some cases a separate program is provided to organise the output from a generalised database-management program, while in others a special-purpose program is used.

Producing specifications by these means can be much quicker than either writing out a draft and having it typed or cut-and-paste methods. It also eliminates the possibility of typing errors.

CARDS — a fixed-structure database-management program

In the last few years, there has been great interest in database-management programs and there are now many excellent programs available. Most computer manufacturers have written their own versions and the larger commercial bureaux can usually offer a choice of several different programs. The principles of two such programs will be described: one that handles only fixed-structure databases and one that can handle variable structures. Although the specific commands may vary between programs, the basic principles and therefore the actions necessary do not change.

A program to handle fixed-structure databases was developed in our own office some years ago and is named CARDS[45]. A fixed structure, as has been noted, is appropriate for information associated with doors, windows, room finishes, personnel and similar situations where there are many different entries, each of which has a fixed set of attributes.

When setting up a database with CARDS it is first necessary to define the structure by giving the titles of the attributes. For example, a personnel file might have the attributes of employee names, position, salary, address, sex, and age It is then possible to enter the information. Each entry in the database must be given a unique identifier so that that particular entry and no other can be accessed at some future time. In a personnel file this might be an internal employee number or possibly the employee's insurance number. In other cases it might be a room number or door number, depending on the type of information to be handled.

CARDS works on the general principle that the entries in question are first extracted from the database, and then a separate process is applied to list them or change them. The simplest form of selection is used when the unique identifiers in question are known. In this case the command to select them is simply the word 'FIND' followed by a list of identifiers, as in

FIND 1003 1005 2003.

where the numbers might be room numbers. The information associated with these entries can then be printed out by typing

LIST ATTRIBUTES.

The program will respond with

'WHICH ATTRIBUTES?'

to which the answer can be the headings under which information is required, or simply

ALL.

if all the information is to be printed.

The entries that have been selected can also be altered by typing the word 'EDIT' followed by the attributes to be changed and the new values, as in:

EDIT LIGHTING='FLUORESCENT'
ILLUMINATION='300 LUX'.

Note that all the rooms selected are changed by the single EDIT command.

More general selections can be made by interrogating the information itself. For example,

FIND AREA>20.

selects all rooms whose areas exceed 20m². A number of criteria can be applied in the FIND command; thus complex conditions can be satisfied. The FIND command can be used to check many points and answer many common questions such as, 'How many half-hour fire-resistant doors are there?', 'Have all the offices got notice boards?', or 'Are we over-crowded in any room?'

The command

FIND ALL.

indexes the entire database, allowing a complete schedule to be printed, or a general change to be carried out.

If the selection is followed by a LIST command, specialised schedules of, say, environmental conditions or services can be obtained from a room-briefing information database. This will aid checking or make a more convenient issue to a specialist consultant. If the selection is followed by an EDIT command, systematic changes can be made quickly and accurately. For example, clocks can be inserted in all offices that do not already have them; a particular floor finish can be changed throughout; and illumination levels can be raised in all workshops.

More complex selection procedures than provided by the FIND command are necessary when the conditions to be satisfied do not necessarily overlap: for example, when the user wishes to select all corridors, all lobbies and all staircases in order to consider the circulation in the building. The FIND command cannot be used in this case because selecting one sort of room would automatically exclude the others. The task is made possible by the ADD command which has the same format as FIND but which adds to an existing selection rather than creating a new one. Thus the circulation areas can be selected by:

FIND NAME='CORRIDOR'.

ADD NAME='LOBBY'.

ADD NAME='STAIR'.

In a similar way, the LOSE command interrogates only the existing selection and removes those entries that satisfy its conditions. If in the above example the stairs on the top storey, level 5 say, are not to be considered, and assuming the convention that the first digit of the room number indicates the level, the stairs can be removed from the selection by the additional command

LOSE NAME='STAIR' NUMBER>4999.

With a little practice, it is possible to perform quite complicated operations with ease. The architect might say: 'We must cut the cost of these finishes; let's change the oil paint to emulsion paint on all the walls. That goes for the polyurethane paint too, so long as it's on a plastered wall; emulsion looks terrible on concrete. Oh, but we'll leave out the offices; we don't want people to have to stare at a dull finish all day.' The computer operator can translate this into:

FIND WALL-FINISH='OIL PAINT'.

ADD WALL-FINISH='POLYURETHANE' WALL='PLASTER'.

LOSE NAME='OFFICE'.

EDIT WALL-FINISH='EMULSION PAINT'.

On occasion, complete entries have to be removed from the database or new ones added as the result of replanning or redesign. Removal is achieved by first selecting entries with the FIND, ADD and LOSE commands, then typing:

EDIT DELETE.

The entries selected will then no longer exist in the database and their identifiers are available for re-use.

Adding items to the database is a little more complicated because not only must the new identifier be given, but data has to be supplied under the attribute headings. To create the new entries the user types 'DEFINE' followed by the list of unique identifiers for the new entries. Thus to add three rooms with numbers 1100, 2100 and 3100 the user types:

DEFINE 1100 2100 3100.

The above command adds the new entries to the database with blanks under all attribute headings. It also creates a current selection list containing the new entries, thus allowing information to be input using the EDIT command.

Obviously, it will often be a long process to type in the information for each attribute; a more powerful form of the EDIT command is therefore provided which can copy data elsewhere in the database file. This takes the form 'EDIT AS' followed by the identifier of some other existing entry. Thus

EDIT AS 1234.

will make all the entries in the current selection list identical in their associated information to entry number 1234.

Optionally, EDIT AS can be followed by the word 'USING' and a list of attribute headings. Thus in a room-briefing information database, the sequence

DEFINE 2001.

EDIT AS 1999 USING LIGHTING TEMPERATURE HUMIDITY.

EDIT AS 2000 USING WATER ELECTRICITY WASTES.

creates a new room with the number 2001, sets its environmental attributes identical to those of room 1999, and its services attributes identical to those of room 2000. All the other attributes remain blank. As database files often contain a large number of entries with relatively low variation between them, the EDIT AS command can greatly ease the initial creation of the database file.

There are a number of short cuts and abbreviated forms that the more experienced user of CARDS may take advantage of. One such is the ability to replace a continuous range of attribute names by the extreme values separated by a hyphen. For example, if a database of doors includes the attributes HEIGHT, WIDTH, THICKNESS, CONSTRUCTION and FINISH in that order and with no intervening attributes, then rather than specify all these names separately in a LIST or EDIT AS command, it is possible to write

HEIGHT-FINISH.

If the structure of the database has been defined in a natural manner with all attributes relating to a certain topic grouped together, then the use of this abbreviated form can save a lot of typing.

There are many other more elaborate facilities available with CARDS, including those to structure the database more efficiently and those to produce properly laid out schedules for issue in various forms, including inverted forms.

The final command of some general interest epitomises the program's philosophy of making things as easy as possible for the user: the HELP command. If at any time the user forgets the correct form of the commands, or even what commands are available to him, he can type 'HELP'. The response to this is a brief description of the options open to him at that stage: a list of commands, a fuller description of a certain command, or a list of attribute names, depending on what activity is currently taking place. The HELP command has been found to be of value even to experienced users, as it is easy to forget the exact details of the working of any program.

System 2000 — a variable-structure database-management program

CARDS is powerful and easy to use within its limitations, but it has the drawback that it cannot deal with multiple entries in a column. If, for example, in a personnel file it was decided to record the qualifications each employee held, there could be from nil to a dozen entries for any particular person. In this sort of situation a variable-structure database is required and a more complex program is needed to handle it. With such a database, there are many different possibilities and a generalised program must be able to deal with all of them without ambiguity; for this reason a variable-structure database-management program is inherently more difficult to use.

To illustrate the greater range of possibilities, we can consider a typical variable-structure architectural database for room equipment. This might consist of a set of named departments, each of which contains a set of rooms. Each room in turn is associated with a name, a number, an area in square metres and a list of the equipment to be provided in that room. This arrangement is illustrated in *Figure 5.11*.

Now, if the user of this database tries to look for a particular type of desk, the reason for his search must determine the way in which the search is performed. He might want to alter the specification of the desk itself, in which case every occurrence of it must be retrieved and altered; he might want to know the location of the desks, in which case the room names are selected at a higher level; or he might want to know the total number of desks per department for budgeting purposes, in which case summations must be performed relative to the topmost level in the database. It can be seen, then, that even with a fairly simple database of four levels and with a straightforward search for a certain data value there are several possibilities. With more complex databases or more complex selection criteria the concepts involved can become very difficult even to understand.

Because a multiple-level database is in the form of a tree, it is meaningful to specify points in the database that are not data locations but structural locations. To make this possible, not only are the attributes named, as in the CARDS program, but also the points or nodes at which the tree branches. Thus in the example given above, the nodes might be labelled 'DEPARTMENT', 'ROOM' and 'EQUIPMENT'. The nodes cannot take any specific values

in themselves, but naming them serves to indicate a route through the database or to isolate a certain section or sub-tree of the database.

One of the most popular variable-structure database-management programs is distributed by MRI Systems Corporation and is called System 2000. This program[53] will be used to illustrate some of the principles involved. System 2000 is an extremely large program and it is not possible to describe all its features. The user's manual runs to over 400 pages, although most users will only use a portion of this for their regular tasks.

Unlike CARDS, System 2000 does not have a double operation system where the objects of interest are first specified and then altered or listed. Rather, each command is complete in itself, the first half specifying the action to take place and the second half specifying the point or points in the database it applies to. Thus, in our hypothetical room-equipment database, the line

PRINT ROOM NUMBER WHERE ROOM NAME EQ OFFICE:

will print out all the office room numbers. Also,

ASSIGN ROOM AREA EQ 20.0* WHERE ROOM NUMBER EQ 1234:

will set the area of room number 1234 to 20 m². These commands are broadly equivalent to the CARDS 'LIST' and 'EDIT' commands respectively, the 'WHERE' clause taking the place of the 'FIND' command in CARDS.

Any mention of a node is assumed to indicate a complete sub-tree of information reaching to the lowest level of the database. Thus the command

PRINT ROOM:

will take each room in turn and print out all the information branching from it, and therefore associated with it. It will not print any information at a higher level, such as that associated with a specific department. Similarly,

PRINT ROOM WHERE ROOM NUMBER EQ 1234:

will list all the information associated with that particular room.

The process of removing information can have two different meanings in a database system. The data value that previously occupied a certain location can be lost, leaving it with no value; or the sub-tree which included that data item can be lopped from its node, in which case even the location itself disappears together with all the other nodes and data items in the sub-tree down to the lowest level.

The first type of deletion is performed in System 2000 by the 'REMOVE' command. For instance, if room 1234 is replanned, the previous value for its area is no longer correct and can be removed by

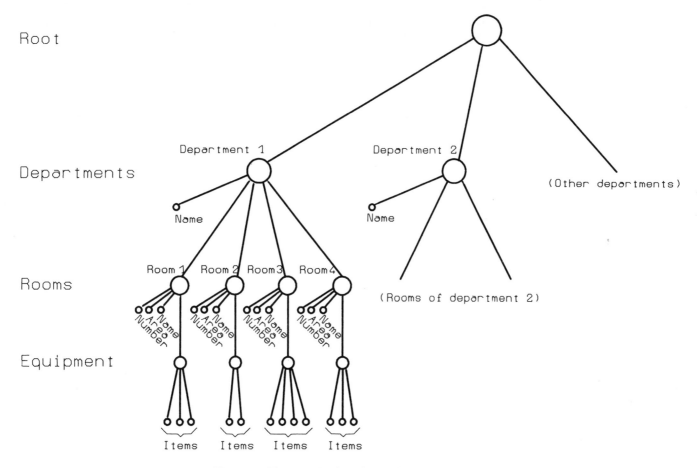

Root

Departments

Rooms

Equipment

Figure 5.11 The organisation of an equipment database

REMOVE ROOM AREA WHERE ROOM NUMBER EQ 1234:

The location itself remains so that the correct value can be inserted later. If room 1234 should disappear completely in the replanning process, then it can be removed from the database together with all the information associated with it by the second kind of deletion which takes the form:

REMOVE TREE ROOM WHERE ROOM NUMBER EQ 1234:

In this case the node below which data removal is to take place, being 'ROOM', has to be specified, together with the particular branch from the node that is identified by having the room number data value equal to 1234.

The opposite process to 'REMOVE TREE' is to insert a sub-tree of information into the database; this is roughly equivalent to the CARDS 'DEFINE' command. The insertion must specify at least some of the data values in the sub-tree and must give the exact location it is to occupy. An example of the use of this command is:

INSERT TREE ROOM EQ ROOM NUMBER *1236* ROOM NAME *OFFICE* END* AFTER ROOM NUMBER EQ 1235:

This command, by specifying the node 'ROOM' and the particular branch from it that is occupied by room 1235, defines the location of the new sub-tree. The pairs of data headings and data values terminated by the word 'END' give some of the information for the new room. In this case the information supplied is its number, which is 1236, and its name, which is 'OFFICE'.

These are the basic processes but they are capable of extensive elaboration to meet special cases. The 'WHERE' clause, for instance, can take complex forms. Thus to find all circulation areas, the following phrase might be used:

... WHERE ROOM NAME EQ CORRIDOR OR ROOM NAME EQ LOBBY OR ROOM NAME EQ STAIR:

Similarly, the phrase

... WHERE ROOM NAME EQ OFFICE AND ROOM AREA GT 20.0:

will access all offices with an area in excess of 20 m². The 'WHERE' clause can be used very flexibly to set up complex and restricted search patterns or to scan the database in various directions.

Although all the commands have been written out here in full for clarity, System 2000 provides a number of abbreviated forms for the more experienced user.

For example, most command words can be shortened to two letters; thus 'PR' is acceptable instead of 'PRINT'. It is also possible to refer to a node or a data item by means of a number assigned to it at the creation of the database. Thus if the item 'ROOM AREA' was assigned the number 10, then 'C10' is acceptable where the full name would otherwise appear. On a larger scale, it is not necessary to repeat identical clauses. The clause 'WHERE SAME' is taken as an instruction to use the same qualifying conditions as in the last 'WHERE' clause. Similarly, the word 'DITTO' can be used to avoid repeating the action clause in the first part of the command.

Where an action is repeated many times with different data values, it is possible to set up a loop that will eliminate unnecessary typing and can also save a significant amount of processing time. For example, at the detail design stage many room areas might have to be changed from the values they had at the briefing stage. This could be done by commands like

ASSIGN ROOM AREA EQ 22.3* WHERE ROOM NUMBER EQ 1234:

ASSIGN ROOM AREA EQ 31.8* WHERE ROOM NUMBER EQ 1235:

and so on, perhaps dozens or hundreds of times. It is, however, possible to set up a loop in this case by using the command

REPEAT/ASSIGN ROOM AREA EQ *DATA* WHERE ROOM NUMBER EQ *DATA*:/:

then just supplying a list of room areas and numbers as in:

22.3*1234*

31.8*1235*

50.2*1236* etc.

This command form is not only very convenient for the user, but also saves computer processing time, because the program waits until it has all the information, indexes it, and then does a single update of the database rather than make the multiple changes necessary with individual commands.

A drawback to such an extensive range of facilities and possibilities is that the form of commands can be difficult to work out and to remember, and therefore use of the program by inexperienced members of staff will be restricted. To help overcome this difficulty, System 2000 allows the user to store complete commands in a database under a name of his own choosing. Thus, for example, a command to output a schedule of total equipment numbers in a properly paginated form might be long and elaborate, but frequently required. The user might therefore store this command, once constructed, under the name 'PRINT TOTALS'; then any future use of this name would automatically invoke the complete original command.

The stored commands can also be organised to accept varying data values; thus commands to perform various common editing or interrogation operations can be stored under meaningful names. By this means, a lot of the most complex work can be done when the database is created, and accessing the program is then made easier for the less experienced user.

Variable-structure databases are much more difficult to handle than the fixed-structure type. They are also normally much more costly in computer time. For these reasons, it is always worth looking at the possibility of introducing some repetition, and placing some restrictions on the data so that it can be handled as a fixed structure. If this is not practicable, then it is important to use one of the more advanced database-management programs that give adequate help to the user.

6
Computer-aided draughting

Advantages of computer-aided draughting

Drawings have always been the architect's main means of storing and conveying information, and as the essential information is spatial this must continue to be so. The architect designs by drawing; the engineer uses drawings as the basis for his calculations; the quantity surveyor takes off his information from them; and the contractor builds from them. The drawing is central to the whole construction process and any benefit offered by the computer in this area will also be central.

Although computer-aided draughting has been possible for a long time, it is only recently that it has begun to be cost-effective. Graphical applications inherently require a lot of processing power and this has meant that they have been too expensive compared with the benefits that they can provide in architectural practice. Fortunately, the continuous fall in the cost of circuitry has brought computer-aided draughting within the bounds of viability.

Computer-aided draughting systems can normally provide equivalents for all the usual manual operations; they also have extra capabilities of their own. The most important of these is probably their ability to use the same drawing many times in different contexts as parts of a larger drawing. At its simplest level, this eliminates the frequent redrawing of standard building components and fittings. At the beginning of a job, a range of drawings of standard elements such as columns, doors, fittings, and services symbols, can be defined and copies of these drawings positioned within the building as required. A typical standard element might be a door plan, such as the one shown in *Figure 6.1*.

This element can be used in any position on a drawing just by giving its associated code to the computer. The orientation can be changed and the element can also be mirrored. Thus a left-hand swing door can also be used as a right-hand swing, a sink can have its drainer on the opposite side, and so on. *Figure 6.2* shows the door element used in several different contexts in a portion of a typical plan. The use of these standard elements can save a lot of time on a large floor plan and can improve the quality of the drawing because the standards can be drawn in detail and very accurately without imposing any time penalty when constructing the main drawing.

At a higher level, copies can be made of entire rooms or even blocks or departments. Thus a standard office layout could be repeated at a number of locations in a building, or a standard ward plan could be used several times in a hospital project. Again, mirror images can be made, giving rooms that are handed copies of the original. In an extreme case, if a plan is symmetrical only one-half of it need be drawn, then a mirrored copy made and the two drawings joined together to form the complete plan. *Figure 6.3* shows an example of the repeated use of a room plan.

Another very useful capability that cannot adequately be duplicated by manual methods is the overlaying of drawings containing different information to make up various composite drawings. For example, the information to produce a drawing of the wall and structure plan can be stored in the computer separately from the information for furniture, sanitary fittings and service outlets. These files can then be combined in a number of different arrangements to make up drawings for different purposes. The walls and structure by themselves comprise an outline plan to give a clear view of the design for evaluation or for the contractor to build from (*Figure 6.4*). The structure plus the service outlets, such as electric sockets and taps, together with the sanitary fittings, gives a drawing for the mechanical and electrical services engineer to work from (*Figure 6.5*). Finally, all the information together in a single drawing gives a floor data plan for a complete view of the design

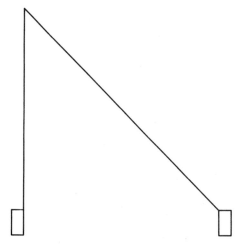

Figure 6.1 A standard graphic element

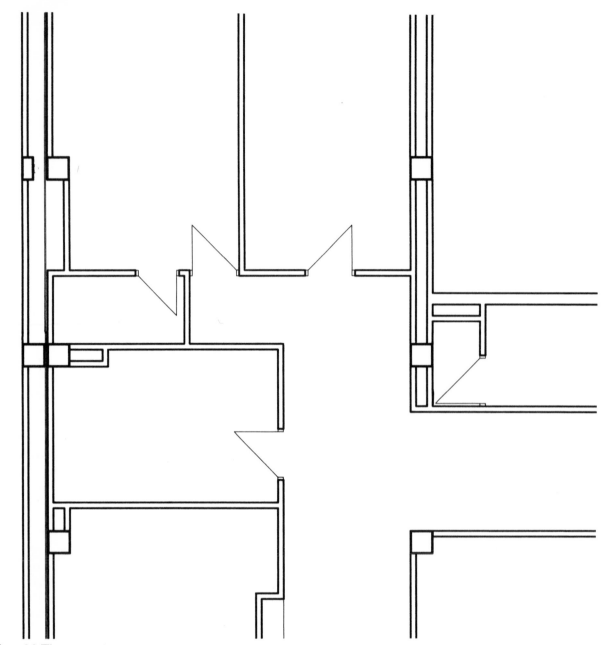

Figure 6.2 The repeated use of a standard graphic element

(*Figure 6.6*). This technique can be used to produce a wide variety of plans with little effort, and can greatly improve communication.

In theory, overlaying is possible with manual methods, but in practice it is little used; multiple layers of tracing paper become opaque, and accurate alignment is almost impossible with drawings of any size. The computer, however, can display several drawings on a screen at once, or output several drawings to the plotter on top of one another, with no loss in clarity and with very accurate alignment. It is therefore quite practicable to build up drawings as several layers.

Drawings can be output at any required scale and automatically trimmed to the area of interest, or combined with adjacent drawings according to the size of the output sheet. Thus it is possible to produce plans of the entire project at a convenient scale, 1:200

say, to give an overall impression. Conversely, it is possible to produce large-scale plans of single rooms or groups of rooms for discussion or detailing.

This technique saves a lot of draughting time at the initial stages because of all the duplicate drawing that would otherwise be necessary. An important additional advantage is that if any changes are made to any aspect of the design only a single alteration need be made to the file that contains that element of information. With manual drawing, if the position of a wall is altered, care must be taken to alter all the other plans that show that wall. This can occupy a lot of time, as perhaps half a dozen sets of drawings have to be kept in step. There is also the possibility of errors creeping in. These problems do not arise with a computer system as only the structural overlay need be altered and the correction will then appear on all subsequent drawings.

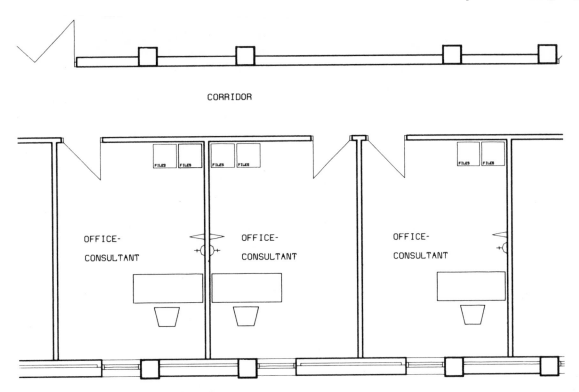

Figure 6.3 The repeated use of a standard floor plan

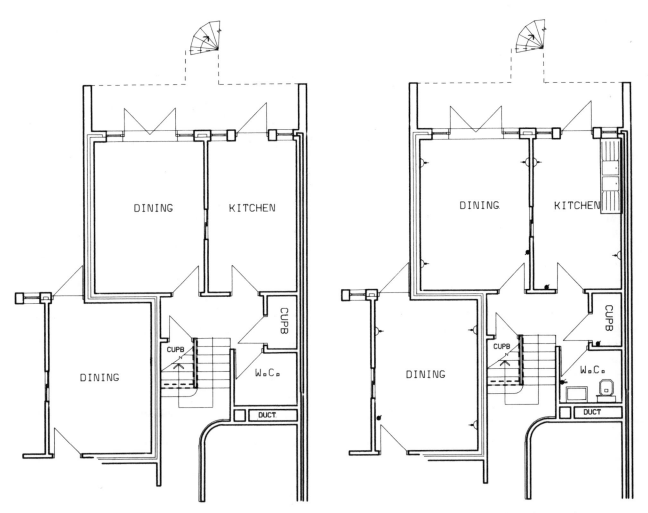

Figure 6.4 A computer-produced structure overlay

Figure 6.5 A structure overlay with services overlay

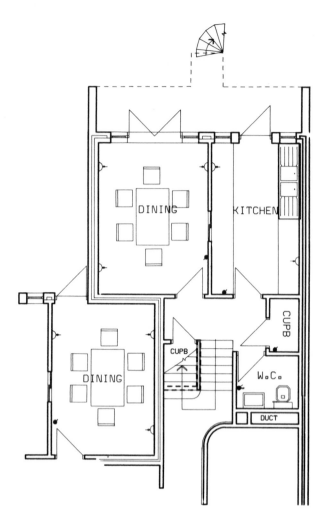

Figure 6.6 A structure overlay with services overlay and equipment overlay

Computer-aided draughting systems can also alter drawings faster than is possible with manual methods. Very few drawings are right first time; most undergo change and refinement as the design progresses. Manual erasure of ink lines involves laborious removal with an eraser or scalpel. The result, especially when a fairly large area is erased, is often very messy. If yet another alteration is required in the same place, the result may be a hole in the paper! It is common practice in most offices to scrap an old drawing to which extensive modifications have to be made and to redraught it. With a computer-aided system, erasure of even single lines is quick and leaves no trace of their former presence. Even quicker erasure is possible if an object that is a pre-defined element is to be removed. A single indication of the object will result in its elimination from the information file and remove all the lines that comprise it.

The increase in speed is yet more dramatic if, instead of being erased completely, an item is moved to another location. This often happens in replanning, where furniture and items of equipment may be rearranged in a room. Manually, of course, this requires erasure and complete redrawing of each item of equipment, but with a computer system all that is required is a simple adjustment of the positional and possibly rotational coordinates of some pre-defined elements in the file. An example of the sort of situation where this facility is especially powerful is adjustment of a partition wall at the detail design stage. The wall will typically have a line of equipment abutting it on either side, so manual erasure and redrawing might take perhaps half an hour. With a computer system the same operations can be performed in seconds.

The convenience of editing can be applied on a larger scale to avoid duplication of effort. One application of this is in the working up of sketch plans produced at the outline design stage. At present, because of the multiplicity of small changes, erasure would be lengthy and would result in a very messy drawing. Also, outline design plans are often produced at a smaller scale than that required for the detail design equivalents. A computer-aided system can make use of the basic sketch plans, provided the changes are not too drastic, and can change the scale as required.

Similarly, if two or more floors of a building are largely, although not completely, identical, it is much quicker to copy one floor and make the relatively minor changes than it is to redraw the plan afresh. In most buildings, the external walls and structural walls and columns will be the same on all levels, so this part of the information file at least will serve as a prototype. Lifts and staircases and many non-structural walls will also often be duplicated throughout.

At another level, computer editing facilities can be of great help in the use of working details, such as those showing the exact construction of wall junctions or of damp-proofing. Many architects' offices have attempted to use standard working details for all their projects, but not many have been successful because each job seems to require slightly different dimensions or different materials or extra features which make it impossible to use the standards. For example, the addition of an extra course of bricks in a wall section detail would mean that half the drawing would have to be erased and redrawn. The computer equivalent is to adjust the vertical position of the upper portion of the wall, which can be done by a single transformation, and draw in the extra brick. Such techniques make the use of standard details much more practicable.

The techniques of copying in different contexts, division and overlaying of information, and editing the information, provide the major increases in draughting speed, but there are a number of more modest, although useful, facilities. For instance, putting text onto drawings by typing is much quicker than stencilling, even for a poor typist. Lines of different styles can be drawn in a single action by selecting the appropriate option, just as a draughtsman selects a pen to give a certain thickness of line.

Thus dashed lines to indicate hidden items or chained lines to define section lines can be drawn just as quickly as solid lines.

The computational and repetitive abilities of the machine can be used to perform many draughting functions directly. For example, planning grids that might otherwise take a full day of tedious work to draw can be produced in minutes. Setting out a pattern of columns, lighting fittings, or other regular arrays can also be automated. Many draughting systems allow semi-automatic dimensioning of drawings; the user indicates the endpoints of the dimension and the machine draws the line and inserts the correct figure for its length.

The amount of information needed to be given to a computer system is potentially a small fraction of the amount transferred to paper by manual methods. There can, therefore, be considerable increases in the productivity of the drawing office. However, the building must be big enough for the overheads involved in using expensive machinery to be absorbed, and for there to be a reasonable amount of repetition at all levels of design, so that the computer's basic strengths can be taken advantage of.

Working methods will have to change somewhat. The results of the draughtman's work are no longer immediately visible; they are held within the computer's storage system, and not on paper. When an alteration to a drawing is necessary, it may be marked roughly on a plotted version but it is counter-productive to spend any considerable amount of effort altering the plot. Eventually, the information file will be updated and a new plot produced; the old plot must then be discarded to avoid confusion. Many draughtsmen find this difficult to grasp, because the drawing on tracing paper has always been sacrosanct and has had to be handled carefully and updated as neatly as possible.

As well as the gains in draughting productivity, it is possible to obtain many beneficial results on the computer that supplement the draughting process. In fact, it is often the production of these supplementary results that provides the justification for the computer system. The possibility arises because the definition of the building shape necessary for producing a drawing can also be used as input data for other programs.

The most common supplementary result is the generation of various forms of textual production documentation. If the doors, windows, and fittings are pre-defined elements, then it is straightforward for the computer to count up how many there are and print out the appropriate schedules. An interface to a standard database program is easy to arrange and all the usual interrogation facilities will then be available. As the schedules tie back directly to the drawing, there will be no disagreements between the two and no need for the consistency checks necessary with a separate database program.

Some computer systems can go further than this and as well as scheduling discrete objects can also calculate quantities of materials. Thus the volume of concrete used in the walls, or the area of window glass, say, can be listed. From these materials schedules, reasonably accurate sketch design costings can quickly be obtained; the designer can therefore check that he is close to his budget figure and will not indulge in any abortive work. These schedules can also be used as the basis for a bill of quantities.

This last facility raises a problem encountered frequently in computer applications; it crosses a line of professional responsibility, because the production of bills is the task of the quantity surveyor. Most private practices are obliged by their clients to work with quantity surveyors who must charge a fixed percentage fee. There is therefore no financial advantage to the architect in producing bills. However, it is quite common today for the quantity surveyor to require longer to cost the scheme than the architect takes to design it and any increase in design time is very welcome. Multi-disciplinary practices, local government authorities' architect's departments and other large organisations with architectural divisions can of course also derive financial benefit from automating bills.

As well as production documentation, other supplementary results are possible that depend on the building shape for part of their calculation. These include most environmental evaluations. Daylight factors are easy to calculate by computer, but this is rarely done because the measuring and typing in of the window size and room dimensions are too onerous compared with the benefits. However, if these dimensions already exist in the computer, then it becomes simple to run a program to calculate and draw out daylight contours, and the architect can check this aspect of the design as he goes along. A similar principle applies to the calculation of heating losses, artificial lighting levels, and acoustic performance.

On the engineering side, some systems are capable of doing structural calculations, laying out pipework, or calculating duct sizes. These and similar capabilities illustrate the ways in which draughting programs can be extended from their basic function to take in more and more of the design and documentation process.

Program classification

The most basic division of computer-aided draughting programs is into interactive and non-interactive types. With an interactive program, the computer continuously monitors the actions of the user and helps him to produce and modify drawings. For example, a line or object will appear on a screen as soon as the user requests it and can then be immediately repositioned or removed if unsatisfactory. Thus the drawing is built up as the sequence of actions and responses progresses. These methods are very fast but require a large investment in machinery.

By contrast, non-interactive methods require the information defining the drawing to be typed onto cards or tape, and then submitted to the machine as a single set of data from which the drawing will be produced on a plotter. This uses the computer much more efficiently, as it is working continuously for a few minutes instead of having to monitor human reactions for hours. Non-interactive methods are thus comparatively cheap in computer costs, but are much more cumbersome in use. The finished drawing must be checked, and any necessary corrections made, by modifying the block of data and resubmitting it to the computer.

Another way to categorise computer-aided draughting systems is into those that work in two dimensions and those that work in three. A two-dimensional system is equivalent in its basic philosophy to manual draughting; the user draws by arranging lines and text on a flat surface. However, if a computer-held drawing contains information about the third dimension, it becomes possible to look at other views of the arrangement. Thus, for example, walls will not be defined in plan as parallel lines, but rather as solids having height as well as width and depth. The user can then choose to look at an elevation, which merely requires the computer to work out the way the wall solids will appear from another angle. There are many supplementary results that require a three-dimensional image for their calculation, including perspectives, heat-loss calculations and pipework and ductwork layout.

The most common way to construct three-dimensional drawing files is to compose them entirely of pre-defined elements rather than individual lines. By providing information on the third dimension of the elements, alternative views of any room can be calculated. As a separate exercise, the user must define the order in which the plans are arranged to make up the complete building, so that elevations of any facade or perspective views can be produced. Computer draughting programs used in engineering applications are true three-dimensional systems, but those for architectural use are normally of the '2½-dimensional' type. In such systems the elements comprising the building are not defined as solids in space, but as rectangular boxes on the faces of which are projected the various views of the element. Thus a cylindrical container would be defined as a circle in plan, and a rectangle in front and side elevations.

This system has advantages and disadvantages. The advantages are that it is much quicker to define elements in this fashion than as true solids, and also that much less computer time is required, as the machine only has to process a fraction of the information required for three-dimensional working. The main disadvantage is that the system cannot give correct results if more than one view of an object is visible at once on any drawing. This will occur when an object is placed in any orientation other than parallel to the three main axes; that is, in a non-orthogonal position. Some 2½-dimensional systems go as far as completely forbidding non-orthogonal positioning, while others will accept it but must inevitably give slightly incorrect elevations.

In practice, this is not often a problem with architectural applications as the structure is almost always made up of surfaces at right angles to each other, and the positioning of the equipment and fittings tends to follow the orientation of the surfaces. *Figure 6.7* shows an elevation obtained automatically from a wall on the plan illustrated in *Figure 6.3*.

A fairly minor disadvantage of 2½-dimensional as opposed to three-dimensional systems is that the range of perspective views that can be obtained is

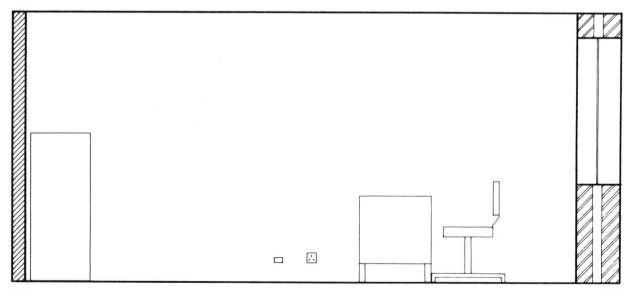

Figure 6.7 An elevation obtained from a 2½-dimensional system

limited, because these always involve viewing several surfaces at once. In practice, where perspectives are obtainable they are limited to showing the structure of the building; thus exterior views and views of room interiors without equipment are possible.

There are other ways of classifying computer-aided draughting systems, but the above divisions of interactive/non-interactive and two-dimensional/2½-dimensional are the ones most relevant to architectural working at present. Computers continue to get cheaper and more powerful; it seems probable that eventually interactive systems will take over from non-interactive, and also that advanced facilities such as 2½-dimensional capabilities and an elaborate range of supplementary results will become popular.

Working methods with interactive graphics

Because of the load that interactive graphics imposes on a computer, the only economic solution is to have a machine dedicated to the task. Ideally, it should serve only a single user. Systems are in use that use a larger machine serving three or four workers, but they need to be very carefully designed if the losses inherent in time-sharing are not to prove prohibitive. More details of viable configurations were given in Chapter 3.

Current interactive graphics systems use a screen to display the drawing. A few early systems used a plotter, but they never became popular for architectural applications because they lacked flexibility; an erasure could only be shown by complete redrawing, for instance. A screen gives flexibility, but at best can only display an area approximately equivalent to an A3 sheet. Therefore, at any readable scale, most drawings will not fit entirely onto the screen.

To display all of a complex drawing at any scale, there must be some means of selecting and displaying particular areas of the complete drawing. Thus if a user works on a number of areas it will seem as if he is moving a larger drawing under a window formed by the screen. The obvious solution of continuous movement from one area to the next is not practicable. This is because a typical architectural drawing contains far too much information for it to be possible to scan and display at anything like the minimum rate of sixteen times per second needed to avoid flicker.

Repositioning can therefore be achieved by moving in jumps of a single screen dimension, or by scaling the drawing down so that the new area is visible, indicating the new centre of interest, then scaling back up. Alternatively, some form of separate overall reference to the complete drawing can be kept and used to pinpoint the new area to be displayed. This reference can be a slave screen that holds the entire drawing at a small scale; indicating a point on the slave screen changes the contents of the main screen. This system is quick and efficient and is not as expensive as might appear at first sight because slave screens cost comparatively little. However, it is a rather clumsy solution to the problem.

Another form of overall reference is a large digitiser on which a plotted version of the complete drawing is laid. Using the special pen, the user can indicate portions of the drawing off the screen and have them brought into view. Several systems using this configuration have been written in recent years, most often using a digitiser of A0 size.

As well as changing position on the drawing, the user may wish to change scale. This enables a draughtsman to work easily at a large scale, or to obtain an overall view of the project by reducing the scale. This facility is unique to interactive computer-aided draughting, and can be very powerful. For similar reasons to those preventing continuous repositioning, the scale cannot be changed smoothly in any reasonable time to give the effect of zooming in or out on the plan as if from a helicopter. Instead, the change in scale must be an abrupt one, a typical jump being to double or to halve the existing ratio.

Given that the screen forms the principal output device by which the computer communicates with the user, there must also be input devices by which the user can make his decisions known. The most frequent input requirements are to indicate a position, to initiate an action, and to select a pre-defined element from the library. An indication of position may be necessary for a number of reasons: for recentring as described above; for pointing to a line to be erased or to an object to be moved; or for indicating two points between which a line is to be drawn. There are a wide variety of devices in use at present to specify positions; the most common ones were described in Chapter 3. Action initiations are needed to inform the system of the process that the user wishes to carry out next so that the computer can interpret his subsequent movements correctly. Thus if the process is to erase, then indication of an object will remove it from the drawing, whereas if the process is to move, indication will release the object from its old location ready for repositioning.

Actions can be initiated in several ways. The most obvious is to type in a command at the keyboard. This has the usual drawbacks of being slow and prone to error. More convenient communication can be achieved by the use of 'function keys'. These are buttons on the keyboard that are not associated with any particular character, and which can be programmed to have any meaning the user wishes. Thus one button might be associated with the action of increasing the scale. The use of function keys is probably the fastest way of initiating processes, but as there are seldom more than twelve function keys available, only the most common actions can be assigned to them and the rest must be typed in.

The use of a 'menu' is a popular means of initiating actions. A menu is a list of alternatives that can be selected by the positional indicator. For example, the list can be written on the screen; touching one of the entries with the light pen or other indication device will initiate the associated action. If the system uses a large digitiser for input, parts of its surface can be used to provide a menu. A digitiser can usually support a larger menu than a screen, on which it is difficult to display more than about twenty options clearly. However, the screen can alter the menu dynamically to break it down into sections or to use more than one level of command. *Figure 6.8* shows a typical screen menu of actions as used in one implementation of the ARK/2 system.

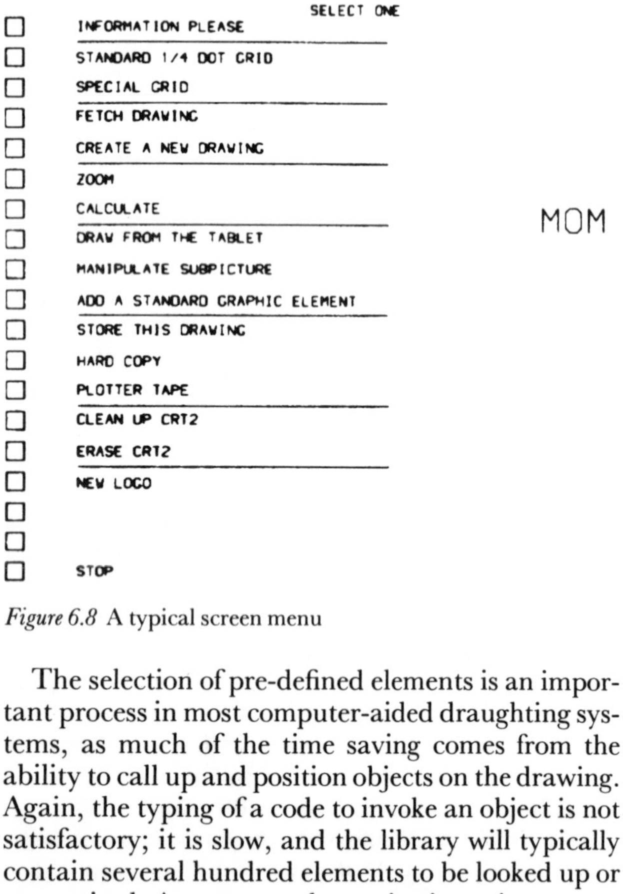

Figure 6.8 A typical screen menu

The selection of pre-defined elements is an important process in most computer-aided draughting systems, as much of the time saving comes from the ability to call up and position objects on the drawing. Again, the typing of a code to invoke an object is not satisfactory; it is slow, and the library will typically contain several hundred elements to be looked up or memorised. A common alternative is again to use a menu to list all the elements available. The number of elements would normally strain the resources of even a large digitiser, so a screen menu with a multi-level structure is often more convenient. The master menu might contain such categories as 'building elements', 'joinery fittings', or 'service outlet symbols'. The indication of, say, 'building elements' would bring up a new list containing the categories 'columns', 'stairs', 'doors', 'windows' and so on. Selection of 'doors' will display a menu of the standard doors available and a final selection of one of the alternatives will produce that element.

One of the decisions that the writer of a draughting program has to make is how to balance the different inputs from the positioning device, the keyboard, the function keys, and the menus. Some systems make extensive use of all these methods while others go to the opposite extreme of putting even the letters of the alphabet into a menu so that the user need never use anything but the positional indicator. Most systems adopt a compromise and emphasise one or two inputs so that the user is not forced to change to another form too often. No currently used solution seems to offer overwhelming advantages and there is little agreement as to what balance is the most convenient. However, research has been carried out on the ergonomics of interactive graphics[62] and one such study found that using a menu was sometimes slower than using a keyboard, but was always more accurate[65].

As well as the major types of input, there are various subsidiary forms: for example, calling up the appropriate drawing at the start of the draughting session; changing the current line weight or the text size; or annotating the drawing. As these are less common than the other types of input they are often relegated to the keyboard.

A large digitiser has several important advantages which have made it a popular choice as the principal input device. It gives a good overview of the plan at all times; space is available for a generous menu; and it is also the best system for putting a copy of an existing drawing into the computer, as is normally necessary when carrying out alteration jobs or drawing up a site plan from a map. Its physical resemblance to a conventional drawing board is claimed to make it more acceptable to the user who is making the transition from manual to computer methods. In my opinion, however, once you have deprived a draughtsman of his pens and instruments and seated him in front of advanced and highly priced machinery there is very little that can soften the blow!

Working off a plotted drawing on a digitiser does have a number of serious disadvantages. The principal one is that by using a fixed drawing some of the benefits of interaction are lost. For example, it is not possible to change the scale while working; movements of the draughtsman's hand across the drawing will always be in the same ratio to the true distance and so the facility of working with great accuracy on a small portion of the drawing will be lost. Similarly, with a 2½-dimensional system, the user cannot choose to work on an elevation rather than a plan without changing the plotted drawing.

Another serious problem is that if the drawing in the computer is modified, there will be a lack of correspondence between the computer version and the plotted version. The solutions to this are to plot out the revised drawing at frequent intervals, which is expensive and time-consuming, or to sketch in the alterations on the plotted drawing, which also takes time and tends to defeat the object of computer-aided draughting.

One fairly minor, but nonetheless irritating, problem with digitiser input is that it is often difficult to make points on the drawing coincident with the correct points on the screen. This is because stretch or buckle in the drawing may not be consistent across a large sheet, and folding the drawing is certain to give inconsistent spacing. If this happens, the user finds that placing the pen on a line does not quite correspond to the true position of the line as shown on the screen. This can lead to more difficult or inaccurate drawing.

Despite the drawbacks, it is demonstrably possible to construct successful systems with large digitisers as the principal input device, and a number of such programs have been used in practice for some years.

The principles of draughting on a computer-aided system show little variation whatever form of input device is used, whether digitiser, light pen, or joystick. There is, however, a distinct dichotomy into the methods used with storage screens and those used with refresh screens. At the most basic level, drawing lines on a storage screen is similar to using ink and paper; once a line is drawn it must be erased and redrawn if it is incorrect. A line drawn on a refresh screen can be moved or changed in length dynamically if necessary.

When working with a storage tube, there will usually be an array of dots or possibly a grid drawn over the screen. The user specifies two dots with his positional indicator and a line will then appear between them. This method ensures true horizontal and vertical lines, where required, that are of exact modular lengths. It may be necessary to resort to typing coordinates if the line is off the grid, but this is unlikely if the building has been designed rationally.

Drawing straight lines on a refresh screen is commonly done by the 'elastic band' method, so called because it gives the effect of stretching an elastic band between two points. The draughtsman first locates a starting point, with a light pen say. As he then moves his pen away a line will appear stretched between the pen and the starting point. Any movement of the pen, whether backwards, forwards, up or down, will completely retrace the line in a new position. *Figure 6.9* shows the effect diagrammatically of

moving the pen from point A to point B, given a starting point S. This process bears little resemblance to manual draughting.

To keep elastic band lines horizontal or vertical and ensure correct lengths, draughting programs commonly only allow the positional indicator to reference intersection points on a grid across the screen. Thus as the user moves the pen, the line changes position or length in jumps rather than continuously. The grid may be visible or invisible; if the latter, the screen is less cluttered but the user has to be careful to count jumps as they occur to check lengths.

With storage screens, different weight lines are indicated by different thicknesses, as with manual draughting. This is usually achieved by defocusing the beam. With refresh screens, different brightnesses are used to indicate weights. As mentioned earlier, as well as a different weight line, the user can specify a different style; the line that appears can be dashed or chained instead of solid.

The methods of positioning and transforming predefined elements also vary with the type of screen being used. With a refresh screen it is possible to call up an element on the screen and drag it to its correct location with the positional indicator. More exactly, the element will continuously position itself at the point referenced and so moving the indicator will bring the element into place. Again, a modular grid can be used. With a storage screen, attempts to drag an element will leave a large smear that will make accurate positioning difficult or impossible. Because of this limitation it must be arranged that elements can be accurately positioned on the first attempt.

The most common method is to assign every element a relationship to the planning grid, which will be displayed on the screen. When positioning an element, it is necessary to indicate two grid lines; the element will then align itself to them in the appropriate manner. A simple example is provided by a square structural column. This will typically be required to be centred on the intersection of two grid lines. When the user wishes to place a column, he need only indicate a point reasonably close to an intersection and the column will appear precisely aligned. This can be a quicker way of locating objects than dragging, if less 'natural'.

A more complicated form of alignment might be assigned to a wall, which could straddle a grid line along its length, or possibly face into a line. Its location along the other axis might be defined by its centring itself over an intersection. A relationship could also be an offset from a line. For example, if walls straddle grid lines, then objects placed against walls will need to be offset from the grid line to half the wall thickness. A typical arrangement of predefined elements on a layout grid is shown in *Figure 6.10*. The columns are positioned within the grid, modular lengths of wall face onto grid lines, and

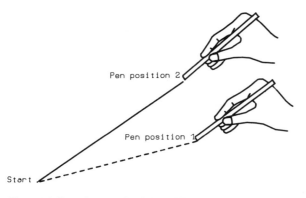

Pen position 2

Pen position 1

Start

Figure 6.9 Drawing an elastic band line

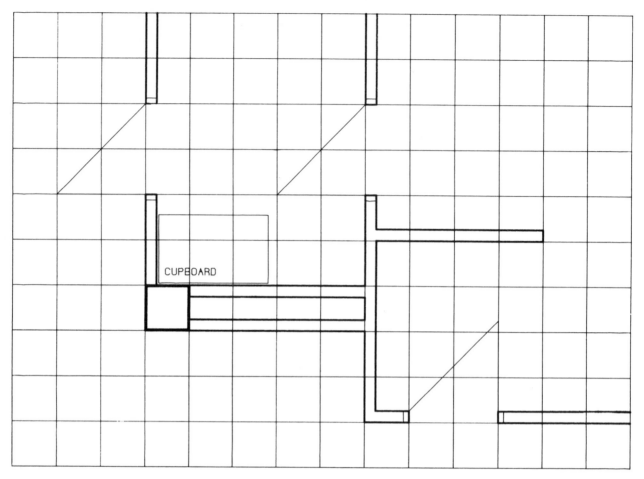

CUPBOARD

Figure 6.10 Arranging elements on a grid

items of equipment have an offset from a line that is either a wall thickness or zero. The problem is that items of equipment will require different offsets if they are to be placed against walls of different thicknesses — structural walls rather than partition walls, for instance. This sort of contradiction will frequently occur with a system of fixed relationships and is difficult to resolve.

A supplementary system of relating elements to a grid is to relate objects to each other. The user indicates which faces of two existing elements are to be adjacent to which faces of the new element. The element will then appear on the drawing in its correct orientation. This method is acceptably fast, especially in such situations as placing a line of equipment against a wall, but of course requires the presence of adjacent elements.

The transformation of elements on a refresh screen can be done dynamically. The function of the positional indicator can be modified so that as the user moves it across the screen the object will rotate as he watches until he is satisfied as to its correctness. Similarly, movement across the screen can be used to scale the element up or down depending on the direction of movement. With a storage screen, dynamic movement is not possible, so the object must be correctly transformed before it appears on

the screen; and it can in some cases be rather difficult to visualise which transformations should be applied to give the required appearance.

The specification of transformations on a storage screen can be done by the sort of methods already described. The use of a menu or of function keys is fast but cannot easily be used for unusual values, such as a rotation of 40°. Typing the instruction gives full flexibility at the cost of some loss of speed. The ideal system is probably to allow both selection methods and typing.

The drawing of arcs and circles can be less straightforward with a computer system than with manual methods, unless the computer has an extra bit of circuitry known as an 'arc generator'. This allows arcs and circles to be defined by a single instruction to the computer, just as straight lines are. Without it, all curves have to be approximated by numerous small straight lines. It is then more convenient to arrange that all curves are pre-defined elements, as otherwise it is difficult to erase or to move them if necessary.

Text is usually input conventionally via the keyboard. It can be scaled to any size and can be of different weights. However, normally only one style of text is provided as, for efficiency, the character set must reside permanently in the computer's memory.

This style is usually not particularly attractive as the characters will contain the fewest lines consistent with legibility, and no curves.

A problem arises with text because of the division of information into overlays. Before text can be put on one overlay, the user must ensure that it does not overlap with the text on any other. Thus if an item of joinery is being labelled on its appropriate overlay, the user must check that it does not interfere with the room name on another, or a door or window reference on yet another. This problem does not exist with manual methods. However, at least one current system sorts out the position of text automatically before displaying it on a screen or plotting it on a drawing.

Although some of the techniques used in interactive computer-aided draughting are more onerous than the manual equivalents, there will normally be a sizeable speed increase overall. Some controlled tests that I have made on various different systems indicate that the average reduction in draughting time is to between one-third and one-quarter of the manual time[70].

The systems that work in 2½ dimensions tend to be less efficient in producing plans than the two-dimensional systems, because separate positioning and transformation may be necessary in the vertical plane. For example, a shelf has to have a fixing height specified as well as being located in plan. Pre-defined elements take longer to include in the library with 2½-dimensional systems as several views must be supplied. Thus the inevitable occasional one-off items will cause more of a delay in updating the alternatives available than in a two-dimensional system. However, the decrease in speed is more than made up for if a reasonable number of elevations are eventually produced.

Working methods with non-interactive graphics

The characteristic of interactive working is one of action and response. The user asks a question and receives an answer, or specifies an action that the machine must take and which is initiated immediately. With non-interactive working the roles of the user and of the computer are completely separated. The user types up a set of instructions to the computer; they are submitted and carried out without further human intervention and finally the results are produced for consideration.

This method of working is obviously not as convenient as creating a drawing on a screen, but it does have certain advantages. The main one is that it is much cheaper in computer time than interactive drawing. Instead of having to buy a dedicated machine costing perhaps £40 000–£50 000 with all its associated difficulties, an office can prepare the data at a terminal or card-punch and send it to a batch or time-sharing bureau. Once in the machine, the data can be processed rapidly and directly to produce the complete drawing. Interactive working, with the need to refer all decisions back to a relatively slow-working human being, is inherently much less efficient.

The other important advantage is that non-interactive working is far more adaptable to changes in workload. If the workload should fall, so will the computing bills if the office uses a bureau service; an office that owns or leases a machine will be losing money. Alternatively, if the workload should rise suddenly, more technicians can be set to preparing the data in parallel; with interactive working all draughting must be funnelled through existing machines. New machines can be purchased, but delivery times are usually measured in months.

The usual method of working is for the architect to produce a free-hand sketch of the building on gridded paper which is then handed to a technician to translate into the computer language. The technician should also be able to identify repeated drawing elements so that they can be used as pre-defined objects. Once prepared, the data is submitted to the computer and a drawing produced. This is checked and the data altered and a resubmission made if necessary. Future alterations will be marked by the architect on the drawing and again given to the technician so that the basic data can be altered to implement the changes.

This method of working will be much slower than interactive drawing. It takes longer to measure the coordinates of an element on a sketch and type in these values than it does to indicate the position of the element on a screen. Other drawing actions are similarly slowed. The method is also very prone to errors. It is easy to miss out a line, to type a dimension incorrectly, or to use the wrong command. As the user cannot see the drawing develop, these errors will remain until the finished drawing is carefully checked.

Some tests that I have made indicate that, despite gains from overlaying and the elimination of repetitive drawing, non-interactive draughting is about one and a half times slower than the manual equivalent[70]. Because of this, the cost-effectiveness of non-interactive systems relies on the production of supplementary results. The most successful systems can produce elaborate schedules, perform environmental analyses, lay out pipework, and do structural calculations.

Another problem with non-interactive draughting is the extreme tedium of preparing the data. Most people find that spending days measuring dimensions and writing out data forms is unbearably boring. It is possible to find staff prepared to do it as a regular job and yet intelligent enough to become competent in the techniques involved, but it is unlikely to become a popular task.

Over the years, there has been a significant shift in

the basic principles of non-interactive draughting systems. This is in contrast to the programming of interactive systems, which has mainly been a development and refinement of principles worked out by Sutherland and other pioneers in the field. In many senses, the early systems tried to copy the actions of a draughtsman. They tended to work in two dimensions and to be general purpose, aiming at duplicating any drawing that could be produced by hand. There were attempts to use these programs in a wide range of applications, including architecture, engineering, and laboratory work.

These systems also mimicked a human draughtsman in that as each line of the drawing was processed it was drawn out and thereafter could not change its length or position. This is essentially because such programs attempt to save operating costs by not keeping a record of every line in the drawing, and so each new line or element in turn is incapable of referring back to earlier lines or elements. This means that, for example, a sink cannot be specified to stand against a wall; its position must be related to a grid line or to a central point. It is therefore quite easy to make a mistake and to have the sink drawn as if it penetrated the wall or stood some distance away.

Thus the early systems simply translated the command language into movements of the pen on the plotter and did not create any sort of data structure within the computer. Without this it is impossible to produce most kinds of supplementary result; the rate of heat loss through a wall, for instance, cannot be calculated unless the computer is aware that a certain pair of parallel lines define that wall. As we have seen, non-interactive systems are rarely cost-effective without results supplementary to the draughting process; these early systems were therefore rarely used in practice.

A characteristic of such systems is that their command languages were usually very clear and easily used. In general, each line of the language began with a word that defined the drawing element to be output, followed by parameters that fully defined the element. Thus a command to draw a circle would be followed by the diameter. The next command might be to move the pen to a new point, which would be followed by two values giving the x- and y-coordinates of the movement. A drawing could therefore be built up one step at a time in a fashion that was natural and easy to use, but rather long-winded.

The main characteristic of modern non-interactive draughting programs is that they maintain a data structure describing the building. The program collects all the information within the computer's storage system and only when all the data has been input does it output the drawing. This obviously puts more strain on the computer, but the increased size of present-day computers and the lower cost of processing make it possible and not particularly expensive.

The presence of a data structure means that the computer can make decisions and help the user. As the program knows which elements are walls, the junctions can be made automatically. Thus a user can simply define two connecting walls and the computer will show the correct L-shaped or T-shaped junction on the final plan; with the older systems, each individual line that made up the wall plan would have to be defined. It is also possible to insert doors and windows into a length of wall; the program will automatically make a correctly sized opening and correctly position the item relative to the wall. Similarly, pre-defined elements can be positioned adjacent to each other or to a wall, and floor slabs and ceiling tiles can be generated automatically. Once a data structure exists, many irritatingly minor actions can be eliminated and the user can define the building at a higher level of detail.

A data structure also makes it possible to produce supplementary results, especially if the draughting system is $2\frac{1}{2}$-dimensional; outputs such as materials schedules or perspectives become possible and add to the potential gains given relatively small increases in the amount of input data. Such a system is therefore particularly attractive in non-interactive working, which must extract every possible benefit to be economic, and which is normally implemented on large computers compared to those used for interactive versions and thus can afford to spend extra time processing data.

Clearly, to define a data structure describing a building and to perform detailed operations such as making wall junctions, the program must be specific to architectural draughting instead of being general purpose. The modern non-interactive system languages therefore require that the user specify the building elements that he is positioning, such as walls, doors and fittings, instead of working in terms of lines and shapes.

The need to cut down on data preparation time has also forced the languages to become much more cryptic. Instead of using simple mnemonic commands such as 'LINE' to draw a line, commands are reduced to single letters; each command will usually carry out several operations and will therefore require many parameters to follow it. This makes the language much more difficult to learn and understand, but it also makes it much more compact and enables an experienced person to work much faster. The modern languages typically occupy only 10% of the space required for an equivalent definition in the older languages.

Data is normally prepared in sections, corresponding to the overlay files on an interactive system. Thus one block will be for the structure, another for the equipment and so on. The sections can therefore be presented in different combinations and with a special control card on the front to set the scale of the drawing to produce a range of results.

MEDALS — a 2-dimensional non-interactive system

One of the best of the non-interactive draughting systems that do not attempt to create a data structure is called MEDALS, and was written some years ago by the Computer-Aided Design Centre in Cambridge, England. MEDALS is an acronym for Modular Engineering Draughting And Library System, and the system is basically general purpose, although it does have some bias towards the creation of architectural drawings. The MEDALS language is used to create two-dimensional drawings and is easy to understand and work with[61].

Each line of data prepared for MEDALS is used for a single instruction. The general form of the instructions is a command word followed by the requisite number of parameters. Optionally, the command word can be preceded by transformation values that can set the starting point of a graphic element, rotate it and scale it. Drawings are built up by specifying displacements or locations in Cartesian coordinates. Conventionally, the point (0,0) or origin will be at the bottom left-hand corner of the drawing and the *x* and *y* values will reference movements horizontally and vertically respectively. The values will usually be in millimetres in architectural practice, but all of these conventions can be changed if necessary.

Perhaps the most basic command is the one to draw a single line. The command word is 'LINBY2', followed by two values giving the total displacement in the horizontal and vertical directions. Thus a horizontal line of 1000mm is drawn by:

LINBY2 1000 0

The line drawn by this command starts at the point at which the pen was left at the completion of the previous command. It is also possible to draw lines to given locations on the drawing, but this is less useful for architects because it involves working out co-ordinate positions instead of measuring the length of lines.

After drawing a series of linked lines, the user may need to move to a different point on the drawing and draw another series or possibly a pre-defined element. The pen is moved without drawing by the command 'MOVBY2' which works in an identical manner to LINBY2 but does not mark the paper. The diagonal lines illustrated in *Figure 6.11* can therefore be drawn by the following instructions, assuming the pen is initially at the point indicated:

LINBY2 500 200

MOVBY2 –500 0

LINBY2 500 –200

Often, on architectural plans, the user needs to draw a long sequence of alternate horizontal and

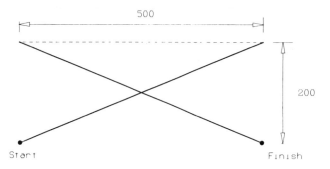

Figure 6.11 Drawing lines with MEDALS

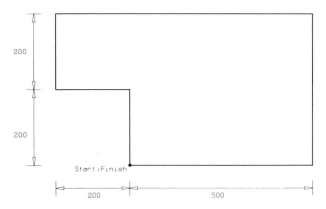

Figure 6.12 Drawing a series of lines with MEDALS

vertical lines. MEDALS provides for this by two commands which require only the lengths of each line in turn; there can be any number of lines. The command words are 'XYXY' and 'YXYX' depending on whether a horizontal or a vertical line is the first in the sequence. Thus the shape illustrated in *Figure 6.12* can be drawn by

XYXY 500 400 –700 –200 200 –200

At a higher level, MEDALS provides some useful shapes and elements that can be invoked by command words. Thus

CIRCLE 1500

draws a circle of 1500mm diameter; the pen is positioned at the centre both before and after the command is issued. Another shape is the rectangle which is drawn by the word 'RECT' followed by values for the width and height of the shape. In this shape the pen starts and ends at the lower left-hand corner. A practical example of the use of this command might be to draw two abutting worktops each of dimensions 1500mm by 600mm as illustrated in *Figure 6.13*. The commands are:

RECT 1500 600

MOVBY2 1500 0

RECT 1500 600

As well as such basic shapes, MEDALS provides many more complex elements, most of which have an architectural application. There are, for instance,

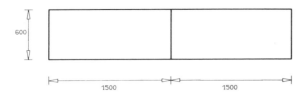

Figure 6.13 Arranging standard elements with MEDALS

command words to draw cavity wall plans, structural columns, and staircases. Parameters must be supplied for most of these; thus the stair plan requires values for the width of step, the tread depth and the number of steps.

To obtain many of the benefits of computer-aided draughting, the user must be able to define his own graphic elements that can be called up and positioned as many times as required. These elements, or modules as they are called in MEDALS, are defined by putting the word 'DEFMOD' followed by the name by which the element is to be known at the head of a set of instructions drawing out the element. The end of the set of data is indicated by the word 'END-MOD'. A useful symbol to have in the library of pre-defined elements might be a simple north point as illustrated in *Figure 6.14*. If this were to be given the name 'NORTHP', the definition of the module would be as follows:

DEFMOD 'NORTHP'

CIRCLE 2000

MOVBY2 –250 –968

LINBY2 250 1968

LINBY2 250 –1968

LINBY2 –500 0

ENDMOD

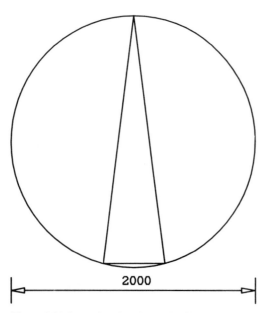

Figure 6.14 A north point drawn by MEDALS

The symbol can now be drawn out wherever the user wishes by the command:

MOD 'NORTHP'

Modules can call other modules, and this can save a lot of repeated drawing if used carefully.

The transformation commands can be used with simple lines and shapes, but are at their most powerful when applied to modules. In default of other instructions, all drawing will commence from the last pen position. If this is not suitable, the user can put the letter 'P' followed by the coordinates of the required starting position in front of the command word. Thus drawing the north point at the top right-hand corner of an A0 sheet at 1:50 scale might be done by

P 50000 30000 MOD 'NORTHP'

Alternatively, a separate move command could be given, but it takes longer and is more difficult to understand when reading the data.

Rotation is specified by the letter 'R' followed by the clockwise rotation in degrees. Thus if true north lies at 5° to the top of the sheet, the north point could be drawn correctly by

R 5 MOD 'NORTHP'

The final transformation is scaling. This is effected by the letter 'S' followed by two values giving the amount of scaling of the element in the horizontal and vertical directions. Usually, both values will be identical, but it can be useful to 'stretch' the length of certain modules, such as shelves or worktops, while retaining the same depth. The north point could be drawn at twice its originally defined size by

S 2 2 MOD 'NORTHP'

If required, more than one transformation can precede the command word. The order of operation is first positioning, then rotation, then scaling.

MEDALS provides many other commands to carry out such functions as writing text, drawing dashed or chained lines, hatching areas, changing the scale of the output drawing, and drawing frames and grids. No supplementary results are provided, although I have obtained a primitive form of scheduling by writing a simple program that reads through the data and counts up the number of each different module. The language is clear and easy to use, but this makes it rather longwinded to prepare data. MEDALS in its present form is therefore not normally cost-effective for architectural applications. At a lower level, however, the basic graphical handling routines which the language controls are powerful and flexible. They are collectively known as GINO, for Graphical Input/Output, and the Computer-Aided Design Centre have sold many sets of these all over the world.

CARBS — 2½-dimensional, non-interactive aspects of a versatile system

CARBS is an acronym in Welsh that translates into English as 'Computer Aids for Design Organisations'. CARBS has its origin in the automatic draughting and billing techniques developed at ICI Ltd between 1959 and 1970 and was first used in Wales as a purely architectural design aid by Clwyd County Council in 1973. The sale and distribution of the system is now organised by the County Architect of Clwyd[64]. Since 1959 the system has been used in many fields of engineering and building design and versions are available for most current computers including some minicomputers.

CARBS was written as a general engineering tool, architectural applications being only one aspect of this. For this reason the system has been designed to hold true 3-dimensional structures as well as working in 2 or 2½ dimensions when this is sufficient. CARBS can be used with interactive or non-interactive input and the various sites use the method most appropriate to their work. However, much of the architectural use of CARBS has been as a 2½-dimensional, non-interactive system, and the techniques involved can be used to illustrate the concepts behind an advanced system of this type.

Non-interactive input is performed via a language known as M&BDL, for Mechanical and Building Design Language. The language is used to create a definition of a structure rather than to manipulate lines and shapes directly. M&BDL is orientated towards architectural applications and can make many assumptions based on the common forms found in building practice. Such assumptions and conventions make the user's task easier for most of the time and can usually be overridden if necessary.

One of the best examples of how the use of conventions can speed data preparation is the definition of walls. These are defined in plan and may be inclined or circular as well as orthogonal. The shape can be described in terms of the length of each wall in millimetres and the direction in which it runs. The direction is indicated by the letters N, S, E or W, standing for north, south, east or west. North can be conveniently taken to be at the top of the drawing and

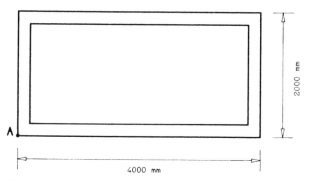

Figure 6.15 A simple floor plan illustrating CARBS input

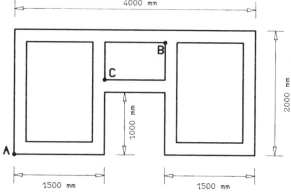

Figure 6.16 A more complicated floor plan illustrating CARBS input

the definition is assumed to proceed in an anticlockwise direction around the rooms. The program automatically forms the correct junctions where walls meet and can distinguish between external walls, usually of cavity construction, and internal walls. The use of this system allows the plans to be defined at a more general level and eliminates the painstaking definition of each small line that would be necessary when using MEDALS.

A simple rectangular room as illustrated in *Figure 6.15* could be defined by the line

> START AT A, E 4000, N 2000, W 4000, S 2000, FINISH

It is not necessary to give simple numbers for lengths. The user can write 'E 4000+250–325', for instance, and the computer will evaluate the result. This avoids the time-consuming and error-prone process of adding up individual dimensions.

Another useful facility is that alphabetic characters can be used to represent constants. For example, if the letter 'T' is set to represent the thickness of the walls, then the more complicated plan in *Figure 6.16* can be defined by:

> START AT A, E 1500, N 1000, E 1000, S 1000, E 1500, N 2000, W 4000, S 2000,
>
> START AT B, S 1000–2T,
>
> START AT C, N 1000–2T,
>
> FINISH

Rather than giving a wall length, it is possible with CARBS to specify that a wall should run up to a certain point on the planning grid. The grid line is enclosed in brackets to distinguish it from a dimension in millimetres. Thus 'W(6)' means extend the wall westwards to grid line number 6; this must be a vertical grid line if westwards has been defined as a horizontal direction. Calculations can be incorporated into grid coordinates in the same way as in dimensional coordinates. For instance, 'E(9–2T)' means go eastwards to a point two wall thicknesses short of grid line 9. Grid coordinates have the advantage of eliminating the cumulative errors that tend to build up when defining a shape as a series of dimensions; they also tie in the drawing to a specific point on the grid.

Before defining the walls, the user has to give their height and also the floor level. Thus the computer can build up a three-dimensional image of the building. Doors and windows can now be positioned and floor slabs and ceiling tiles can be generated and inserted automatically. By these means the definition of the building is made quick and easy. A typical floor plan of 40 rooms could be defined by about 50 lines of coding for the wall definitions, 80 lines for the rest of the structure, and about 10 lines per room to fit them out and annotate them. To some extent this terseness has been achieved at the expense of immediate intelligibility. It takes a fair amount of training and practice to be able to use CARBS efficiently but, once learned, it is a very powerful tool.

Over the years, the CARBS team have built up an extensive library of pre-defined elements. Each item in the library is given a unique code and, if using the 2½-dimensional facilities, the user should give plan and elevational views of the object and can also define sections. The object can be associated with a full description to supplement the code, can be given a cost, and can be classified under the headings the user may require, such as structural elements, services symbols, or contract fittings. New elements can be defined as required for individual jobs and can be positioned on the drawing relative to the grid or to each other. If the application should require the full three-dimensional facilities of CARBS then the shape of an object must be defined in three dimensions in a single description.

To an extent, the definition of an element can vary with its nature. For example, an electrical socket is merely a symbol. A desk, however, is an entity with three dimensions, and a rostrum is a linear component whose length is undefined until it is put into position.

Once the data has been prepared and input, the computer has all the information it needs to produce drawings. Plans can be produced, with certain classes of information present or absent as required; outside elevations or elevations of any internal wall are possible; and as the component definitions include sectional views, sections can be obtained when required. CARBS can also produce structural, foundation and drainage drawings from the information available. Perspectives can be produced, although there will be depth limitations if components have been defined in 2½ dimensions rather than three.

As well as drawings, CARBS can provide an extensive range of supplementary results and in fact, despite its power, the production of drawings alone would not normally be cost-effective. One of the most useful of the results at the production documentation stage is the production of detailed schedules. Schedules of materials can be output, giving, say, the volume of concrete needed, the area of glazing, the length of skirting, or the number of doors. The program is aware of the nature of materials and will adapt the form of output to suit. Schedules can also be produced of the items within the building, classified as required. The fuller description and the classification that can be associated with pre-defined elements makes this possible. A full schedule would have items grouped according to their classification, and each group would be automatically costed separately.

The various schedules produced can be processed by a separate program that uses standard measurement conventions to produce automatic bills of quantities. At present, Clwyd, using their dimensionally rationalised traditional systems, can produce about 60% of their superstructure bills without human intervention, and even higher figures have been reported by organisations using CARBS on industrialised building systems.

There are other programs in the CARBS system that perform such functions as environmental performance evaluations and analysis of costs in use. This information together with the capital-cost estimating and perspective-drawing facilities is used extensively at the design stage by most users. In addition to M&BDL, CARBS offers a powerful data-interface facility which enables the system to be linked to specialist design programs. A typical application using this facility is to analyse structural components, to size them automatically, and to produce a full geometric definition. Other specialist programs in the engineering field include those for the design of heat exchangers, reinforced concrete, car components and simulation systems.

CARBS is a highly developed system and its non-interactive capabilities are possibly the most advanced of their kind to date. Its wide range of uses in building and engineering, both interactively and non-interactively, also suggest that it is a very versatile system.

DAISY — a 2-dimensional interactive system

We have developed in our own office an interactive draughting program called DAISY (Draughting Aid Interactive System) which can be used to illustrate the ways in which such systems can work. DAISY is a two-dimensional system, and although it is capable of producing a certain number of supplementary results it essentially relies for its justification on improving the productivity of draughtsmen. The program is implemented on a Tektronix 4081 stand-alone graphics device and makes use of the extensive library of graphical manipulation subprograms that the manufacturer provides.

The program does not use a digitiser. The drawing as held in the computer is displayed on the screen and worked on directly. We believe this to be preferable to working at second hand via a plotted output. Positional input is provided by a screen cursor controlled by a joystick. When the cursor has been guided to the correct position, this can be communicated to the computer by pressing a button next to the joystick. Most actions are initiated by the twelve function keys provided; these also have a secondary use in calling up pre-defined elements. The less-used commands are typed in at the keyboard. The effect is that for the greater part of the time the user will move the joystick with his right hand and push the function keys with his left; there is therefore little swopping between input devices.

At the beginning of a session with DAISY, the user must call up the drawing he wishes to work on. This will normally be made up of several overlays. If the user is to carry out any modifications to the drawing, therefore, he must declare which overlay is to be modified, and which overlay provides background information. Thus if the client has asked the architect to add a few extra sinks, the sanitary fittings overlay will be the object of modification and the structural information overlay will provide a background. If this distinction were not made, the program could not decide which overlay to assign the additional items to.

As changing drawings occurs relatively infrequently, it is implemented by typing. The drawing to be modified is retrieved by typing 'DISPLAY' followed by the name of the overlay, and the other drawings are retrieved by typing 'BACKGROUND' followed by a list of names that provide the necessary additional information.

The drawings initially appear at a scale of 1:100, as this shows the greater part of most architectural drawings. It is too small for accurate working, and so the user must first select the portion he wishes to work on and enlarge it. This is done by the function keys to 'RECENTRE' and to 'SCALE UP'. Pressing the RECENTRE key will cause the cursor to appear on the screen, and the joystick can be used to position it over the centre of interest. The confirm button can now be pressed and the drawing will be redisplayed, shifted so that the required point is at the centre of the screen.

The SCALE UP function key can then be used to increase the scale of the drawing. Scaling up and down are done in steps to the next standard value. Thus, one step up from 1:50 scale is 1:20, while one step down is 1:100. In general use, the available range is from 1:2000 to twice full size. Repeated pressing of the SCALE UP and SCALE DOWN keys can therefore bring the required amount of detail onto the screen.

At the most elementary level, the user can now add lines to the drawing by the 'elastic band' method described earlier. Pressing the DRAW function key causes the cursor to appear. It can then be moved by the joystick to the required starting position of the line and the confirm button pressed to tell the computer to begin drawing. As the cursor is moved away, the line will appear stretched between the cursor and the starting point. The confirm button is pressed again when the line is complete to the user's satisfaction; it is then added to the file of information.

The drawing process does not end there, because the user can go on immediately to draw another line from the end point of the previous line. In this way, a sequence of linked lines can be drawn very quickly. The drawing process is terminated by pressing the confirm button twice at the end of the last line. A grid setting is normally in operation during the drawing of lines. It has been found that grids of 5 cm and 10 cm are the most useful, but the setting can be varied as required. Resetting the grid is done by typing in the new value.

More powerful is the ability to call and position elements stored in a library file. A typical file will contain several hundred elementary shapes and configurations. Most of the entries will have been made up by drawing individual lines, although it is possible for elements to use other elements in their definition. Thus a counter unit could be made up of a worktop and cupboard and drawer units or, at a higher level, all the information for a standard room could be defined and thereafter positioned as often as necessary. Each element is identified by a code name of up to six characters.

To invoke an element, the user presses the CALL function key, which is the twelfth and last in line. The response to this is that the names of the last twelve elements used are written on the screen above the function keys. The user then has the option of pressing a function key to call the appropriate element or, if none of them is associated with the one he wants, to type in the new name at the keyboard.

In practice, it is found that most of the elements used will be associated with a function key, because it is natural to carry out a single process at a time, such as laying out the structure or positioning service outlets. The process will tend to involve a restricted set of elements of which a dozen will meet most requirements. The most common action of all is to press the CALL key twice, thus reusing the last element. The element selected will appear at the centre of the screen and will be 'attached' to the joystick. Thus as the user moves the joystick, the element will be moved into the required position. When that position is reached, pressing the confirm button will release the element from joystick control and add it to the picture information file. Rotation and mirroring of the element can be done by two function keys provided for the purpose. Rotation is performed in steps of ninety degrees clockwise; so repeated pressing may be necessary. Non-orthogonal rotations, or scaling of the element, are performed by typing at the keyboard.

The final important source of additional information is the inputting of text to annotate the drawing. Pressing the TEXT function key causes the computer to take the next line typed in as an annotation and to place the entire line under joystick control, as with elements. The ROTATE function key can also be used with text to alter the direction of writing.

Few drawings remain unchanged throughout their existence and so DAISY provides facilities to remove and to modify sections of the drawing. Removal is effected by pressing the ERASE function key. This causes the cursor to appear, and it must be placed over a point on the line or element to be removed. When the cursor is positioned correctly, the user presses the confirm button. The line or element is not removed at once, however, because there might be some confusion if two lines were very close or if one element were drawn over another, as when a shelf is over a desk. Instead, the line or element which the computer thinks the user is indicating begins to flash on and off on the screen. The confirm button must then be pressed again to verify that the object is the correct one; if it is not, the cursor must be moved to a less ambiguous location and confirm pressed again. It is not possible to remove a single line of a pre-defined element; the indication of any line is taken as referencing the entire object.

Rather than completely erasing an element, it is sometimes required to adjust its position. This can be achieved by pressing the MOVE function key. The element must be selected by joystick and confirm button as for erasures but, once identified, it can be moved about and transformed in exactly the same way as an element retrieved via the CALL key.

The Tektronix 4081 has a screen that combines the characteristics of storage and refresh modes. The bulk of the drawing is usually in storage mode so that flicker is eliminated and any amount of information can be held on screen. Only elements being moved about and lines being drawn are in refresh mode. Thus when a line or element is erased, it is removed from the file of information but its image remains on the screen. In a similar way, when an element is moved to a new position, its old appearance still remains as well as its new one. After a time, therefore, the user may become confused as to what is and what is not actually present. When this happens, the pressing of the REDRAW function key will erase the screen and redisplay the information file to give a true picture.

The last function key, marked CANCEL, is used to terminate operations in progress. It can be used to reject an element called up in mistake for another, or to terminate the erasure process.

The facilities described are the principal ones that DAISY supports. In use it has been found to be fast and productive, typically three to four times as much as a manual draughtsman, and yet easy to use: benefits which cannot always be reconciled.

As a two-dimensional system, DAISY cannot produce many of the more sophisticated supplementary results. It can, however, provide most of the schedules that an architect would be concerned with, including door, window and equipment schedules. An auxiliary program takes the picture file and also an outline drawing showing the boundaries of the rooms or departments or other areas of classification. The program can then scan the picture file and assign the elements to the appropriate room. The outline drawing also contains the names of the areas in question, so that schedules can be produced in the required form. By selecting the appropriate overlays to be given to the program, schedules of doors, contract fittings and other items can be obtained.

ARK/2 — a 2-dimensional interactive system

ARK/2 was one of the first viable uses of interactive graphics in the architectural profession and was a remarkable achievement at the time. It was written in the offices of Perry, Dean and Stewart of Boston, Massachusetts and went live in 1970. It is now marketed by Decision Graphics Inc. The name ARK/2 comes from the words 'Architectural Kinetics — Man and Machine'[73]. In Britain, ARK/2 was acquired by the Percy Thomas Partnership in 1975, after a careful investigation, and has been used by them on many projects including three major hospitals[68].

ARK/2 is a two-dimensional system. The user works at a screen, as with DAISY, but the screen is of the refresh type rather than combined refresh and storage. This gives a less cluttered result when moving or erasing items as there are no spurious images. However, there is an upper limit to the complexity of drawing that can be displayed. The Percy Thomas Partnership report that they use up to 100 standard elements in a single drawing, and then link them together at the plotting stage to produce the final result on paper[74].

Points on the screen are indicated by a cursor controlled by a small digitiser that usually rests under the user's right hand.

ARK/2 supports about a dozen programs to carry out various tasks. To create or modify a drawing, the program COMPROSPACE must be executed. When this is running, a menu is displayed on the right-hand side of the screen called the Master Operational Menu (MOM), one version of which was illustrated in *Figure 6.8*. Selections from MOM may bring up other menus in a logical hierarchy. For example, the 'Draw from the tablet' (i.e. digitiser) option brings up a menu of the various elementary drawing functions available. These include straight lines, which can be forced to be horizontal or vertical, rectangles, circles, arcs and text.

Certain other selections require the user to type in information at the keyboard. For example, the option labelled 'Add a standard graphic element' will ask the user to input a 5-digit reference code for the required element. The general effect is that the user's attention is on the screen for most of the time and the use of the keyboard is kept low.

The 'Calculate' option in MOM allows the production of supplementary results involving measurement. By indicating the endpoints of a line via the digitiser, the length can be obtained, which allows quick evaluation of dimensions or of circulation path lengths. Indicating the corners of a room or other space will calculate the area of the space and, by multiplying by a vertical dimension, volume calculations can be made automatically. The ARK/2 teams report that they find these facilities very useful for such tasks as cost estimating and calculation of materials.

The other programs in the system cannot strictly be classed as supplementary results, because they require separate data input rather than direct work on the drawing files. The program 'COMPRO-VIEW', for example, requires the outline of the building to be entered via the digitiser and from this data will produce perspective views. Other programs exist to manipulate bubble diagrams, to produce schedules and specifications or perform critical path analysis.

By the standards of the computer world, where change is very rapid, ARK/2 is a well-established and well-tried system. In the time it has been used it has become very reliable, as the errors in programming have been eliminated; it has also become adapted to easy use.

BDS — a 2½-dimensional interactive system

In its lifetime, the integrated set of programs now known as Building Design Systems (BDS) has undergone radical changes in scope and in the machinery on which it is implemented. Development originally started in the UK in 1971 when the firm of Applied Research of Cambridge and the Oxford Regional Health Authority wrote a program to define buildings constructed with the Oxford Method industrialised system. The program, which at that time was called OXSYS, could be used to produce a definition in 2½ dimensions. From this definition, drawings could be made and a wide range of supplementary results were obtainable including bills of materials, structural calculations and various environmental analyses.

At that time, the program was implemented using a time-sharing service on a large computer. As was discussed in Chapter 3, interactive graphics requires a dedicated machine, and the users of the program complained of slow response and high costs. In 1975,

therefore, the program was rewritten for a minicomputer with the cooperation of the National Research Development Corporation[71,72].

BDS is generalised enough to cope with traditional building methods as well as industrialised system building. Each user is provided with a workstation consisting of a storage screen for graphical output, an A0 digitiser as the main input device, and a teleprinter to provide keyboard input and textual output. In a typical configuration, two or three workstations share one of the more powerful minicomputers on a time-sharing basis. There is, therefore, some inefficiency due to the computer's swopping its attention between users, but this is minimised by the fact that the machine is dedicated to a single application and can therefore be tuned to a certain specification; also, it only has to support two or three users rather than the forty or more that a typical commercial time-sharing service will handle. The fact that the computer is much more powerful than the ones installed in stand-alone graphics systems means that it is much more suited to the calculation of supplementary results, which is one of the strengths of BDS. A typical workstation is pictured in *Figure 6.17*.

Figure 6.17 A BDS workstation (courtesy Applied Research of Cambridge)

The philosophy behind BDS is that it is an integrated computer-aided building system that can help the architect at all stages of the design. The production of drawings is simply one aspect of this, although owing to the nature of architectural information it is the principal one. To supply all the supplementary results, the data has to be arranged logically, and a good deal of information has to be supplied besides purely spatial information.

To define a building, the user must first divide it into self-contained 'functional zones'. There can be many different types of zone, such as rooms, suites, activity areas, departments, or building blocks. Definition of the boundaries of the zones allows the program to produce results broken down by area; thus a cost analysis might for example be on a department-by-department basis. Various properties may be assigned to zones. They may be named, given a cost target, or assigned environmental standards. Again, these properties are used in the production of various supplementary results.

The library of pre-defined elements is similarly structured logically and contains information in addition to the graphical information. The library is called a 'Codex' in the BDS program and follows an hierarchical structure. It is divided into families of items such as beams, cladding, and partitions. The families can be divided in turn into subfamilies; thus cladding might be broken down into wall panels, fascias, and external doors. Finally, the subfamilies contain the individual components. As BDS is a 2½-dimensional system, views from front, back and the sides may be defined as well as the plan view. Three sections may also be given. In addition to the graphical definitions, the user can assign any number of other properties to the component, including a description and a cost.

After these preliminaries, the user can begin to define the building. The usual first step is to locate partition walls which will normally face onto the perimeters of the room functional zones that have already been defined. This gives a basic outline plan which can be plotted and put on the digitiser. The plan then becomes a reference sheet on which the detailed positioning of the components can be indicated. The digitiser can also have a menu of components placed on it, from which items can be selected; or the component code can be typed in at the keyboard. As the screen at a BDS workstation is of the storage type, the position and orientation of the item must be defined before it can be added to the information file for the building. This is done by relating reference points or sides of the object to points on the existing drawing, which may be grid lines, zone perimeters or other components.

By these means the building can be defined quite quickly, the only serious restriction being that components may not be placed in non-orthogonal orientations. Because of the elaborate structure behind BDS, it is not as easy to use as the majority of other interactive systems. The command systems of DAISY or ARK/2 are concerned only with transcribing graphics and therefore can be made simple enough to be mastered within hours. The user of BDS, however, has to have a reasonable awareness of the organisation of the data, and therefore requires more training. Given the requirement for an integrated system with a variety of supplementary results, this problem is probably unavoidable.

A wide variety of drawings can be obtained from the building definition, including plans, sections and elevations of any internal or external wall. It is also possible to obtain perspectives of the structure from any viewpoint, internal or external. The components on the drawings may be labelled if required, and the system has the useful feature of sorting out labels so that they do not overlap on the plotter.

Other results obtainable include bills of quantities, schedules of components and of materials, costings, mechanical ventilation design, circulation analysis, and environmental performance checks. The programs that comprise BDS are continually being extended by a full-time team at Applied Research of Cambridge and will no doubt in time become even more versatile.

RUCAPS—a 2½-dimensional interactive system

RUCAPS is the acronym of Really Universal Computer-Aided Production System. The program was written in the office of the Gollins Melvin Ward Partnership and is now marketed by the firm of GMW Computers Ltd. RUCAPS does not aim to be an integrated system like CARBS or BDS, but rather concentrates on the rapid production of drawings to justify itself and so might be considered closer in its working philosophy to ARK/2 or to DAISY.

The output device of RUCAPS is a refresh screen and the input device is an A0-size digitiser. The designers of the program have tried to confine all input to the digitiser because they feel that the use of a pen on a board is the most natural and easy to accept, and that joysticks and light pens are contrived solutions. The digitiser supports an extensive menu which can initiate actions and manipulate drawing elements, and which includes the letters of the alphabet and the ten digits; the user can therefore pick out commands by touching the appropriate letters and numbers with the pen. This use of what is effectively a single input device and a single output device makes the system easy to learn and use, and facilitates fast working.

The first implementation of the program, which is still in use, was as a stand-alone system where a minicomputer served a single workstation. More recently, the RUCAPS team have developed a system in which the minicomputer can support at least two graphics terminals without any degradation of response time. This is possible because the terminals used have a certain amount of processing capability of their own. This configuration has the advantages that the machinery cost per user is reduced and that plotting and scheduling can take place at the same time as the terminals are in use. The terminals are from Imlac International Ltd's DYNAGRAPHIC range which has been designed for this type of application.

The user works at the digitiser by first indicating on the drawing opposing corners of the area of interest. This area then appears on the screen so that the user can see the effect of his actions. Pre-defined elements are then called up as necessary by spelling out their code names on the alphabet menu and are fixed by indicating their relationship to grid lines. Options on the menu provide facilities for transformations, including non-orthogonal rotations.

The usual variety of drawings from a 2½-dimensional system are then obtainable, including plans, sections and elevations. Supplementary results are not considered important to RUCAPS, but simple scheduling is available in the form of lists of com-

ponents used and in schedules of continuous construction quantities.

RUCAPS has proved efficient in practice and has fulfilled its commitment to the fast creation and production of drawings. One of the first schemes to which it was applied was the planning of 1 200 000 m² of educational space in association with another firm. A team of three to four operatives produced the equivalent of 675 manual drawings in eleven months and brought the estimated requirement of 16 500 man-hours of draughting time down to about 6800 man-hours[63].

7
Visualisation

Principles of visualisation

It is an interesting contradiction that although the most important aspect of architectural design is the attractive disposition and massing of three-dimensional solids, an architect develops his design almost entirely from two-dimensional plans and elevations. Some rough perspectives will normally be drawn at the start of the design phase, but they will not usually be to scale or very detailed, and often have aerial viewpoints to show the site plan. Essentially, the architect relies on his spatial sense to tell him that the building is acceptable from other viewpoints.

Properly drawn perspectives or detailed models are sometimes produced to present the building to the client and others whose spatial sense may be less well developed; but because they are expensive to provide and difficult to modify, they are nearly always produced after the design is finalised and play no part in the generation of the design.

The methods of generating a representation of a building by computer, techniques known as 'visualisation', can be used to produce views from any point and from any angle very quickly. These views can help the architect in generating a pleasing design; they can also be used in presenting the building to the client and to the other members of the design team, thus increasing involvement from an early stage.

Computer visualisation can sometimes offer results otherwise unobtainable without a great deal of effort. For instance, it can give representations from unusual viewpoints from which it would be difficult to calculate perspectives, or which would be inaccessible to a modelscope. Once the initial data has been input, generation of perspectives is fast and cheap, so that many views can be produced with little effort. The designer can therefore 'walk round' his building and see it as an observer would after completion. Some visualisation programs can show the shadows cast by a building at different days of the year, different times of the day and at different latitudes. If a building has strong shadows this information is very valuable to the designer but would require extensive calculations to draw manually.

If data is provided for the internal walls it is also often possible to obtain perspectives of interiors.

From these, the architect can see the effect of walking through his building: a consideration that is often neglected when designing.

Building schemes that are difficult to represent manually because of their nature can often be handled easily with the help of a computer. For example, a large housing estate might contain only a few different types of house. Manually, a view of the estate would require each house to be drawn separately; but a set of computer data need only define each type of house once, then give the positions at which they are found.

Certain unusually shaped buildings can be represented much more easily by computer methods: for example, the geodesic dome popularised by Buckminster Fuller. An accurate manual perspective of such a dome requires long and tedious calculations, but as the structure is so formalised the data defining it to the computer need only occupy a few lines, and as many perspectives as necessary can then be generated with little further effort. The computer perspective in *Figure 7.1* was produced in the UK by

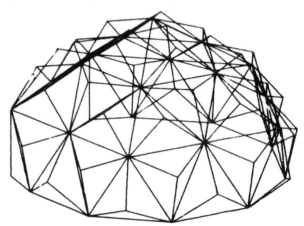

Figure 7.1 Perspective of a classroom at Kennington Road Primary School (courtesy Lancashire County Council)

Lancashire County Council architect's department and shows a school classroom that was built of glass-reinforced plastic modules. Most designers would find it difficult to visualise this structure without pictures of some kind, and as these would be so tedious to draw manually it might have been necessary to design a more conventional building instead of experimenting with new concepts and materials.

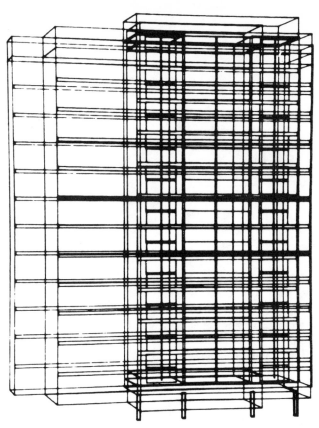

Figure 7.2 A wire-line perspective (courtesy the Computer-Aided Design Centre)

Figure 7.4 A half-tone perspective (courtesy the Computer-Aided Design Centre)

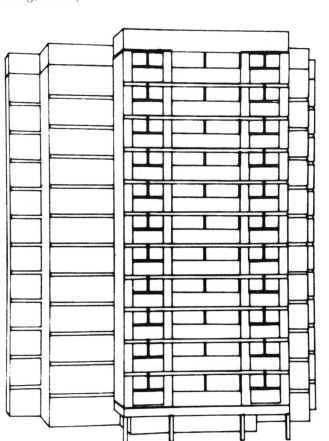

Figure 7.3 A hidden-line perspective (courtesy the Computer-Aided Design Centre)

There are several different forms of computer visualisation currently available. The simplest and cheapest is known as a 'wire-line' perspective. The effect given is as if the object were transparent, with the lines that are normally hidden being shown. A typical wire-line building perspective is shown in *Figure 7.2*. A simple mathematical transformation will convert lines in space into lines on a two-dimensional plane, representing the object as seen from a particular viewpoint and in a particular direction. The generation of this sort of perspective is therefore quick and cheap by machine as relatively few calculations are involved.

To remove the hidden lines and show the object as if it were opaque, the computer must perform many more calculations and therefore image generation will be slower and more expensive. In the worst case every line will have to be compared with every plane surface to see if any plane hides it. Over the years, a lot of effort and ingenuity has gone into solving the problem of hidden-line removal; it is now well understood, and it is unlikely that there will be any great improvements on the methods now used. However, even the best of these is comparatively slow. The equivalent hidden-line perspective of the building in *Figure 7.2* is shown in *Figure 7.3*. This view cost about ten times as much as the wire-line perspective, but given the relatively low cost of processing today, the

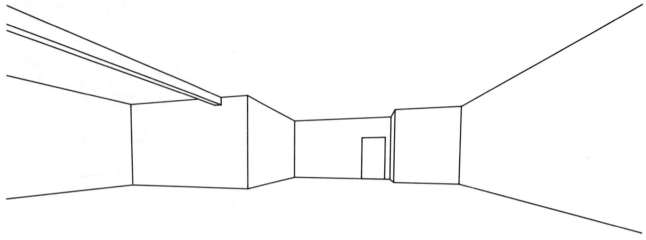

Figure 7.5 An interior perspective

resultant figure is still not excessive and will become less as time goes on.

By using a different technique to that needed for hidden-line removal and by sending the result to a screen rather than to a plotter, it is possible for the computer to generate a shaded perspective with half tones giving a very realistic impression similar to that of a black-and-white photograph of a model (*Figure 7.4*). The usual method of generation is to take 'slices' through the object, in a direction and of a thickness corresponding to the scan lines of the screen. This method therefore takes each region of the screen in turn rather than each line on the object. Despite this, the same basic principles apply as for hidden-line removal.

The generation of interior perspectives is no different in principle from the production of external views, although useful savings in computer time can be made by only submitting the data for the rooms in question, as otherwise the program must deal with many more lines that could not possibly appear on any perspective view. A typical hidden-line interior perspective is shown in *Figure 7.5*. When looking from one room into another it is often more helpful to see the hidden lines than to have them removed, as a better idea of the circulation patterns can be gained. Most visualisation programs provide the option of retaining the hidden lines to give a wire-line drawing. The presence of many extra lines can be confusing, so some programs provide the useful compromise of showing the hidden lines dotted, while leaving the visible lines solid.

A lot of work has been done in recent years on producing computer-generated images in colour. Some of the results can be very impressive in showing such things as flow patterns and cartoon images, or presenting the results of computation in an easily absorbed manner. Some use has been made to present building views in colour, but so far the results have been disappointing; the colours tend to be flat, lacking the subtle variations of brickwork or grass, and they also tend to be garish because of the difficulties of colour specification by program. In future, however, such images may well become of acceptable quality.

Until very recently, visualisation techniques have been implemented by programs in general-purpose computers. Since the advent of cheap micro-processors, however, it has been possible to build special machines to display views. Among the firms currently producing such machines are the Evans and Sutherland Corporation. Their device is a high-resolution colour-television screen driven by a small computer provided with extra circuitry to generate representations of three-dimensional objects. The machine can recalculate and display coloured and shaded perspectives thirty times a second. So an object can be shown in continuous motion, and an architect could revolve his building on the screen and see it from all angles. This would be impossible with a conventional computer; even a large machine would require several seconds to perform the calculations necessary for a single view. Regrettably, the cost of such ingenious and attractive machines is far too high for an architectural firm to justify. It is likely, however, that in a few years they will be cheap enough for the larger practices to be able to afford one.

Within a computer, all information must ultimately be stored in the form of numbers. The representation of a three-dimensional shape is usually held as the spatial coordinates of every corner point on the object, together with information linking the points together. This method requires curved lines to be approximated by a number of straight lines and curved surfaces by a number of plane facets. Early visualisation programs required the user to calculate and type in the spatial coordinates of the corner points[78]. This was extremely tedious and error-prone, and so the programs were seldom used in practice. The modern equivalents have sophisticated data-collection methods, often requiring much more space in the computer than that needed to calculate the perspectives themselves.

Despite the great improvement, the basic problem of computer visualisation techniques remains the effort of collecting the data that defines the building. This takes so long that it normally dwarfs the cost of the computer runs to produce the perspectives and will almost always take longer than the manual drawing of a single view. So computer visualisation is not usually cost-effective if only one or two views are required: for example, when the design has already been finalised and a perspective is required for presentation, or when the building is an infill between existing structures, and only a couple of views are necessary. A survey by the Design Office Consortium found that the break-even point between manual and computer methods lies at about three or four views[76], although this varies with the nature of the building.

If the building contains a lot of arbitrary massing or detailing, the effort of data preparation may be so high as to make it almost impossible for computer visualisation to be cost-effective. As an example, we might take Sir Denys Lasdun's National Theatre on the South Bank of the River Thames in London (*Figure 7.6*). This building consists of many masses of different shapes; the amount of data required to represent it would be considerable. However, even fine detailing can be represented economically if it is repetitive. *Figure 7.7* shows a view of King's College Chapel produced by Applied Research of Cambridge. As most of the window bays are identical, only one prototype was needed; the computer was instructed to reuse the same data along the facade. Furthermore, the bays themselves are symmetrical about the vertical axis, so it was finally only necessary to prepare data for half of one bay, and this was automatically mirrored to represent the other half.

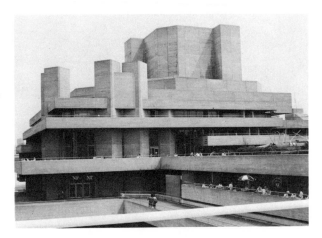

Figure 7.6 The National Theatre

The other serious drawback of computer visualisation techniques is that the quality of the result is much worse than that of the manual equivalent. The amount of detail cannot be very great; it is therefore necessary to define the building in broad outlines, avoiding the intricacies. This is because, to keep the cost of calculations to a reasonable level, all the data has to be held within the computer's own memory. If some of the data were stored on a magnetic disc, it would have to be scanned once for every line in the data. As disc accesses are much slower and more expensive than memory accesses, the time and cost of the calculations would greatly increase.

Unfortunately, a computer's memory is severely limited and much of it will be required to hold the visualisation program itself; therefore the amount of data that can be stored is comparatively small. Most visualisation programs cannot handle more than 500 plane surfaces, and as even a single doorway might be made up of over 100 surfaces, there is little scope for detail. Curved lines and surfaces exacerbate the

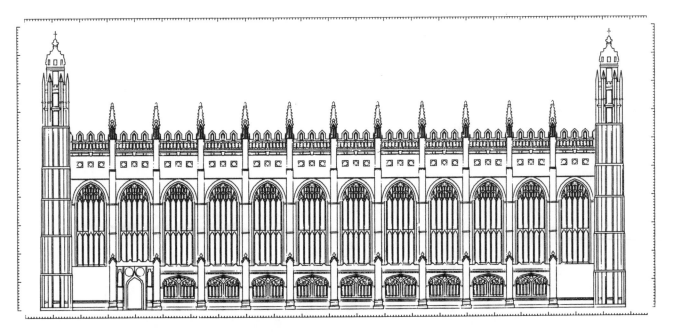

Figure 7.7 King's College Chapel (courtesy Applied Research of Cambridge)

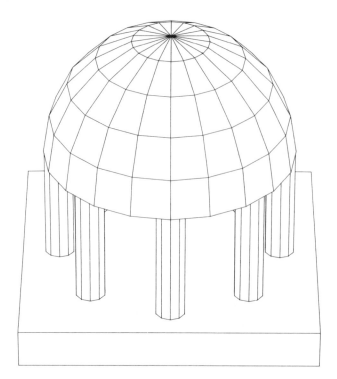

Figure 7.8 Computer visualisation of a rotunda

problem, as their generation into straight-line and plane-surface approximations adds greatly to the amount of data to be processed; it is therefore often necessary to use crude approximations.

Although most programs accept these limitations in the interest of reducing costs, there is at least one program that uses the magnetic disc as auxiliary storage for large amounts of data. It can handle complex buildings containing thousands of planes. The penalty paid is that it takes the computer several hours to produce a hidden-line perspective of an object of such complexity. Usually it is impracticable to include fine detailing.

Curved surfaces not only cause problems in calculation, but also mar the quality of the output. They will be shown as a multitude of facets, giving an ugly tessellated appearance to domes and similar features, and a striped appearance to circular columns and barrel vaults. The computer visualisation of a rotunda in *Figure 7.8* illustrates this problem.

The finish on a computer perspective will not be as good as that of most manual efforts. Almost all programs require every line in the data to be given the same weight, so that the output will be entirely in a single pen thickness; a human draughtsman will almost automatically draw such features as doors, windows and facade details more lightly than the rest to balance the emphasis of the design. Also, there will normally be no question of putting in trees, figures, cars and the other small details that add finish to a perspective or model. With floor plans and working details, the lack of finish does not matter so much

because these drawings convey information; a perspective drawing, however, is expected to be a representation of reality and so a loss in quality is far more noticeable.

In practice, the poor quality will not usually hinder the designer, who will be more interested in the overall impression of the building. A computer perspective will not normally be good enough for publication or formal presentation; but savings can still be made by using the computer output as a basis for manual finishing by 'working up' the drawing with shading and detail.

Shaded pictures produced on a screen suffer from the same problems of lack of detail and finish, and for the same reasons. Further, because of the poor resolution of the screen, the amount of detail on the output may be degraded even more. Subjectively, however, a half-tone image is much more satisfactory than a line drawing and therefore will often be considered adequate for presentation where a plotted result would not.

Data-collection methods

The most popular method of data collection used by modern visualisation programs is to make available a range of elementary solids such as boxes, cylinders, and pyramids. The user's data then dimensions these shapes and fits them together, so constructing a block model in much the same way as a child uses a toy building set to build up complex models from simple shapes. An example of this is shown in *Figure 7.9*. A simple representation of a church with a steeple can be exploded into a box shape for the nave, a differently proportioned box for the tower, and a pyramid for the spire.

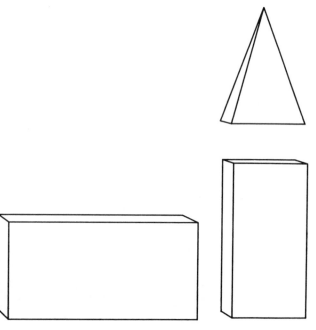

Figure 7.9 Defining a church with elementary solids

The use of shapes conveniently avoids the tedious and error-prone calculation of the coordinates of each corner on the building. The data is much easier to collect and can be understood at a glance. Shapes can be modified or reassembled if required, to represent an evolving design. Curved surfaces such as those on columns and domes are dealt with merely by providing cylindrical and hemispherical solids which have plane facet approximations already applied.

Most perspective programs using this method of data collection allow shapes to be positioned so that they interpenetrate. This can save a lot of trouble with junction conditions. For example, two pitched roofs meeting as shown in *Figure 7.10* can be defined as simple solids with triangular cross-sections interpenetrating as indicated by the dotted lines. If interpenetration were not possible, an irregular junction shape would have to be specially defined.

Even greater savings can be made with more complex objects, especially those containing curved surfaces. For example, an inflatable structure will typically consist of a dome with one or more tunnel entrances that form airlocks. With interpenetration facilities this is defined simply as a hemisphere with smaller hemicylinders embedded in it, but would require a lot of calculation to define in any other fashion.

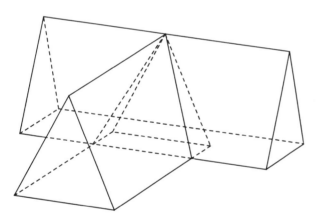

Figure 7.10 Interpenetration of solids

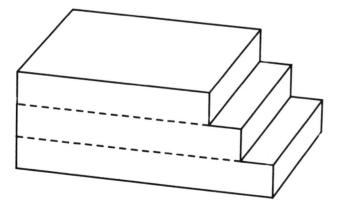

Figure 7.11 Redundant lines in an assembly of solids

A problem with assembling shapes is that if two or more are adjacent, there may be redundant lines where they join. For example, the flight of steps in *Figure 7.11* is easily assembled by stacking rectangular slabs but parts of some lines, as shown dotted, are redundant. A few programs have facilities for detecting that two surfaces are coplanar and eliminating the boundary lines.

Most programs have the important ability to reuse a complex shape once it has been constructed. For instance, if a building has several entrances, the flight of steps described above could be defined as a standard module and located where necessary in the same way as an elementary solid.

Modules can be scaled up or down and independently along each axis; thus the flight of steps can be of different width for a wider entrance, or of different pitch or tread, or a combination of these. A scaling factor of minus one forms a mirror image of an object. This is useful if a building or part of a building shows symmetry; a module of one half can be constructed then joined with its mirror image to form the complete shape.

The actual assembly of shapes may be done in several ways. One popular method is to provide a special command language in which an instruction will specify a shape, dimension it and locate it in space. This is easy to use and understand, but a special-purpose language is often so specific to its job that it cannot utilise the other powers of the computer and so can sometimes make data collection more difficult.

Because of the possible limitations of special command languages, some data-collection methods for visualisation consist of a set of subprograms that can be invoked from a conventional general-purpose computer language. Fortran is the usual choice because of its modular characteristics and numerical abilities and also because of its universality. Each subprogram will generate a particular shape and the parameter values give the dimensions and the location in space. By calling the subprograms as required, the data will be built up in exactly the same way as with the special command language, but the user can also use the other facilities provided by the computer.

Computational capabilities are often useful, for example in positioning shapes according to a mathematical formula or generating a shape that can be defined by an equation, but they are rarely found in visualisation command languages. Such languages may also lack the ability to repeat the same process again and again, so it will not be possible automatically to lay out regular arrays of shapes, which is often useful with regular and symmetrical buildings. Decision-making capabilities are also usually absent, so it is not possible to include useful aids, such as checks that all shapes above ground level are supported by other shapes, or other restrictions corresponding to building applications.

A general-purpose language can perform all these operations, but of course is only usable by a reasonably experienced programmer. However, it will usually be found that a command-language system is adequate for defining buildings, which are rarely susceptible to mathematical analysis; it is also much easier to use.

Command languages and subprograms in general-purpose languages are both non-interactive methods of working which, as in draughting, are cheap and do not require a dedicated machine, but do not make it possible to see the building appear as the data is built up, so that the process is prone to error. With the growth in the number of minicomputers, interactive methods of shape arrangement are beginning to appear. The user can select from a menu of elementary shapes, call them up on the screen, and move them into position using the positional indicator. Correct alignment can be done visually rather than by computation and so is much faster. A comparison by the Design Office Consortium found that one interactive program could define a complex office block in a twentieth of the time required with a non-interactive language. Interactive methods are also much less prone to error, which also implies a speed increase with complex models.

The disadvantage of interactive methods is of course the high cost of a graphics device. An architect does not often require perspectives and it would not make economic sense to buy the machinery just for this purpose. However, if the office already owns an interactive graphics device for draughting, this approach would probably be preferable to other methods.

The various methods of assembling block shapes are the usual means of data collection for visualisation programs. There have, however, been recent experiments based on a completely different principle, that of supplying simple projections of an object from which the computer can calculate the three-dimensional shape. One method uses a digitiser to input the coordinates of a plan and two elevations of a building. Given the orthogonal projections, it is not difficult for the machine to match up points on each, making some allowance for the inaccuracy of manual draughting, and generate a data file. This method can be very fast indeed as it does not take long to digitise a few dozen points and, as plans and elevations will usually be produced anyway, there is no need for additional work.

Systems are in use using projections other than orthogonal, but working on similar principles[81]. This approach is interesting and appears promising, but at the time of writing no program based on it has been in regular productive use.

The CADC visualisation programs

The Computer-Aided Design Centre in Cambridge,

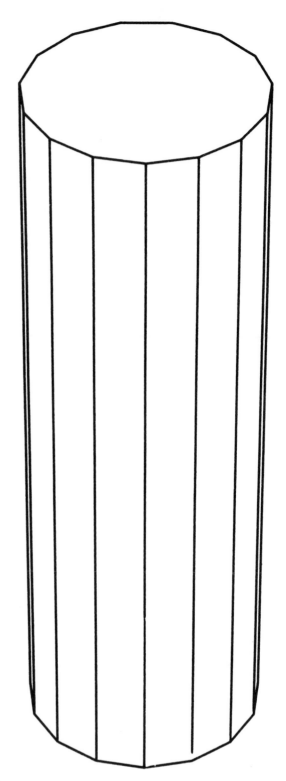

Figure 7.12 A cylinder defined by THINGS

England, has produced a set of interconnected visualisation programs. The principal components of the suite are a program called THINGS that collects the data, a program called HIDDEN LINES that produces hidden-line perspectives, and a program called GREYSCALES that can generate half-tone images on a screen[77].

THINGS is a versatile program for assembling shapes. A wide range of elementary solids is provided, together with facilities for the user to define his

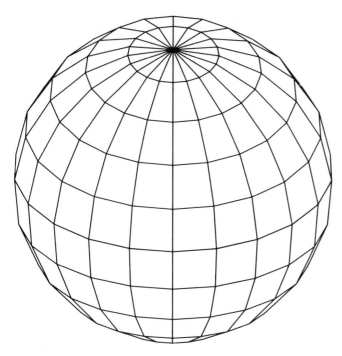

Figure 7.13 A sphere defined by THINGS

own. THINGS is usually used as a set of subprograms invoked from a Fortran program. However, it also has its own command language which is similar in syntax to the MEDALS draughting language described in Chapter 6. The THINGS language is an advanced example of its kind and illustrates the way non-interactive shape assembly works in practice.

The elementary shape most frequently used is the rectilinear solid, named **BOX**. The user must supply with this command word the width, depth and height of the solid. Thus a tower block 50 m wide, 20 m deep and 30 m high can be generated in outline by

> BOX 50 20 30

On a different scale, a square structural column might be generated by

> BOX 0.3 0.3 3

A cylindrical shape is defined by its radius, its height, and the degree to which it approximates to a true cylinder. This last parameter is necessary because visualisation programs cannot handle curved surfaces; a 'cylinder' must really have a polygonal cross-section and the last parameter gives the number of sides of the polygon. A large number will clearly give a better approximation to reality but will require more processing time and computer memory. Another point is the relative size of the cylinder on the final drawing; the larger it appears, the more sides it should have to give a reasonably accurate representation. A cylindrical column of half-metre radius and a height of three metres might be adequately approximated by a fifteen-sided solid as illustrated in *Figure 7.12*. It can be defined in the THINGS language by

> CYLIND 0.5 3 15

Similarly, a sphere will be made up of trapezoidal facets, and THINGS requires the user to specify the number of these. For convenience, this is done by specifying the number of lines of latitude on the sphere. Therefore to define a 'sphere' of fifteen metre radius and with facets bounded by ten lines of latitude and twenty of longitude the user should write

> SPHERE 15 10

The resultant shape is illustrated in *Figure 7.13*.

A shape that can be used in a variety of situations is the 'pyramid', which is a solid with a rectangular top and bottom. Obviously if these are of the same dimensions then the resulting shape is an ordinary box, but by varying the relative sizes a number of differing effects can be produced. The command word is 'PYRAMI' and must be followed by the width and depth of the bottom, the width and depth of the top, and the overall height. Thus to define a flat-topped 'Aztec' pyramid as shown in *Figure 7.14*, with a 20 m square base, a 7 m square top, and a height of 25 m, the user should write

> PYRAMI 20 20 7 7 25

By making certain of the dimensions zero, different shapes can be produced. A gable-end roof can be regarded as a pyramid with a rectangular base, say 8m by 5m, and a rectangular top of dimensions 8 m by zero. If the height from base to ridge is 2.5 m the shape is defined by

> PYRAMI 8 5 8 0 2.5

This roof is illustrated in *Figure 7.15*. Similarly, a typical hipped-end roof as shown in *Figure 7.16* could be defined by

> PYRAMI 8 5 4 0 2.5

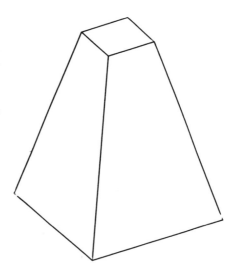

Figure 7.14 An Aztec pyramid defined by THINGS

A conventional 'Egyptian' pyramid can be considered as a shape having a square base, of perhaps 50m on each side, and a square top of 0m on each side. If the height is 55 m, the pyramid's definition is

PYRAMI 50 50 0 0 55

The resultant shape is shown in *Figure 7.17*.

The solids described so far are symmetrical, but it is also possible to define asymmetrical shapes. One of

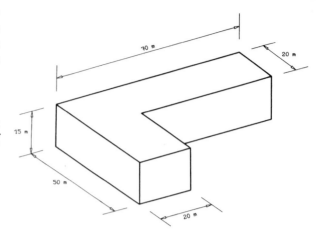

Figure 7.18 A prism defined by THINGS

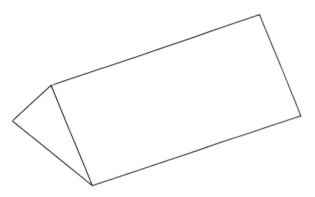

Figure 7.15 A gable-end roof defined by THINGS

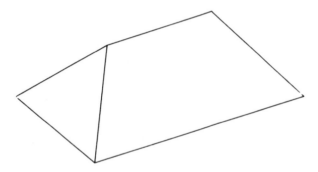

Figure 7.16 A hipped-end roof defined by THINGS

the most useful for the architect is a solid with an irregular cross-section which is constant along its entire length. Such a shape, if the cross-section is made up of straight lines, is known as a 'prism'. Many modern buildings can be represented in general terms by a prism with a rectilinear cross-section; the outside perimeter is often irregular, but it is the same shape at the roof as at ground level, the roof being flat. The form of the command is the word 'PRISM' followed by pairs of coordinates giving the vertices of the plan shape; there may be any number of these. The final parameter gives the overall height. The L-shaped building illustrated in *Figure 7.18* can be defined in outline by

PRISM 0 0 20 0 20 30 70 30 70 50 0 50 15

These are some of the more commonly used shapes, but there are a number of others available, such as the cone, the hemisphere, and the hollow cylinder. It is also possible to define an object of arbitrary shape as a collection of facets; this would usually be used for complex curved surfaces such as car bodies.

By assembling these elementary solids, objects of great complexity can be built up. This is done by prefixing each elementary solid definition with positional and possibly rotational transformations. Positional transformation is invoked by the letter 'P' followed by the required distances in the x, y and z directions from the base point. Thus stacking one cube on top of another, as shown in *Figure 7.19*, is done by:

BOX 2 2 2

P 0 2 0   BOX 2 2 2

Note that THINGS does not remove the redundant lines.

An object can be rotated about any axis by the letter 'R' followed by the number 1, 2 or 3 to specify one of the three possible axes of rotation, and then the amount of rotation in degrees. Rotation is relative

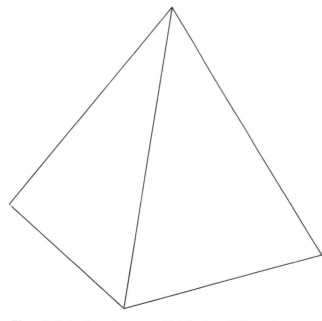

Figure 7.17 An Egyptian pyramid defined by THINGS

to a basic alignment that every object possesses. For example, a cylinder is positioned upright in default of other instructions and could be used directly as a column, perhaps; if it is to be used horizontally (as a water pipe, say), it could be rotated by 90° about the third axis which runs from the foreground to the background. This would be done by:

R 3 90 CYLIND 0.5 3 15

An example of a simple assembly might be a basic house shape. A house could be defined as a box surmounted by a pyramid for the pitched roof. The chimney could be represented by a smaller box that pierces the roof. THINGS allows interpenetration, and in this example saves the definition of a special prismatical shape to form the visible part of the chimney. The house illustrated in *Figure 7.20* can therefore be defined by the instructions:

BOX 10 20 10

P 0 0 10 PYRAMI 10 20 0 10 10

P 0 0 18 BOX 1 1 3

Assembled shapes are most useful when they can be used repetitively. Our house shape might be used dozens of times in different positions to form an extensive housing estate. To preserve a shape for re-use it must be defined as a module, or 'thing' as the THINGS program calls it. A module is created by putting the command 'DEFTHI', followed by its

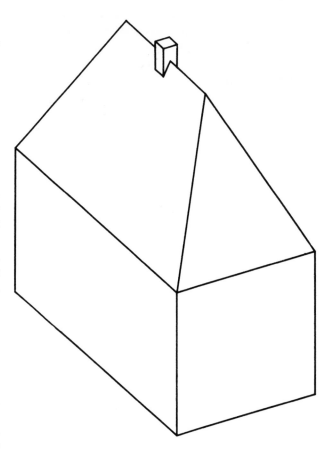

Figure 7.20 Assembling a house with THINGS

name, in front of a set of instructions defining it. The end of the definition is marked by putting the command 'ENDTHI' after the last instruction. Thus to make the simple house into a module called 'HOUSE' the user should write

DEFTHI 'HOUSE'

BOX 10 20 10

P 0 0 10 PYRAMI 10 20 0 10 10

P 0 0 18 BOX 1 1 3

ENDTHI

The specification THI 'HOUSE' is now an elementary solid like BOX or PRISM. It can be positioned and rotated as many times as required to build up the housing estate.

An extra transformation that is useful with user-defined modules is a scaling factor. Placing the letter 'S', followed by three numbers giving the scaling factors along the three axes, in front of a command word will scale the solid by those factors. Thus to get a house twice as big as the defined one in all dimensions, the user can write

S 2 2 2 THI 'HOUSE'

Positional, rotational and scaling transformations can all be applied at once to any shape or module.

When the user has defined his building, he can either link into the HIDDEN LINES program to get

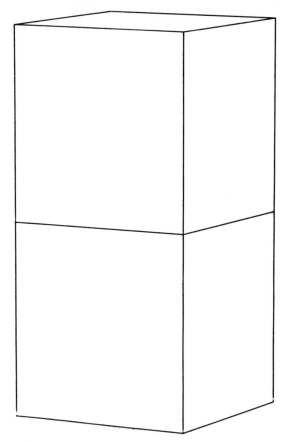

Figure 7.19 Assembling solids with THINGS

a line perspective, or into the GREYSCALES program to get a half-tone image. Both these programs are broadly similar for the user; they require a few instructions defining such things as the viewpoint, direction of view, and the scale the image will appear at. They also have extra facilities including the ability to produce stereoscopic pairs of images, and axonometric projections rather than perspectives.

The Computer-Aided Design Centre has several other programs for visualisation, including one to generate data defining a ground shape from digitised contours and one to produce a perspective for photomontage given details of the camera and the photographer's position.

AUTOPROD

AUTOPROD is a visualisation program written by Colonel F.A.N. Hitch of AUTOPROD Computer Graphics and now marketed by GMW Computers Ltd[80]. It is a very versatile and flexible program and is in widespread use. At the time of writing it has been implemented on eight different makes of computer.

There is a choice of four methods of data input. At the most basic level, it is possible to provide a list of the coordinates of every vertex on the object to be visualised and information on how they will join up to form planes. This is rather slow for human use but does allow the definition of arbitrary shapes. The second form of input is an elementary command language. This can only manipulate rectangular prisms placed in orthogonal alignments and hence construct simple block models. It is primarily intended for the beginner to try out the various picture options.

The third form of input, and the one most commonly used, involves writing a Fortran program to invoke AUTOPROD subprograms. Subprograms are available to generate a range of shapes and to organise them into a complex structure. There is a wide range of elementary shapes including some less common solids such as slotted structures, troughs and meshes. The shapes can interpenetrate freely and the user can either allow AUTOPROD to generate the lines of interpenetration or define his own. Edge lines on shapes can be omitted as required; thus redundant lines can be removed where surfaces meet. There are also facilities to generate automatically only the horizon lines on curved shapes such as domes, so that a facetted appearance can be avoided.

As well as the standard shapes, AUTOPROD subprograms are available to generate shapes by defining the cross-section of the shape at points along its length. It is also possible to assemble modules from elementary shapes and give them reference numbers by which they can be recalled as required.

The last form of data input is a command language that allows a user to define a structure by naming shapes and specifying their positions. This does not offer all the AUTOPROD facilities but enables a designer with no knowledge of Fortran to use the system.

AUTOPROD is especially versatile in its output options. There are fifteen different projections available, including the usual perspective, axonometric and isometric views, and also basic animation and stereoscopic pairs. Views can be obtained from inside as well as outside the structure. It is not possible, however, to obtain half-tone images like those produced by GREYSCALES. A view is controlled by up to 47 parameters and the program can hold a viewing specification while the user changes one or two of them; this is valuable in tracking past a building, or altering the viewing angle to try different effects.

AUTOPROD is far more versatile in both data generation and output definition than THINGS with HIDDEN LINES, and indeed possibly more than any other existing visualisation program. The wide range of options available means that AUTOPROD can give a finish and precision to its output that are often otherwise unobtainable. However, the very scope of these options means that to use AUTOPROD to the full requires a good deal more training than is necessary with less sophisticated programs.

The Leeds Polytechnic modelling system

The computer unit of the School of Architecture and Landscape at Leeds Polytechnic in the UK has since 1974 been developing a system for modelling buildings[75]. There are two main elements of the system, a set of programs which can create and manipulate a database containing a description of a building and its site, and a library of routines which can investigate and analyse the description in various ways. The principal analysis available at present is of thermal performance, but it is intended to add a wide range of evaluations.

Building definition is performed by a fast interactive method, and one of the output options is the production of perspectives. The system is therefore very useful for visualisation. As the package is orientated towards architectural applications, facilities are provided that are extremely useful to designers but which are not available from THINGS with HIDDEN LINES or from AUTOPROD.

The system is currently implemented on a minicomputer driving two storage-tube screens. Building shapes are constructed space by space; the spaces may be rooms, activity areas or complete floor plans. The designer sketches a space plan on one screen, or chooses from a menu of standard plans. He then puts it into position by using the other screen which initially holds the site plan and on which the model is

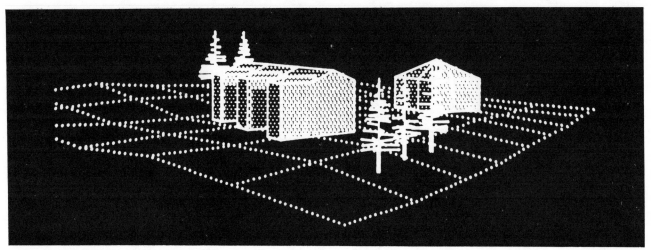

Figure 7.21 An output from the Leeds Polytechnic modelling system (courtesy Leeds Polytechnic School of Architecture and Landscape)

constructed. A roof can be added to the space before it is put into position, and again this may be sketched in or may be chosen from a menu of standard roofs. This input procedure is easy to use and can be very fast, especially on the more complex schemes where it is difficult to grasp the whole shape mentally. The ability to specify spot heights on the site plan and have the spaces automatically level themselves to it also eliminates the definition of the ground shape that can be a major task with other systems.

While the underlying definition of shapes is generalised, the current interactive method of definition imposes some limitations; the spaces must be prismatic in shape and can only be rotated about the vertical axis. This is adequate for most modern buildings but not all, and might in theory discourage more imaginative solutions. There is also no facility for automatic curve generation; curves must be sketched in on the screen where required.

The program has a very high capacity, which makes it suitable for the large amounts of data needed to define buildings. A magnetic disc is used to store most of the data and this allows the structure defined to contain over 5000 planes, a capacity about ten times that of most other visualisation programs. However, owing to the inherent inefficiency of this approach, such a complex building would require several hours of computer processing time for a single hidden-line perspective. Spaces may later be

removed from the data by pointing at them with the positional indicator; this makes error correction and modification quick and easy, which is often important at the early design stages.

The only form of visualisation available is perspective views, which may be taken from the exterior or an interior of the scheme. It is possible to vary such parameters as the focus point and the direction of view. The program is therefore very unsophisticated compared with AUTOPROD, but it does have some extra output features that give realism to architectural modelling. For example, a shaded drawing may be produced as well as a simple line drawing. The sun's position is specified by day of the year, hour of the day and latitude, and the output will show the correct tones and the shadows cast. This information can be extremely valuable to a designer. The system also allows the user to position standard tree shapes where required; obviously they will not be exact representations but their presence will add realism to the outputs. *Figure 7.21* shows a shaded output as displayed on a screen.

To a certain extent the package sacrifices accuracy and flexibility in the interests of speed and subjective realism, but this is a trade-off that most architects would accept. A major drawback is that it is necessary to purchase a minicomputer to use the program, but of course it could be used for other purposes besides visualisation.

8
Job management

The need for job-management systems

During the construction process the contractor must control large numbers of men, large quantities of materials and a great deal of plant and machinery. All these resources are expensive, and if the contractor is to remain competitive they must be tightly and efficiently controlled. By contrast, during the design process only a handful of architects and technicians are employed, and they use virtually nothing in the way of plant and materials beyond drawing instruments and paper. As so few resources are employed, control is relatively simple and does not have to be particularly strict. However, buildings are getting larger and more complex and are requiring bigger design teams; also, there is strong pressure from clients to finish the building as early as possible. Both these factors make project control more difficult. In addition, the costs of employing staff are still rising and the office that does not make the fullest use of its employees will find its already narrow profit margins eroded still further.

A typical control system will specify when tasks should be carried out and how many men will be needed at each stage of the project. It should also be able to reschedule these tasks to take account of the number of staff actually available and their specialist skills. Such techniques will allow the administrator to look ahead and prepare for each task as it falls due, and to specify deadlines accurately. This should help to cut down on the last-minute rushes and late-night working that happen so frequently in many offices and must harm the quality of the design. The administrator will also be able to keep his staff fully employed by organising transfers between jobs at different stages and by knowing when to employ new staff and when to refrain from replacing leaving staff. This last advantage is especially important in an architect's office as professional staff do not expect to be hired and fired with the fluctuating workload, and temporary staff are expensive and require training before they can be of their greatest use.

Another important benefit of formal control systems is that they will pinpoint the 'critical' tasks that must be finished on time if the completion date is not to be delayed. Thus the administrator can make sure that these activities start on time and have sufficient staff, if necessary by delaying the completion of non-critical activities. Conversely, it is only by speeding up the critical tasks that the completion date can be brought forward; therefore if the project is running late or needs to be hastened for some reason, attention can be accurately focused on the most relevant activities and not wasted on tasks that have leeway in their completion time.

The sort of results described can also be obtained by a seasoned administrator on the basis of knowledge and experience, and if such a person is available it may well be more efficient to control the project manually rather than use a computer program. However, if a sufficiently experienced person is not available, use of the computer can ensure adequate results and avoid gross errors and oversights. This is a good example of the way a computer can 'de-skill' fields previously needing years to master. An expert in almost any technical subject can program a computer to follow the best procedure in every combination of circumstances and to evaluate the most accurate formulae, however laborious. His experience is then available to anyone with access to the program, who need only be familiar with the broad outlines of the subject to achieve good results.

Principles of critical-path techniques

The control technique most commonly used is the 'critical path' method, although there are others. This method of project analysis has been around since 1957 and is in widespread use to control all sorts of complex activities from building to the space programme. It can be applied by manual methods, and in fact this was often done before computers became commonly available; but because of the large number of laborious, if elementary, calculations involved it is much more suitable for computer evaluation.

The critical-path method relies on two basic assumptions: first, that the task to be analysed can be split into a number of distinct smaller tasks; and secondly that, apart from the first activity, each task cannot start until certain of the others have been completed. These assumptions are not always valid, as will be seen, but most projects can be expressed in

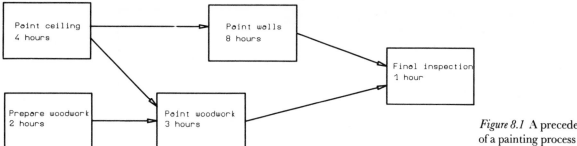

Figure 8.1 A precedence diagram
of a painting process

this way with relatively small amounts of distortion and can then be analysed in a number of useful ways.

As a very simple example, we can take part of the construction process: the task of painting a room. This can be split down in many ways at all levels of detail. For example, a contractor would probably find it most useful to specify painting a room as a single task to be carried out by one man, whereas a time-and-motion investigator might require a detailed analysis down to the level at which taking the lid off a paint pot is a separate activity. For our purposes, we can divide the task into: painting the ceiling, taking four hours; painting the walls, taking eight hours; preparing the woodwork in the room, such as the skirting boards and window and door frames, which might take two hours; painting the woodwork, taking three hours; and a final inspection that takes one hour.

Having determined the best division of the task into subtasks, the best order for the activities must now be decided. The first constraint is clearly that preparing the woodwork must precede painting it. The next is that the ceiling should be finished before the walls or woodwork are started, to avoid the risk of splashing completed work. Lastly, the final inspection must follow the completion of the painting of the walls, ceiling and woodwork. This information can be expressed as a diagram, using boxes for each activity and linking arrows to represent the order in which they are carried out (*Figure 8.1*). Note that no link has been drawn between painting the ceiling and final inspection, although it was one of the constraints. Such a link is unnecessary because painting the ceiling precedes painting the other surfaces and they precede final inspection. It would not be wrong to draw in the link, but it would save computer time not to, and make the diagram clearer.

This network can now be analysed, and it can be calculated that the total length of time for the project will be thirteen hours. Also, the activity of painting

the woodwork can start at any time between the fifth hour and the tenth hour of the project without delaying its completion. The usual terminology is that this activity has five hours 'float'. However, the activities of painting the ceiling, painting the walls and the final inspection must start as soon as the preceding activities are finished and must not take longer than their scheduled times if the project is not to over-run. These activities are said to be 'critical' and to lie on the 'critical path': the longest path through the network.

The activity of preparing the woodwork is a little different. It could be delayed by up to seven hours from the start of the project without delaying the completion time, i.e. it has seven hours float. But if full advantage is taken of this float, then painting the woodwork becomes critical; it must start as soon as the woodwork has been prepared and must not be delayed. If the activity of painting the woodwork is not to be interfered with and is to retain all its float, then preparing the woodwork can only be delayed by up to two hours. Thus although its 'total float' is seven hours, its 'independent float' is only two hours.

The diagram we have been using is drawn with the activities given prominence and is called a 'precedence diagram' or 'activity-orientated diagram'. It is also possible to draw out the network giving prominence to each distinct point in time. With this method, the points at which activities start and finish are usually represented by circles in which start and finish times can later be written in. The activities are then shown as arrowed lines which indicate the relationships between the points in time. To illustrate this we can draw out the room-painting project in this form, known as an 'arrow diagram' or 'event-orientated diagram'. The arrow diagram is shown in *Figure 8.2*.

Note that in this form a dotted line has had to be included to indicate a relationship where an activity links to more than one following activity. This line is

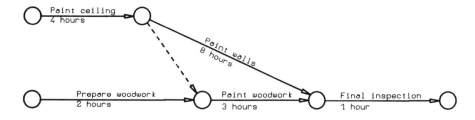

Figure 8.2 An arrow diagram
of a painting process

regarded as a 'dummy activity' having zero duration. Arrow diagrams are neither as clear nor as easy to construct as precedence diagrams, and are in fact being supplanted. However, they were used for many years before the introduction of precedence diagrams and are still in widespread use.

So far we have only considered relationships where one activity commences on the completion of others: a finish-to-start relationship. There are others, however. For example, if the work progress is being recorded, the time at which painting begins should be noted. Obviously this cannot be done until the task has started and therefore this is a start-to-start relationship, which is shown diagrammatically in *Figure 8.3*. More frequently, one activity is dependent on the start of another after some delay. For instance, all the woodwork does not have to be prepared before it can be painted; provided enough men are present, one man can fill and prime the woodwork and another can paint it after it has dried, say one hour. But in this case there is also the constraint that painting the woodwork cannot finish until at least one hour after the preparation of the woodwork has finished. This situation is frequently encountered; one activity runs parallel to and slightly lagging behind another. This is illustrated in *Figure 8.4*. A delay time can be put on other types of relationship as well, to allow for postage time, setting or curing times, and other events that need not be specified explicitly.

Critical-path techniques impose a formalism in specifying activities and their relationships that is not always present in practice. It is, for example, impossible to specify properly a process of feedback or continuous refinement. An architect often works by scribbling a design, then redrafting it in a slightly changed and more detailed form; he continues this process until he has a result that satisfies him. The

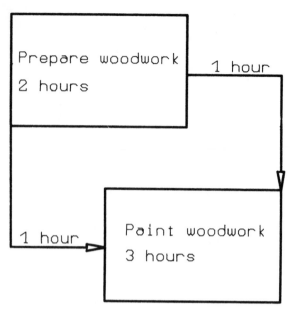

Figure 8.4 A parallel relationship

only ways that this can be specified by the critical-path method are either as a single activity, or as a fixed number of steps. There is no way to make one activity loop back into itself or into any other activity that has already commenced.

Another rather unnatural restriction is that it is only possible to express links between activities relative to their starting and finishing points. Thus it is not possible, for instance, to show directly the architect sending the quantity surveyor information halfway through the production of the working drawings. Instead, either the activity of producing working drawings must be split into two activities with a link to the quantity surveyor's activities at the end of the first stage; or there must be a start-to-start link between the architect's and the quantity surveyor's activities with a delay time on the link to give the effect of a later start to the following activities.

Construction of a network is greatly simplified by drawing out the diagram of activities and their relationships first. The whole project can then be seen in a pictorial form and loops or omissions and other mistakes are much easier to detect. Some programs allow the network to be redrawn on the computer plotter from the input data, in which case it is not necessary to draw the initial network very carefully. Otherwise, it will be necessary to draw neatly and legibly and to lay out the activities with plenty of space between them to allow for the inevitable future alterations. When changes are required, because of a change in policy or because of a hold-up during the project that affects subsequent activities, it is usually essential to be able to refer back to the network diagram to understand the implications of the alteration.

Construction of the network can also be simplified by the use of composite activities. This entails replacing a single activity in the network by a number

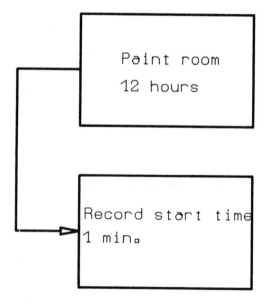

Figure 8.3 A start-to-start relationship

of activities forming a subnetwork of their own. For instance, a network might contain an activity entitled 'prepare production documentation' which can obviously be replaced by a network of its own. This facility is provided by many critical-path programs. It means that a skeleton network can be defined at a general level by the project manager; the activities can then be replaced by detailed networks, prepared in isolation by the appropriate specialists, to give the final complete set of data. While this facility is often useful, an architect's projects are rarely complex enough to need it.

Practice is needed to construct good critical-path networks. The user has to train himself to express reality in the formalised critical-path conventions. He has to decide on the level of detail of the network; too many activities will be confusing while too few will be unhelpful. The way the activities are linked can also be a problem; putting in links that are not strictly necessary will make the project appear too rigid and lacking in float time, while putting in too few links may give the impression of more leeway than there actually is. The technique is not difficult to master, however, and the amount of information to be collected is not high. It will usually be possible to prepare the data for a typical job in a day or two.

The data-preparation time can be reduced to a few minutes if an existing network can be used. This could be a network from a previous similar job that can be used again with small modifications, or it could be a standard network that is applicable to a range of jobs. In the UK, two generally accepted guides to the management of building construction are the RIBA Plan of Work and the Department of Health and Social Security's Capital Projects Code. The Capital Projects Code, usually abbreviated to CAPRICODE, is orientated towards the construction of medical buildings such as hospitals and health centres.

In our office, we have constructed standard critical-path networks, based on these job-management guides, for several different sizes of building. When a new commission is received, the most appropriate standard network is taken and modified to suit any special requirements for that particular job. A reasonably accurate barchart showing the tasks to be done and the deadlines to be met can then be produced very quickly. Most offices have a preferred way of organising jobs, which may not correspond exactly to the Plan of Work; these policies can be embodied in a standard network and then automatically used when applied to a scheme.

The data preparation does not end with the specification and ordering of the tasks to be done. It is common for the logic of the network to allow several activities to go on at the same time, even if there are not enough staff available to carry them all out at once. They must therefore be done in some order, so reducing float time or increasing the time taken to complete the project. For this reason, another factor must be introduced into the critical-path analysis: the allocation of resources. Resources are most often people possessing the skills required to carry out the tasks in question, but they can also be materials, or even money. For example, a contractor will only have a certain number of bricklayers available, and this will set a limit on the number of bricks that can be laid in the times specified. He may only be able to take delivery of a certain number of bricks in any given week and this also sets a limit to the amount of bricklaying that can be done. Thus in this case both the bricklayers and the bricks represent resources associated with certain activities.

Critical-path programs allow the user to specify the resources required for each activity and also the total number of resources available. When scheduling the activities, the program will shift the starting dates of activities within their float times, or if necessary increase the time of the project, to accommodate the activities within the resource limits. As well as ensuring that these limits are not exceeded, the program will also attempt to level out the use of the resources so that, for example, the same number of men are used throughout the entire project. The advantage of this is that consistent use is made of the resources available. It is also possible for the program to report on what resources are required and when: the number of men needed, the right time to order the minimum quantities of materials, and so on.

Some of the more versatile programs allow a variable amount of resources to be utilised over the period of a single activity. For example, painting might require one man for the first day to make preparations, two men on the last day to touch up mistakes, and five men for the intervening period. On a long activity this will obviously give more accurate results than averaging out the number of workers required. With most programs, the limits on the resources can be varied over the project period. Some programs also allow two limits to be specified, the first a 'normal' maximum and the second a limit that could be obtained by taking on temporary staff, paying extra for earlier delivery dates of materials, and other expedients that might be necessary to meet deadlines.

Where resource allocation is provided, it is very easy to associate costs with each resource. Thus bricklayers are paid a certain amount each month, painters a different amount, cement costs so much per cubic metre and so on. Comparatively little extra information need be supplied as there are not usually many different resources. Given these unit costs and the resources needed for each activity, the program can easily calculate the total cost of the project, so that it can be checked that the budget will not be exceeded. The program can also print out the costs incurred month by month; this is important when money is tight and cash flow is a problem, or at a time

SIMPLE DESIGN PROCESS

```
                                              79
                                              JAN                    FE3              MAR              APR
              ACTIVITY TIMES                  1    8   15   22   29   5   12   19   26   5   12   19   26   2
              ACTIVITY NAMES                  •    •    •    •    •   •    •    •    •   •    •    •    •   •

AR01          PREPARE SKETCH PLANS            *XXXXXXXXXX
CL01          CLIENT APPROVAL                 *         XXX
AR02          PREPARE 1:200 FLOOR PLANS       *         OOAXXXXXXXXXXXXXXXXXXXXXOOOO
AR03          PREPARE 1:50 ROOM LAYOUTS       *         XXXXXXXXXXXXXXXXXAXXXXXXXXXXXXXXXXXXXX
CN01          CONSULTANTS DEVELOP SCHEME      *                                OOOOOOXXXXXXXXXXXXXXXXXXXXX
QS01          Q.S. COSTS SCHEME               *                                              XXXXXXXXXX
AR04          FINAL PRESENTATION              *                                                         X
                                              •    •    •    •    •   •    •    •    •   •    •    •    •   •
```

Figure 8.5 A barchart output from a critical-path analysis program

of high interest rates. Costs can also be broken down by resource type so that, for example, the possibilities of saving money by using different materials can be investigated.

A fault of many critical-path programs, so far as the architect is concerned, is that they are too complex. A major construction project or a space travel programme may involve thousands or tens of thousands of separate activities. Projects of this size require management specialists and computer programs that are large, flexible and have numerous options such as subnetworks, variable-cost resources, and probability limits on activity times. In a typical architectural practice the situation is quite different. A building design programme can be adequately defined by a hundred or so separate activities and rarely requires as many as a dozen architects and technicians; the material resources used are negligible. Most offices will not be able to justify a full-time project manager who can become familiar with the intricacies of a complex program, and he would not require most of the facilities provided anyway. It is therefore better for the architect to choose relatively simple and easy-to-use critical-path programs rather than comprehensive ones that will create more problems than they solve.

Outputs from job-management programs

A wide variety of outputs is possible from most job-management programs. Perhaps the most familiar, and certainly one of the most useful, is the barchart or Gantt chart. This presents in pictorial form the time-span of the tasks to be carried out and can show deadlines very clearly. The conventional practice of colouring the activities or proportion of activities that have been completed gives an immediate impression of the progress of a project.

The barchart illustrated in *Figure 8.5* is a fairly typical example of this form of output as produced on a computer printer, although for clarity it is here applied to a very small network. The 'X' symbols represent the activities themselves and the 'O' symbols the float or leeway that they have. Each activity is positioned within its float as far forward as it can go without interfering with the float time of any following activity. Thus when the activity is executed it is obvious if it will reduce float in the rest of the network and, if this is so, the network can be reprocessed to give revised outputs.

The activities on the barchart, and on most other forms of output, can be ordered in a number of ways. The most common is in the order of their starting dates, as in the illustration. This is convenient because the next task to be undertaken is always obvious. Other orderings can be useful in different circumstances. For example, ordering by finishing dates shows immediately which tasks should be completed by a certain time; ordering by float times puts at the top of the list the activities that must be most precisely controlled; and leaving the order of output the same as the input data allows quick correlation with the network diagram. It is also usually possible to specify that certain activities belong to different groups, and to split up the barchart or other output between these groups. This is most commonly done by trades, so that the architect's activities will form one separate section, and the quantity surveyor's another.

All outputs can be produced over a limited time span if required. Thus a typical output might omit activities completed before the current date and only stretch for six months from the current date. This

SIMPLE DESIGN PROCESS

CODE	ACTIVITY DESCRIPTIONS	DURATIONS	EARLY STARTS	LATE FINISHES	ACTIVITY STARTS	ACTIVITY FINISHES
AR01	PREPARE SKETCH PLANS	• 10	MON 1 JAN 79	FRI 12 JAN 73		
CL01	CLIENT APPROVAL	• 3	MON 15 JAN 79	WED 17 JAN 73		
AR02	PREPARE 1:200 FLOOR PLANS	20	THU 18 JAN 79	THU 22 FEB 73	MON 22 JAN 79	FRI 16 FEB 79
AR03	PREPARE 1:50 ROOM LAYOUTS	• 40	THU 18 JAN 79	WED 14 MAR 73		
CN01	CONSULTANTS DEVELOP SCHEME	20	MON 19 FEB 79	MON 26 MAR 73	TUE 27 FEB 79	MON 26 MAR 79
QS01	Q.S. COSTS SCHEME	• 10	THU 15 MAR 79	WED 28 MAR 73		
AR04	FINAL PRESENTATION	• 1	THU 29 MAR 79	THU 29 MAR 73		

Figure 8.6 A datelist output from a critical-path analysis program

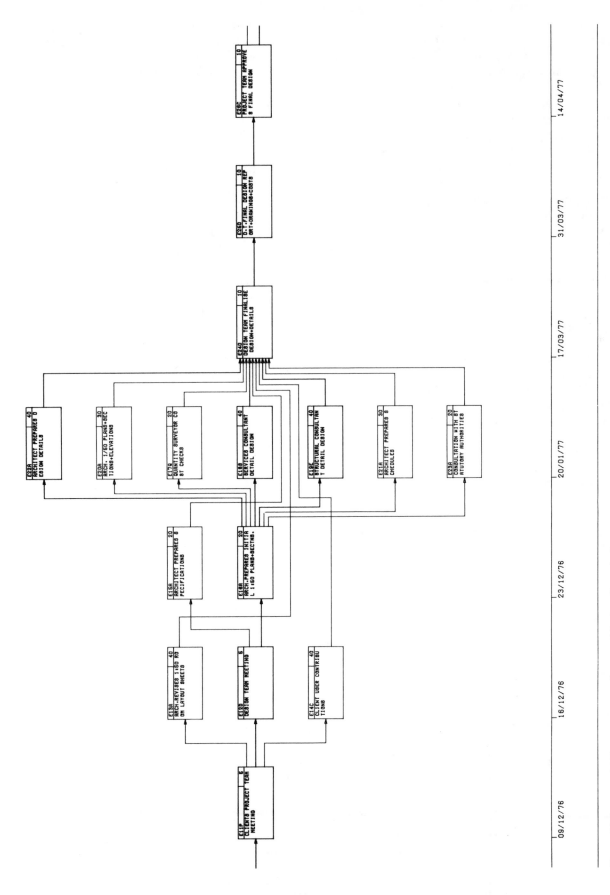

Figure 8.7. A network-diagram output from a critical-path analysis program

focuses attention on the immediate situation and is often less confusing than presenting the entire project.

A more convenient form of output for desk work is a list of activities with their important dates. The example in *Figure 8.6* shows the earliest starting and latest finishing dates for each activity and, if the activities are not critical, the latest starting and finishing times each one can have without interfering with subsequent float times. This output is much more compact than a barchart and precise dates can be noted much more easily than by reference to the date scale on a barchart; it does not, of course, give such an immediate pictorial impression.

Some job-management programs allow the user to specify scheduled starting dates for some activities. Deadlines can thus be incorporated in the network and the float times for the preceding activities will automatically adjust themselves. A useful application of this is to specify a finishing date for the project so that, when the network is processed, the appropriate starting date will be calculated. The problem with scheduled dates is that it will sometimes be impossible to meet them given the network specification. This is indicated by the float times' becoming negative in one or more cases. A float time of minus one day, for instance, means that at least a day has to be saved somewhere to meet the deadlines.

One extremely useful form of output that unfortunately is not often found in critical-path programs is the ability to redraw the network diagram on the computer plotter. Network diagrams take a long time to draw initially because it is not clear how the activities should be laid out on the paper. Therefore drawing a neat diagram has to be done in two stages: an initial sketch to see the organisation, and a complete redrafting with the activities in order of starting times and with the minimum of links crossing, to avoid giving a confusing impression. Several drafts of complex networks may be necessary. Alteration of the network diagram can be a lengthy business as well, especially if it is decided to show one section of the project in more detail by breaking down activities into more specific tasks. This is fairly common if the project is badly delayed and decisions have to be made on speeding it up, but clearly it involves redrafting the remainder of the diagram.

Thus a network-drawing facility can save a lot of time. Some critical-path programs have it as one of their optional outputs and there are also separate programs on the market that can interface with the original data file and produce a diagram independently of a network analysis. A portion of a typical output from such a program written in our office is shown in *Figure 8.7* and illustrates Stage E of the RIBA Plan of Work, the detail design stage.

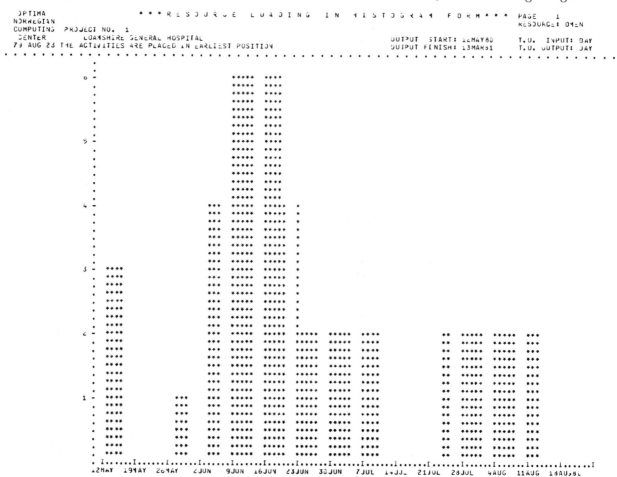

Figure 8.8 A resource-requirement output from a critical-path analysis program

The above ouputs show the progress of the activities, but it is also possible to obtain outputs showing the use of resources and the costs involved in the project. One of the most useful forms to show both of these is the histogram. This is a familiar type of data presentation that uses vertical bars of different heights to represent different resource levels or costs. By studying these a manager can see how many men of what skills will be required in the next time period, and can redeploy the remainder. He can also see what materials must be ordered and what they will cost. A typical histogram of resources is shown in *Figure 8.8*. It illustrates the variation in the number of draughtsmen required over a period of 15 weeks on a certain project. This output was produced by the OPTIMA program developed by the Norwegian Computing Centre.

Data preparation — a worked example

There are many different network-analysis programs in existence. A survey by Internet (UK) and Loughborough University of Technology[89] investigated almost a hundred available in Britain, all with minor differences. Because of this proliferation, data preparation will be illustrated here in a generic manner that can, with slight modifications, be adapted to any critical-path analysis program.

Figure 8.9 shows a network of part of the design process, on a much cruder level than would be used in practice. The diagram shows that the first activity is to be the preparation of sketch plans, taking ten days. When complete they are sent to the client for approval, a process expected to take three days. When approval is given work can start on the floor plans, to take twenty days. The preparation of the 1:50 scale room-data sheets takes place in parallel with the floor plans, but cannot start until the floor plans have started, and cannot finish until the floor plans have finished. This activity takes forty days. The consultants can begin their work when the floor plans are finished, plus two days delay for packing and postage. The consultants' work takes twenty days and there is then another two-day delay before

their drawings are back with the architects. The quantity surveyor can cost the scheme after the room layouts are finished and takes ten days. When this is complete, and when the consultants' drawings have arrived, the final presentation can take place and is to last a single day.

Each activity is given a brief description such as 'Prepare 1:200 floor plans', so that the outputs will be readily intelligible. It is also given a short identification code of four characters, which is used in preparing the data and eliminates typing out the description every time an activity is referenced.

The most basic part of the data is the activity-relationship table. This gives the identification code, description and duration of each activity and the codes of the activities that follow it in the network. It also specifies the types of link and any delay times. Using the abbreviations 'F', 'S' and '–' to represent finish-to-finish, start-to-start and finish-to-start links respectively, we can write out the network as a relationship table (below) for typing into the computer.

Code	Description	Duration	Following activities	Link type	Link delay
AR01	Prepare sketch plans	10	CL01	–	
CL01	Client approval	3	AR02	–	
AR02	Prepare 1:200 floor plans	20	AR03	S	
			AR03	F	
			CN01	–	2
AR03	Prepare 1:50 room layouts	40	QS01	–	
CN01	Consultants develop scheme	20	AR04	–	2
QS01	Quantity surveyor costs scheme	10	AR04	–	
AR04	Final presentation	1			

If resource scheduling is to be included, two other sets of data must be included: a resource-schedule table to specify the different resources and their limits, and a resource-assignment table that specifies how much of each resource every activity will require. The resource-schedule table, in a similar fashion to the activity-relationship table, gives a description and a code to every resource. It also gives the maximum amount of that resource available, and the time

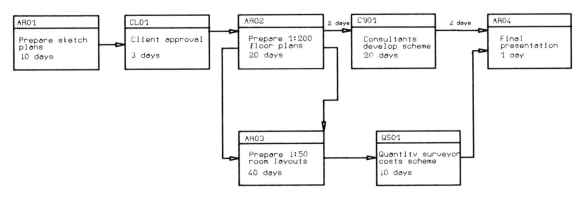

Figure 8.9 A network of a simple design process

from which that maximum applies. Thus if the available amount of a resource will vary over the project time, this can be specified by putting in several start dates with the appropriate maximum. The resource-schedule table may also have an entry giving the cost of that resource in the appropriate units; in our example all the units are man-days.

It is not necessary to specify all resources, or indeed any at all if resource scheduling is not considered helpful enough to be worth the extra effort. In our example, the network is for the architect who wishes to optimise the use of his own staff, but is not concerned with the number of staff the client, the quantity surveyor and the consultants must use. The only matter that affects the architect is the time these others need to carry out their parts of the design. Therefore only the activities carried out by the architect need have resources detailed or assigned; the program will then schedule the other activities as if they had no resource restrictions.

For the purposes of our example, we will assume that the office is able to assign to the job one architect, costing nominally £50/day, and two technicians, costing £40/day each. A partner of the firm will also be available at the final presentation and his time is costed at £100/day. These staff represent resources that are available for the entire project duration; it is not therefore necessary in this example to specify varying levels of resource availability over the duration of the project, although in general this would be possible.

Code	Description	Number available	Cost/day
ARCH	Architect	1	50
TECH	Technician	2	40
PART	Partner	1	100

The next block of information to be given is the resource-assignment table that specifies which resources, and in what amounts, are needed to carry out each activity. For convenience of data preparation, the activity codes and the resource codes are used rather than their descriptions. The table illustrated has a column simply giving the total quantity of each resource required by any activity. As explained earlier, some programs are in fact able to vary the resource quantities over the duration of individual activities.

It might be expected that the sketch-plan preparation will involve only the architect. The preparation of the 1:200 floor plans is estimated to need an architect assisted by one technician. The preparation of the room layouts requires two technicians to develop the design and the final presentation needs the architect and the partner.

Activity code	Resource code	Resource quantity
AR01	ARCH	1
AR02	ARCH	1
	TECH	1
AR03	TECH	2
AR04	ARCH	1
	PART	1

Obviously there is a problem here: by assigning more manpower the activities can be completed earlier, up to a point. The usual course is for a reasonable balance to be struck between too short a duration and too many men, which is inefficient and can give poor results; and too long a time with too few men, which gives good results but may delay the project. After studying the output from the first computer run the manager can often see that better balances may be struck in certain activities: this insight is one of the advantages of job-management programs and enables the use of resources to be optimised.

As well as this basic data, the user must supply a set of parameters giving miscellaneous information that applies on a more general level. This will include the time units in which the data is prepared, the public holidays on which no work will be done on the project, the project title, its start date, and the outputs required.

The example given has been a very simple one; with so few activities it would not in practice be worth using computer analysis. A realistic network for the design of a building would normally contain about a hundred activities, and at this sort of complexity a formal approach can often give better results than an intuitive one.

9
Simulation techniques

The uses of simulation

Not all buildings are concerned with people, but most of the ones that an architect is called on to design will be. The architect is expected to provide adequately for the people who use his building; they should not have to queue for long periods for the lifts, or jostle each other in the corridors, or crowd the rooms, or overload any other facility. At the same time, the architect has a responsibility to his client and, except for the very occasional prestige job, must not be over-lavish in his provision of facilities that will make the building more expensive to build and to run.

At present, the architect relies on experience to judge the correct amount of provision for each area. This may be his own experience of what has worked in the past, or it may be that of some other designer's embodied in existing buildings that can be observed or in planning guides that can be studied. In general, this is a good method of working, but it suffers from a couple of serious drawbacks. First, any departure from a solution that has worked before leaves the architect with no point of reference: he cannot be sure that his new design will work. Therefore, original solutions are discouraged and the basic designs tend to remain unchanged.

Second, because designs remain unchanged, the less obvious mistakes can become 'fossilised' and carried forward from one building to the next. For example, studies a few years ago showed that teaching rooms in universities were on average used at only one-fifth of their capacity, despite overcrowding in some rooms, and that this was largely due to an unsuitable range of room sizes[93]. These had been carried down from building to building because it had not been practicable for any designer to set up long, elaborate and costly studies into utilisation factors. So previous solutions which worked, but which were inefficient, were used. Similar errors must exist in many other types of building and can only be eliminated by systematic analysis.

It is clear that what the designer needs is some way of predicting how a building will perform in practice. He can then test new and adventurous designs and tailor the building to the user, thus optimising the use of the budget. This can be especially important when designing a building such as a hospital or a university when there are usually very stringent area and cost allowances. As there is so little scope for playing safe by over-provision, the designer must be certain that all facilities are adequate but not wasteful.

It can be argued that fitting a building too closely to its function can remove flexibility and make it inefficient if its use should change. This is true, but with greater insight into his design the architect should be able to see where the bottlenecks might occur and so allow for them. He can also predict the effects of changes in use or an increase in the number of users.

Principles of simulation

A few years ago, there was no practical method for predicting the cumulative effect of many people acting independently. In general, problems involving many elements, each behaving in an arbitrary manner, cannot be solved 'analytically', i.e. in a fixed number of sequential steps by applying rules and evaluating formulae. The behaviour of human beings is normally such a problem. Finding a solution therefore entails the analysis of hundreds of separate interacting variables. This has been done by hand in the past, but is so onerous that it was never really viable as a technique. It is not sufficient just to take a handful of variables and multiply up the result, because individual cases may have a disproportionate effect; many variables must be considered if random quirks are to be evened out. Since the advent of cheap computing, however, these problems can be solved quickly and cheaply. The computer can model the actions of many people, each behaving in a random manner and interacting with others, and can print out the total demands on any facility over a given time span. This technique is generically known as simulation.

Various methods have been developed to simplify the construction of these models. Using such methods, the architect can test various points of his design and modify it and retest until it works well enough to satisfy him. Simulation is most often used in architectural applications to predict the movement

101

of people, but can be used in any situation involving random entities or variables, such as cars, aircraft, or outbreaks of fire. These techniques have been used for lift siting, circulation analysis, canteen design, car-parking provision, airport terminal layout, supermarket design and the solving of many other diverse design problems.

The answers that the architect gets from simulation are not feasible layouts, or even comments on how suitable the design is for its purpose. They are descriptions of what happens, from which the architect must decide the adequacy of his scheme. For example, if modelling supermarket checkout points, the computer will output a description of the queues that formed, giving the fluctuations in length over the day. It is then up to the designer to decide if the figures are acceptable. If the average queueing time is over five minutes, this might be considered too long and the architect might try the effects of revising the model to add an extra checkout point or increasing the shop assistant's productivity by providing more mechanisation.

However, if queues are very short or form infrequently, the designer can try eliminating a point or arranging that the assistants take on extra duties such as packing the purchases or stocking the shelves. By these means, the optimum provision of staff and equipment can be determined, and armed with these facts the architect can produce a layout without having to guess at figures or rely on existing solutions.

As with the critical-path technique, it is helpful to draw a diagram of the model network to give a visual impression. It is also necessary to identify individual activities and join them in sequence. The similarity ends there, however, as simulation models are typically made up of separate but interacting networks, which often have looping and feedback characteristics. This can be made clearer by constructing a model for the specific example of a single checkout point. At the checkout, there are two interacting networks. The first of these is the customer network which is entered again and again by individual customers. The process of checking out might be divided roughly into the individual activities of queueing for service, waiting while the goods are totalled, and paying.

The other network describes the assistant's activities. Only one assistant is present, so this network forms a loop with the same activities being carried out for every customer. There are two basic activities: totalling the prices, and taking the money, which includes giving change if necessary. When these activities have been carried out for one customer there is a decision point, indicated on the diagram by a diamond shape. At this point the assistant checks if a customer is waiting in the queue, and if so goes through the network again. Otherwise, the check point is entered again after a short lapse of time. This formal way of expressing the fact that the assistant is

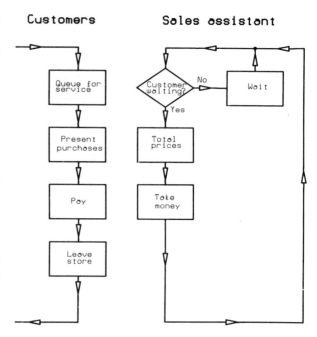

Figure 9.1 A simple simulation network of a checkout point

waiting for the next customer is necessitated by the nature of simulation on a digital computer in which the lapse of time must be modelled in discrete intervals of, say, one second. The diagram of this model is shown in *Figure 9.1*.

The model is an oversimplification, of course. The assistant might have to perform additional activities such as dispensing carrier bags, giving trading stamps, or restocking the till with change. If these occupied a significant amount of time they would have to be included in the model. Activities can optionally be broken down in more detail. Thus taking the money and giving change could be separated, instead of being considered as a single transaction, and statistics collected on both tasks. The network might also be made more informative by considering special cases. Thus if a significant proportion of customers pay by cheque, the network could divide to simulate the mix of cash and non-cash customers. The average time needed to write and verify a cheque is considerably longer than that needed to present cash and receive change; considering cheques as a separate case could therefore yield figures that would be valuable when attempting to speed the paying process. This refined network is illustrated in *Figure 9.2*.

The model can be extended in various ways as well as refined — to model the customers' selection time in the store and the number of items selected, for example. This would give information on how large the body of the store needs to be and how much stock need be carried. It is up to the user to decide what information he wants to collect and construct the model accordingly.

Inspecting the simpler model, it can be seen that there are three points at which data has to be supplied

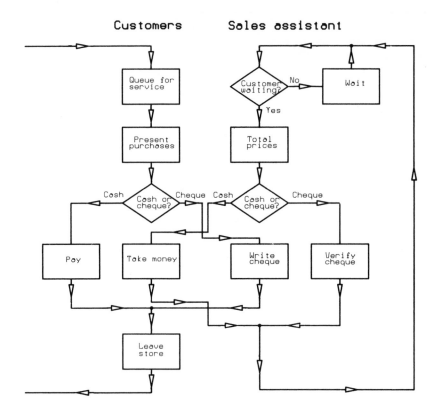

Figure 9.2 A more detailed simulation network of a checkout point

on activity rates. The first is the rate at which customers join the queue. This will obviously vary throughout the day and throughout the week. In this case there may be peaks at mid-morning and mid-afternoon with much larger peaks on Saturday. The model could therefore be provided with a reference table giving the intervals between customer arrivals at the queue throughout a typical day. These intervals are expressed as a histogram in *Figure 9.3*. In

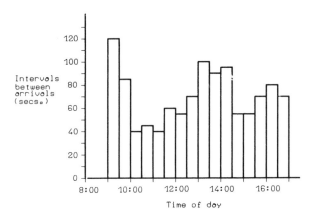

Figure 9.3 A histogram of customer arrivals in a typical day

principle the intervals can take any value, but for simulation they must be rounded off to whole numbers of the discrete time units in which the model is constructed. This need not be a restriction as the units can be made as fine as required, although computer costs will increase proportionately. Units of single seconds should be more than adequate in this example, and much coarser units might well give acceptably accurate results.

The arrival of customers is determined by such things as working hours and social conventions; therefore the histogram does not show symmetry or mathematical consistency and the only way to gather data describing it is actually to perform a survey for at least one day. This task can be considerably eased, however, if only the peak time is modelled. In a supermarket it might not be possible to get extra help just at the peak hours: the same number of assistants would be employed throughout the entire day. If this were so, the designer might find it sufficient to model the peak time alone to see how the model behaved under the worst conditions. Peak-time arrival can often be expressed simply as a pair of limits: customers might be said to join the queue at random intervals between 40 and 60 seconds.

While this is a useful simplification it would not be suitable for all cases. The designer might well be prepared to accept that long queues will form at peak times if they are short for the rest of the day, as this will enable him to make considerable savings in most facilities. To provide an adequate basis for such a decision, an entire day would have to be modelled.

The second activity on which information must be supplied to the model is the speed at which the assistant totals the prices. Observations must be made on the speed of a typical assistant, which will of course vary with the number of items. Because of the nature of the task practically any time may be observed, and the results are conveniently expressed as a curve from which the percentage of occurrences of a given range of times can be read off. This curve is shown in *Figure 9.4*. The time the assistant takes to total items and the intervals between customer arrivals are continuous variables, because in principle they can take any value. The number of items to be totalled is a discontinuous variable because it can only take whole-number values.

As can be seen, the average time taken is about 30s, the values falling off smoothly and sharply towards zero and smoothly but slowly towards infinity. This sort of curve is said to be 'positively skewed'; it indicates that most orders fall into a narrow band, in the lower number, but a few are very quick, involving only a few items, and some are lengthy, perhaps indicating a large number of items or difficulties in assigning prices. Negatively skewed distributions, where most observations are recorded in the higher numbers, are much less common. One example is the time of arrival of office workers, which tends to build up towards the official time of starting work, and then falls off rapidly, most people arriving in the ten minutes before the starting time. A curve illustrating this is shown in *Figure 9.5*.

The third piece of information to be supplied is the length of time needed to pay. Like the previous variables it is continuous in nature, but because of the type of transaction the distribution of times is symmetrical. The average is about 15s, and the time varies slightly either side of this, reflecting the different numbers of coins or notes taken and returned as change. *Figure 9.6* shows the distribution diagrammatically.

Given these sets of information, the computer can simulate the activities. This model could be defined in about a dozen lines using one of the more advanced simulation languages. The processing costs for such a small model would be very low. It is quick and cheap to model typical interactions, so that many of the questions that vex the designer trying to provide for such situations can be resolved with little difficulty.

Over the years a number of different methods have been developed for describing simulation models to a computer. By far the most popular has been to provide special languages. Simulation is not a 'natural' activity for a digital computer, which inherently works in a series of sequential steps; most high-level languages are designed to reflect this. Thus conventional languages encourage the programmer to arrange his problem so that it can be solved one step at a time. Simulation, which essentially attempts to model numerous simultaneous and interacting activities, is most unsuited to such a representation.

Simulation languages must therefore be completely different, and able to represent a network of activities rather than a linked series. So even an experienced programmer can be completely lost when he first encounters simulation techniques, since they require him to think in a radically different manner. However, simulation is not basically any more difficult than any other computational technique and with some practice it becomes easy to set up a model.

Simulation languages fall into three broad types. The earliest was a set of subprograms that could be invoked from a conventional high-level language, usually Algol or Fortran, which are orientated towards numerical applications. Such languages never became very popular because describing a simulation network in a sequential language is difficult and can distort the model. A more advanced type that is still in widespread use is a programming language developed expressly for simulation and which can therefore reflect the organisation of an activity network quite easily, but at a lower level follows the rules of a conventional programming language. The advantage of this is that all the normal facilities of the computer are available and therefore data can be generated, interfaces with other programs can be arranged and so on. A popular example of this type of language is called SIMULA; it was written as a simulation aid but is heavily indebted to Algol at a detailed level.

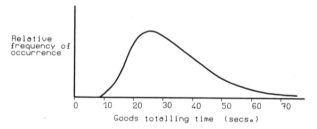

Figure 9.4 The distribution of goods totalling times

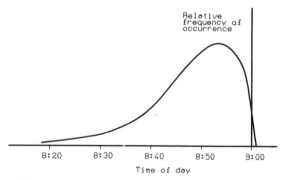

Figure 9.5 The distribution of staff arrival times

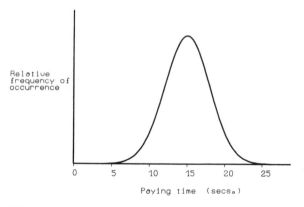

Figure 9.6 The distribution of paying times

The most recent simulation languages have cut the last ties with sequential programming. They involve the direct specification of such things as queues, the order and timing of activities, and the different resources needed for a task. These languages are very specific to stimulation and hence often lack facilities that are occasionally useful; usually, however, they are quite adequate and are very terse in use.

As an exercise, I have modelled the same network in a number of different simulation languages. The results were broadly that the model description occupied 200 lines of a general-purpose language equipped with simulation subprograms, 80 lines of a language with a simulation bias, and only 27 lines of a special-purpose simulation language. The computer costs in running the models were lower for the more general-purpose languages, but because it is so much easier to create and modify a model in the special-purpose languages they are almost always more cost-effective in practice[104].

Other methods of defining models have been developed. Programs have been written in which a network can be drawn on the screen of a graphics device and the computer will automatically build a simulation model from it. Data can be given to the model by plotting graphs on the screen rather than by the typing necessary with language methods. Interactive methods have the advantage that there is no intermediate step between drawing the network and running the simulation; they are therefore quicker and easier to use. Altering the model or the input data is also easier and less error-prone. Results can be displayed on the screen so that the designer can, for example, actually see the queue lengths fluctuate during the day[97].

Despite the attractiveness of interactive graphics for simulation, very few such programs have been written and they have never become popular. This is possibly because simulation is a 'number-crunching' task; it requires a lot of processing power but little input or output. Such a task is much more suited to a large computer than to the minicomputers usually used to drive graphic devices.

Whatever method is used to define models, large networks or very long runs modelling days or weeks of activity can be expensive to process. Because simulation does not fit in well with the working of digital computers it can sometimes actually take longer to model an activity network than the elapsed time in real life. An example of this is the simulation of calls passing through a telephone exchange. Thousands of calls may go through every hour, occurring at random intervals and lasting for random lengths of time. A computer simulation can be very valuable because it gives an idea of the load on the exchange and the effects of malfunction. However, because the exchange has hundreds of lines handling calls in parallel while the computer has to consider each call in turn, a computer simulation typically takes two hours to model a single hour of exchange operation, despite the vastly greater speed of the computer.

Fortunately, most simulations performed by the architect will only involve a few thousand activities at the most and can on average be carried out for perhaps £5 a time: a small sum compared with the savings from a better design.

Data-collection techniques

The drawback to simulation may appear to be that a lot of time has to be spent taking observations to supply the basic information on the distribution of individual activity times. In practice, however, this is not usually a serious difficulty. The most important reason for this is that one set of observations can be used in a wide variety of situations. For example, once the serving times have been established for a typical assistant, they can be used in any supermarket design analysis and possibly in other situations as well, such as totalling food items in a self-service canteen or transactions in a bank. Similarly, money-taking and change-giving times can be used in many situations and at all levels of customer demand, and still keep their validity. As most architects tend to specialise in a fairly narrow range of building types, a 'library' of useful observations can be built up to cover most of the activities that need to be modelled.

A second way of saving data-collection time is to make use of the laws of probability. Many observations using continuous variables will eventually settle down into a smooth curve; in some cases the curve's shape can be completely predicted from only a few observations. The distribution of goods-totalling time is inherently a smooth curve and if the user is aware of this, or can deduce it with reasonable certainty, he need only take enough observations to give him the rough outline; he can then draw in the smooth curve that would eventually result after many more observations.

A knowledge of the expected shape of the curve is both a powerful and a dangerous aid to gathering

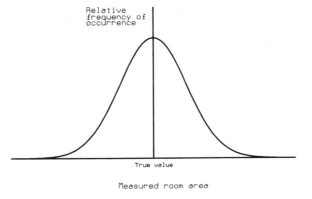

Figure 9.7 The normal distribution applied to area measurement

data. There are formulae for various standard distributions that can be applied to a wide variety of circumstances. The most generally applicable of these is the 'normal' distribution, a symmetrical distribution that can describe the observations in hundreds of everyday activities or occurrences. It used to be known as the 'Law of Errors', because one of its earliest uses was to describe the errors made by a large group. For example, if a large number of people were to measure the area of a room, the normal distribution would predict the amount of error made by different people. The curve is shown applied to this example in *Figure 9.7*. Another similar example of a normal distribution is shown by the distances that darts land on the dartboard from the point aimed at.

There are many other situations that are normally distributed, or closely enough for simulation purposes. The life of light bulbs and fluorescent tubes is one example; the average may be perhaps a thousand hours, but the overall picture is the normal curve and servicing statistics can be predicted on this basis. As another example, the heights of the population and their girths approximate closely to the normal distribution and these facts can be used when simulating the amount of space needed for a group of people.

The mathematical expression of the normal distribution is complicated, but many simulation languages allow the user merely to state that some random occurrence is normally distributed with a stated average and scatter around the average, and the program will then automatically generate a typical sequence. Otherwise, tables exist from which the user can easily derive his own values to give to the program as data.

Another very useful expression is the Poisson distribution. This shows how events that have an equal chance of occurring at any time or at any place will occur when observed a large number of times.

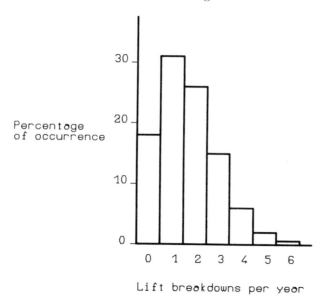

Figure 9.8 The Poisson distribution applied to lift breakdowns

For example, the number of goals scored at football matches follows a Poisson distribution. The number of flawed bricks in a load will closely approximate to an observation from a Poisson distribution. One use for the architect might be in predicting the occurrence of fires in a building. Assuming that fires have an equal chance of breaking out at any time during the working day and in any room, their frequency and position can be modelled and used in a simulation that tests the efficacy of the means of escape and fire-fighting precautions. *Figure 9.8* gives an example of a Poisson distribution recording the incidence of lift breakdowns, which could be incorporated into a lift simulation. In the diagram, the curve is positively skewed, but in fact the Poisson distribution has no set shape, unlike the normal distribution which always has a bell-like configuration; it may follow a wide variety of forms depending on the average value and the scatter about the average.

There are several other distributions which can be used, but all such formulae must be treated with great caution when applied to simulation. There are two reasons for this. First, it is very easy for someone who is not a trained statistician to choose the wrong distribution and therefore obtain misleading results; the user must be certain of the correct distribution before applying it. Second, in real life unexpected quirks and fluctuations often occur; and although it may seem obvious in theory to use a certain distribution, it may not be what actually occurs in practice. Unless the situation is clear cut, it is in general better to play safe and observe an actual activity.

GPSS — an advanced simulation language

One of the most popular simulation languages is GPSS, which stands for General Purpose Simulation System. GPSS is completely specific to simulation and allows the user to translate his network diagram almost directly into a simulation model, single instructions in the language being equivalent to complete activities[98,105].

GPSS calls the entities that move through the network 'transactions'. Most often, transactions will be people going through a sequence of activities, but they could be cars in traffic or crates in a warehouse, if these were the situations being simulated.

Transactions can use two kinds of resource: facility resources and storage resources. A facility is an item that can be used by one transaction at a time. It may be an item of equipment: for example, a petrol pump in a garage simulation. A GPSS network can specify that a transaction makes use of a facility for a given time and later transactions are delayed in the network until the facility is free. A facility can also be a person handling a transaction — a clerk in a bank simulation, for example. Statistics are automatically gathered by GPSS on such factors as the number of times each facility is used, the average time they are used for, and the proportion of the total time they are in use. From these figures, the user can see if facilities are being used intensively enough and if they are over- or under-used.

A storage resource is something that a number of transactions can use at once, up to a certain limit. In architectural applications, it would very often be a room; in a canteen simulation, for example, the dining room would be a storage resource with capacity equal to the number of places provided. When the room is full, subsequent diners are prevented from starting to eat. GPSS will organise this automatically; when it notes that a storage is full, later transactions are delayed and prevented from entering. Statistics are gathered on the average contents of each storage, the average time the transactions use them and so on.

As well as providing resources that transactions can use, GPSS provides for queues of transactions waiting for facilities or storage resources to be free or to accommodate other delays. A queue differs from a storage resource in that it does not have an upper limit; transactions enter a queue and wait their turn until the earlier transactions have been able to move on. GPSS collects statistics on the maximum length of queue, its average length, and the percentage of time it does not form at all.

GPSS works with the broad concepts of performing actions for certain lengths of time, using certain resources, and waiting in queues. Statistics are gathered automatically and printed out at the end of the simulation. This makes GPSS definition much shorter than the equivalent in less specialised languages. It also means that it is straightforward to translate a network into the appropriate activities and match them back up later if modifications are necessary.

An activity instruction in GPSS is called a 'block' and may optionally start with a name by which it can be referenced. The second parameter is a short mnemonic that defines the sort of activity to be modelled. For example, QUEUE is an instruction that will set up a queue at that point. The mnemonics ENTER and LEAVE arrange respectively for a transaction to make use of a storage resource and to leave it; typically they will be used to model people entering and leaving a room. In general, transactions move from one block to the one defined immediately after in a simple linear sequence. However, it is also possible to skip to a block that is out of sequence by giving its name. GPSS can often automatically select paths for the user; it can, for instance, specify that any path not blocked by other transactions can be used. This would be appropriate in a simulation of, say, a railway train where passengers enter the first compartment that has a free seat.

Subsequent parameters vary with the type of instruction, but might give the lengths of time the activity is in progress, or the conditions necessary for a transaction to commence an activity or to go elsewhere in the network. Some instructions do not take part in the actual flow of the simulation but give associated information. For example, a STORAGE instruction defines the capacity of a storage resource. Other declarative instructions may be supplied to give data on, say, the length of time that activities take to perform.

The principles of GPSS can be made clearer if we apply it to an actual example. Taking the supermarket checkout point used earlier, it is first necessary to identify which resources will be used by the simulation. There are no storage resources, as we are not here concerned with how full the supermarket gets, or how many baskets and trolleys are used. There are a number of facilities (the assistant, the till, the scales etc) but only the assistant concerns us in this example as we wish to find if the work is within the capacity of one person. Information will also be gathered on the queue for service, to ensure that the waiting times are not excessive.

A network of the simulation can now be drawn in a form appropriate to GPSS with each box in the diagram corresponding to a single GPSS block. The GPSS diagram is often simpler than other representations because the details of the behaviour of facilities and the paths taken by transactions can usually be adequately handled by the assumptions the program makes, although these can be overridden where necessary. The network as redrawn is shown in *Figure 9.9*.

The first activity is the arrival of a customer at the checkout point. The second activity is the process of joining the queue. At the head of the queue a block indicates the customer's engaging the assistant's attention. The next two blocks clock up the times for totalling goods and for paying and receiving change. After this, the process of releasing the assistant's attention is specified and then the process of leaving the queue. The last activity is the process of leaving the network; this has to be specified to GPSS so that it can remove the transaction from its memory. The original network diagram in *Figure 9.1* has an extra decision point where the assistant waits if the queue is empty; this does not have to be explicitly specified to GPSS as it will automatically schedule the assistant to serve the next customer, if there is one, and will otherwise note the unoccupied time.

Having drawn the activity diagram a person familiar with GPSS can write the program directly. The command that initiates a transaction and so simulates a customer's joining the queue is GENERATE. Obviously, the program needs to know the intervals at which a customer can appear, and this can be specified by referring to a separate table of observations such as the one shown in *Figure 9.3*. If it is sufficient to model only peak-time activity, then we can specify directly a pair of time limits between which a customer will appear. The number of

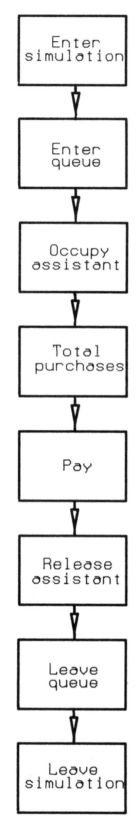

Figure 9.9 A GPSS network

customer arrivals to be modelled is specified later. Usually, it is better to specify a higher rather than a lower number so as to give the random fluctuations a chance to settle down to a set of figures that are reliable over a long period.

The final form of the command is:

GENERATE 50,10

Translated, this means that customers will arrive every 50 s, plus or minus 10 s, and will then enter the next activity. The multiplicity of commas is an unfortunate feature of GPSS that makes it difficult to read. However, it is always possible to refer back to the original diagram which corresponds exactly with the program and so check or revise the model.

The GENERATE command can take slightly different forms, either towards a more complicated arrival pattern by reference to a table as previously mentioned, or towards a simpler pattern where a transaction occurs exactly every 10 s, say. This latter form might be more appropriate to a machine manufacturing an item or the arrival of a product on an assembly line. There can also be a number of GENERATE commands, each initiating its own stream of transactions; this facility could be used when simulating customers entering a store through several doors, some of which are more popular than others.

The next action is the process of joining the queue. This is simply described to GPSS by:

QUEUE 1

This means that a transaction arriving at the block will be added to queue 1. Statistics are gathered automatically and printed at the end of the simulation under the title of queue 1; the number is redundant in this case, of course, but an elaborate simulation might have many queues.

The next process that a customer must perform is to 'gain control' of the assistant. Any subsequent actions carried out by the current customer are assumed to require the assistant who is therefore not available for use by any other customer. This implies that the next transaction in the queue cannot pass this point and will not advance through the simulation until the assistant is explicitly freed by a subsequent block. The form of the compound is:

SEIZE 1

This means that the current transaction will use facility number 1 (the assistant) until further notice. Again, a larger model might use many numbered facilities. The SEIZE command, like the QUEUE command, accumulates statistics on the use of the facility it references.

The next two activities, the assistant totalling purchases and the customer paying and receiving change, have a lot in common. They both involve the customer and the assistant for a length of time that varies at random but which cumulatively corresponds to observations already made and illustrated in *Figures 9.4* and *9.6*. The form of the commands is:

ADVANCE FN1

ADVANCE FN2

These mean that the transaction is delayed for a length of time given by an observation from the curve FN1 and then for a length of time from the curve FN2. FN1 and FN2 are defined elsewhere in the data.

The curves, or functions as they are called in GPSS, can take several forms and represent either continuous or discontinuous variables. In both the examples, the result is a continuous variable: the time taken to carry out the activities. When a function is invoked, it returns a time at random, but many such times will conform to the curve of observations it is using. GPSS requires the curves to be presented so that, for any activity time, we can read off the percentage of occasions on which this time was not exceeded. This implies that if percentage figures are selected at random, a suitable set of times will be provided for the simulation. This sort of curve is known technically as a 'cumulative frequency curve' and an example applied to totalling time is shown in *Figure 9.10*.

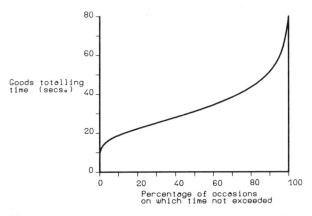

Figure 9.10 Goods-totalling times as a cumulative distribution

The information defining the distribution is supplied by the FUNCTION specification. This instruction is declarative; it does not take a direct part in the simulation but is called upon during the run. In the example, function 1 defining goods-totalling time uses the random-number generator built into the language to reference a set of percentage-points/totalling-time pairs defining the cumulative frequency curve. Specifically, the line might read:

1 FUNCTION RN1,C7

This means that function 1 uses random-number generator RN1 to index a continuous distribution defined by seven pairs of readings. The readings themselves must follow this line. Function FN2 is defined similarly.

Having completed the processes, the assistant may be released for the next customer by:

RELEASE 1

The current customer then leaves the queue via a block of the form:

DEPART 1

These commands affect the statistics on facility 1 and queue 1 respectively.

The last command in the network is to remove the completed transaction from the simulation. This is done by:

TERMINATE 1

The number following the word TERMINATE is added to a total used to determine how long the simulation will run.

In general, simulations can have any number of TERMINATE instructions so that transactions can exit the system at several points. In a supermarket, a proportion of the customers will not purchase anything and will leave without passing through the checkout; simulating this would require a separate termination block.

The model is now complete, but there are two other necessary lines to give information to GPSS. One is:

START 500

This line can be positioned anywhere and has the effect that when the TERMINATE instructions have reached a total of 500 the simulation will stop. In the example, this means that a total of 500 customers will pass through the checkout point. The other line is required to indicate to GPSS that all the information has been presented. It takes the form:

END

The entire simulation, therefore, can be represented by eight lines to describe the model itself, and perhaps six lines to provide data and system information. If the functions required exist in a library of observations, an experienced user can construct the model in minutes. Otherwise, a few hours would have to be spent in gathering data, but this could probably be used again in future simulations.

Figure 9.11 shows part of the output from a GPSS run using the values for goods-totalling and paying times described earlier. From the facility statistics it can be seen that the assistant was occupied for over 92% of the time, but this is an expected result at peak times. The queue statistics are more informative: the longest queue consisted of five customers and the average queue length was 1.4 customers. The average time spent in the queue was about 72 s. The designer

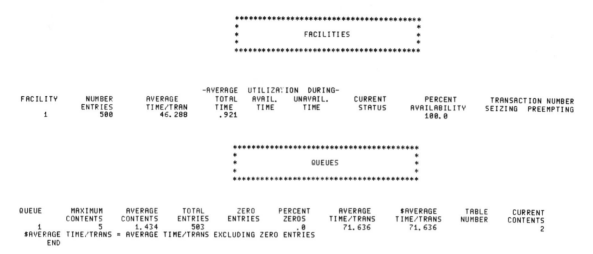

Figure 9.11 An output from a GPSS simulation

might conclude from this that the queue times are short enough for the design to be satisfactory.

If it is felt that the basic statistics printed are not sufficient, GPSS commands are available to specify that certain queues and resources be analysed in more detail, or to print out statistics in the course of the simulation.

The model can easily be altered to try out different solutions and arrangements, and this often means the difference between being reasonably confident that a design will work and making a guess. Simulation cannot, however, usually be said to save the architect money; its justification is a better design and better use of the client's budget. Despite its unfamiliarity, simulation is a powerful technique and with the growing use of computers I would expect it to become one of the most popular design aids at an architect's disposal.

There are many other GPSS commands that are provided to model different situations. Some can be used to check the length of queues or the number of transactions in a storage resource, and to route transactions according to the results. It is also possible to cause a transaction to execute a sequence of activities a given number of times; this could be used to model a worker on an assembly line. It takes a long time to learn the use of these and the other commands in GPSS, and the detailed construction of models is probably best left to the office specialist in computing matters. Provided the designer has a working knowledge of the principles of simulation he can outline a network from which a computer model can be defined.

Simulation packages

Over a period of time, most firms will build up or acquire ready-prepared simulation models for particular situations and certain buildings that only need minor modifications in the capacity of storage resources or the number of users to be applicable to any project. A firm that specialises in hospital building might construct a package that models the traffic between departments such as the pathology laboratories or the central sterile supply given a certain number of patients, or the assignment of nurses to wards of different types, such as geriatric or intensive care.

Some organisations are marketing simulation packages to model various standard situations. The provision of lifts is a popular one and about a dozen models are available at present. The user supplies data on the number of lifts, their speeds, their capacity, door-opening and closing times, and other statistics usually obtainable from the manufacturer's catalogue. These packages often have a choice of lift strategies built into them, such as an express lift to certain floors, or certain floors having priority in summoning lifts. The user can test combinations of lift siting and strategies and so optimise the performance[94,95].

The cost of lift machinery is significant in most buildings: typically 2% of the total cost. It is therefore not difficult to make large savings by optimising the lift provision and this will only involve a few hours of the architect's time and a few pounds in computer costs. A byproduct of some of these packages is that the congestion in lift lobbies can be checked: as these typically form 2%–5% of the total circulation space, important savings can be made here[101].

Lift simulation is applicable to almost any sizeable building but some packages are specific to certain types of building. An example of this is an airport-terminal simulation package named AIR-Q marketed by the Architecture and Building Aids Computer Unit, Strathclyde, Scotland. This package accepts a variety of spatial configurations and manpower provisions and tests them against variations in aircraft schedules. It can, therefore, be of the greatest use when designing or extending airports[100].

An interesting package at a more abstract level of operation is MIBS (Movement in Buildings Simulator) marketed by Applied Research of Cambridge. This package requires as input a network of movement patterns: entities move between the nodes of the net in different numbers and at different speeds. Running the simulation will reveal bottlenecks in some branches and under-use of others; so by changing their characteristics the flow can be made faster. In concrete terms this might be equivalent to shortening the length or increasing the width of some corridors to shorten walking time. MIBS has proved flexible enough to handle many different flow problems, including mechanical handling in warehouses and libraries, passenger and baggage movement in airports, and pedestrian movement in hospitals[91].

10
Environmental analysis

The need for environmental analysis

In recent years analysis of the environment in a building has been turned over almost entirely to the mechanical and electrical services engineer. The architect has normally relied on experience and rules of thumb to produce an adequate basic design and the engineer has worked out the details of the lighting fittings and the heating and ventilation plant needed to service the design. Occasionally he would advise the architect to change some details if it would give significant advantages in simplicity or cost savings.

In a period of cheap energy, this policy was normally sufficient. The architect might quite reasonably be generous in his specification of window sizes, say, and a larger heating plant could be provided to compensate for the extra heat losses; the costs of constructing and running the building would not be greatly influenced. Thus when energy saving was not an important requirement of the design, the weak liaison with the engineer did not particularly matter.

However, since the 1973–74 energy crisis, some priorities have had to change radically. Energy in all its forms is now expensive and seems likely to stay that way in the foreseeable future. There is now great pressure on the architect to design buildings that will require less energy and therefore cost less to run, and this may strongly influence the basic design of the building. The building may become more compact, have a different shape, a different orientation, and less glazing. In this new situation, close liaison with some source of environmental analysis is vital; the current method of sending the design to and fro between the engineer and the architect for analysis and refinement is clumsy and inefficient, and may well lead to a poor compromise, or to the engineer having undue influence over the design.

The problem has been made more acute by energy-saving legislation that affects building design. The UK Government's Department of the Environment has recently introduced new Building Regulations[114] that require non-domestic buildings to meet certain strict insulation criteria. Some flexibility is allowed, but normally the maximum U-value for walls, floors and roofs is 0.6 and the maximum single-glazed area allowed is 35% of the total wall area.

Legislation also exists to enforce environmental standards. The Factories Act and the Offices, Shops and Railway Premises Act are the major instruments in the UK. In any case, user expectations of comfort have been steadily rising and most people expect their workplace to be adequately heated and ventilated winter and summer; they also expect reasonable standards of acoustic isolation and privacy. If the building is not to be very expensive to build and run, therefore, careful analysis of its environmental performance is essential.

A solution to the problem may well be provided by the use of the computer. Most of the analyses required for environmental design are straightforward, if mathematically complex. The formulae and the standards required have been the subject of much research and have been published in the UK by such bodies as the Building Services Research and Information Association and the Chartered Institution of Building Services[110]. Their guides provide a reliable basis for calculation which can readily be given to a computer. The architect can therefore evaluate his building and, provided he knows the basic principles involved, alter it until it satisfies his requirements. The computer can comment on the adequacy of the daylighting, specify the amount of artificial lighting required, give the size of the heating plant taking into account all gains and losses, and even print out a comparison between different fuels for the heating plant in respect of their capital cost and running cost. If the architect has a teleprinter terminal in his office, and they are very cheap to rent, he can use one of the many programs available and quickly test the environmental factors and integrate them with the other principles and concepts of his design.

Program structure

Environmental analysis is a computer application which, like visualisation or critical-path analysis, can often be counter-productive because of the amount of data to be specified. In itself, the data is easy to collect as most of it consists of simple parameters such as structural dimensions or U-values which can be measured or taken from standard reference tables.

Despite its simplicity, data collection tends to be a long and tedious process because there are so many items of information to be supplied.

In the past, programs tended to deal with just one aspect of environmental performance: daylighting was a popular choice, and such subjects as solar gain and noise transmission were also tackled. Such programs still exist, but the current trend is towards programs that analyse a wide range of factors at the same time, or sets of programs that analyse different factors but use the same basic set of data. This is possible and convenient because a lot of the data values are common to many analyses. Room dimensions, for example, are required for lighting, heating and acoustical calculations. Also, most of the environmental factors influence each other. For example, the level of natural light governs the amount of artificial lighting required during the day, and both the area of glazing and the heat gain from lighting fixtures affect the thermal balance.

Programs that analyse single factors may be slightly faster and give an extra place of accuracy than manual methods. For instance, a survey by the Design Office Consortium into daylighting analysis programs[106] indicated that they can be a little faster than daylight protractors, Waldram diagrams and other manual methods; but the process of measuring and checking dimensions and the often lengthy procedures needed to access the computer will make traditional methods more popular with most designers. However, for a relatively small extra effort in data preparation the complete environmental performance can be evaluated and this will be dramatically more cost-effective.

At an even more inclusive level, most of the integrated computer-aided design systems offer environmental analyses amongst their other results. For example, the CARBS and BDS programs described in Chapter 6 require the user to define the building to the computer as a three-dimensional structure. This data is used in the production of a variety of results, including the evaluation of environmental performance.

This approach is obviously very simple and cost-effective because almost no extra data need be collected and the user also has the benefits of the automatic production of drawings. There are a couple of drawbacks, however. The first is that the user has to take the radical step of changing his whole manner of working from manual to almost completely computer-orientated techniques, and this might be considered unacceptable.

The other drawback is that the results can often only be obtained when the building has been defined in some detail and so a lot of work will already have been done on the design, which may be wasted if its performance is inadequate. It may, for instance, be necessary to have sized and positioned all the windows before an accurate assessment of heat loss can be made. In contrast, a program orientated towards this type of calculation may allow data to be input at a much more general level; thus glazing could be expressed as a percentage of the surface area, for instance. This latter approach may be much more preferable at the sketch design stage.

Lighting analysis

Of the many aspects that go to make up the environment, daylighting is perhaps the most basic and the most complex. It is complex not because the formulae to evaluate it are particularly difficult, but because the presence of windows has psychological and aesthetic implications that cannot be evaluated objectively. Given a window description and other data on, say, external obstructions, a computer can easily calculate the daylight factors at any point in the room; these can then be checked for adequacy and in any case are often the subject of legislation[106]. The size of the window will also affect the amount of heat loss and solar gain experienced; thus the architect may wish to reduce the sizes and rely on permanent supplementary artificial lighting, retaining the windows largely for the psychological effect they have on the occupants. The computer can calculate and put a price on the savings made by this and similar decisions.

The calculation of artificial lighting levels is much more straightforward as the subjective elements are less marked. Given the daylighting levels, the computer can calculate the level of artificial lighting required for any time of day or year, according to the standards laid down by, say, the Illuminating Engineering Society[117]. If the architect specifies a standard lighting fitting the computer can then go on to calculate the number required, the total wattage they will consume, and the amount of glare they produce at various points in the room[119].

Thermal analysis

The most important financial aspect of the environmental performance of a building is of course the heating or cooling necessary to maintain comfort. Again, recommended standards exist against which the performance can be measured; thus evaluation is straightforward although the measurement is mathematically complex owing to the number of factors involved, most of which vary constantly.

The computer can calculate heat losses through the fabric: typical U-values for various structural materials will often be built into the program to save data-preparation time, but alternatively they can be taken from one of the standard works of reference. The greatest heat losses will be through the fabric but there will also be losses due to ventilation; data on this must therefore also be supplied.

There will be heat gains from the occupants, from machinery, if present, from the lighting fittings, and from solar gain. This last will of course vary not only with the season and time of day, but also with the building's position and aspect and with the amount of shading from surrounding buildings and from its own shape. Another source of heat gain will be the thermal lag of the structure and its contents, as they take in heat when the building is warmed and give it up if the heating is switched off, as it often will be at night.

Because of all the variables, the calculation of the thermal balance of a building involves long calculations, but as the required standards are clearly set out there is little scope for subjective assessments: the subject is therefore ideally suited to computer methods. A typical program can perform all the calculations in a few seconds and specify the plant required to deal with the largest heat losses and gains that would be encountered[108]. If the architect decided from this summary that the plant was too large and expensive, he could ask for a breakdown giving the heat losses through each surface and from this he might specify more insulation for the walls, a smaller glazed area, or a different orientation for the building.

This analysis can be performed at any level of detail. Thus the designer can define the building envelope only and find the performance for the whole shape; he can then modify the shape or try other ideas until he has decided on the best general form for the building and has a fairly precise knowledge of how much it will cost to run. At the outline design stage, he can define individual rooms with varying needs and conditions and optimise at this level. This method of submission and evaluation can give the architect much greater insight into the environmental implications of the design than is usually available.

Programs also exist to evaluate the trade-off between the capital cost of different heating systems and their running costs[116]. For example, electric heating is cheaper to install than gas heating, but costs more to run. From the figures provided, the architect can decide which fuel would suit the building best.

Sunlight analysis

Solar gain is one of the factors in thermal analysis. The internal heat gain can arise in two ways. The sun's rays may fall on external surfaces and appear as a heat gain internally at some later time, depending on the U-value and thermal lag of the fabric and on the difference between the internal and external air temperatures. Alternatively, the rays may fall directly on internal surfaces through unshaded windows. This latter aspect can usefully be considered as an analysis in its own right, because sunlight has a psychological effect on the occupants of a room quite apart from the temperature change. The analysis can also be valuable in climates where solar heat gain is a major factor.

Programs are available that will calculate the parts of a building that are shaded at a particular time of day and day of year for the appropriate latitude. The shading may come from surrounding buildings or from the building's own facade, including window recesses. From the results the designer can see which rooms receive direct sunlight and at what times[125]. This could be important for different reasons: in England, for example, an architect might be concerned that every room should receive some direct sunlight on each day of the year, while in Mediterranean or tropical climates he might be concerned to shield the windows from as much direct sunlight as possible.

Air-conditioning analysis

Air conditioning of a building usually costs even more than simply heating it. There are also extra design problems because of the need to provide bulky ducting and position vents to provide the requisite number of air changes without creating draughts.

Computer programs exist that can calculate the heating and cooling loads on an air-conditioning plant in a very similar manner to those that calculate heating plant capacity. Again, the many sources of heat gain and loss with their different cycles according to the time of day and thermal lag can be consolidated into a total loading cycle given a design internal temperature and a range of external temperatures[121,122]. In addition, many air-conditioning programs can size pipe and duct networks, giving a compromise between wastefully large ducts with low air speeds and small ducts with high air speeds which need a lot of energy to drive. In large modern buildings service ducts take up a sizeable proportion of the total volume, and so a quick and accurate method of calculating minimum duct sizes can easily pay for itself.

More elaborate programs exist that can calculate air movement patterns throughout a building. A study of the output from these will give the designer insight into the movements and speeds of the air currents so that he can position vents where they will be most effective and can eliminate draughts and pockets of stagnant air. In some buildings an understanding of air movement patterns is vital to an adequate design. In hospitals, for example, sterile areas should have higher air pressure than their surroundings to prevent cross-infection from airborne viruses. Similarly, a kitchen area should have lower air pressure to prevent the escape of steam and cooking smells. Smoke control during fires also depends on correct air pressures. Given data on the ducting network, computer programs can plot isobars on a plan of the building from which checks can quickly be made that the design air pressures will be met.

Acoustical analysis

The last important aspect of environmental performance is the acoustical behaviour of the spaces. There are several different considerations, acoustic isolation being perhaps the most important. Normally this is the amount of interference with speech from outside sources or from other sources within the space. Noise-criteria curves have been published that lay down standards for acoustic isolation by giving the maximum permissible background noise over the range of frequencies for different activities. Several computer programs exist that take data for external noise sources, calculate the way they will be transformed by passing through the building fabric, integrate them with internal noise sources from conversations and from business machines such as typewriters, and then match the result against the noise-criteria curves. These programs often have standard spectra for certain commonly met noise sources such as traffic noise and aircraft noise to simplify data preparation.

With the current popularity of open-plan offices, the considerations of aural privacy have become very important. If the office is to operate efficiently and comfortably there must be a minimum of interference between conversations and telephone use at different points, and the annoyance from typewriters and other machines must not be excessive. With computer analysis, the architect can check the number of people he can reasonably expect to work in a certain space and can check the effectiveness of screening or absorbent surfaces.

When designing rooms for people to listen to speech or music the consideration of reverberation time becomes important. A balance must be struck between sound clarity, which implies a short reverberation time, and sound reinforcement, which involves longer reverberation times. The ideal requirement unfortunately varies between speech, which needs clarity most of all, and music, which needs reinforcement varying with the type of music performed; organ music needs more than chamber music, for instance. Again, quite simple computer programs can calculate reverberation time given the room dimensions and the finishes on the surfaces[109]. Absorption coefficients for different materials can be held in the computer and this will simplify data preparation. The output will advise on the appropriate amount of extra absorption needed.

In theory, the behaviour of sound within a room is also well suited to computer analysis. Calculation of the amount of direct sound and the amount of reflected sound at any point in a concert hall is laborious; the slow and expensive alternative is to build a scale model and measure the effect of injecting high-frequency sound. The calculations could be done much more cheaply and quickly by computer, and checks could easily be made on echoes or focusing

of sound waves. Alteration of the data is comparatively simple; thus a range of different solutions such as adding reflectors or changing surface absorbency could be tested where manual calculations or alteration of a model would be prohibitively slow. Surprisingly, however, there do not appear to be any programs of this type in existence. It is possible that the number of applications is too small to justify the expense of writing a program, but whatever the reasons there appears to be a gap in the market here.

In general, acoustic evaluation seems to be the least used of the environmental analyses, and many package programs that handle all the other aspects of the environment omit this one, or handle it in a cursory fashion. It is not clear why this should be so; perhaps architects give insufficient consideration to this matter. Alternatively, it may be because acoustic analysis cannot be properly performed until the surface finishes have been specified, and this traditionally occurs very late in the design process; thus analysis cannot influence the room size or shape without involving a lot of abortive work.

ESP — an integrated environmental analysis system

The Architectural and Building Aids Computer Unit, Strathclyde, Scotland, have developed a suite of inter-relating programs for a wide range of environmental analyses[111]. The suite is collectively known as ESP, which stands for Environmental System Performance. ESP can be used at different levels of detail; at the sketch design stage the architect can investigate the performance of different building shapes and at the detailed design stage make checks on a room-by-room basis. To make this possible, the data is arranged so that it can evolve naturally with the design just as an architect works from a broad concept to a detailed scheme.

The data for the ESP program must be prepared as several separate sets. The first set, the Geometry File, defines the shape of the buildings and the positions of the internal walls, windows and so on. The file is in three sections. The first gives the broad outline by defining the buildings on or adjacent to the site as a number of blocks. The second section describes the internal details of each block, giving the floor levels and the positions of the walls that enclose the rooms for which results are required. The third section defines the size and positions of the windows.

At the sketch design stage the internal wall details and specific window details will not normally be given, and the building will be regarded as a set of large block shells. From this data can be calculated the overall energy consumption of a building of a given form and with a given percentage of glazing. Later, more detail can be added to give a fuller and more accurate evaluation. Buildings adjacent to the site will usually be left as block shapes in the Geometry File because they are not to be analysed but may shield some sunlight or daylight from one of the buildings on site. The structure of the Geometry File not only allows definition at any level of detail, but also allows buildings to be moved or re-orientated on site with the minimum of data changes. Walls, floors and windows are all defined relative to the block shells, so even at a late stage the effects of changing location or aspect can be investigated by altering a single line in the data.

Having defined the physical form of the building in the Geometry File the user must specify the characteristics of the materials from which it is constructed. This is done by a separate set of data called the Thermal Properties File. The data in this file is used when calculating such factors as heat flow through the surfaces, the amount of sunlight absorbed, and the thermal lag of the fabric. A lot of parameters are required, including those for density, specific heat, and conductivity. The amount of solar transmittance of the windows must also be specified.

The third set of data to be supplied by the user is the Project File which gives parameters applying to the whole scheme. It includes the site latitude and also figures for incidental heat gains from such sources as the occupants and any machinery installed. The Project File typically occupies only a few lines. There is a fourth file that contains climatological data, but this will not normally involve much preparation time as it contains a range of standard yearly figures for representative localities, one of which can be chosen by the user. Only if the building is in an unusual climate or if the designer wishes to test the effect of very extreme conditions will it be necessary to gather data for this file.

Having prepared the information, the architect can thoroughly test the energy performance of his scheme and also obtain results for natural lighting

WORKING PLANE HEIGHT = 0.5 M

6.0	14.0	21.3	20.3	16.1	21.3	23.5	17.1
5.3	8.0	10.5	11.0	11.0	12.8	15.3	19.1
4.3	5.3	6.3	7.0	7.7	9.3	13.4	23.8
3.6	4.1	4.7	5.2	6.0	7.6	11.8	22.7
3.3	3.6	3.9	4.3	4.9	6.0	8.7	14.6
3.0	3.2	3.4	3.7	4.1	4.7	5.7	6.4

Figure 10.1 Daylight factor levels predicted by ESP (courtesy ABACUS)

and acoustic behaviour. Artificial lighting analysis facilities are currently under development. The package is normally run interactively with the results displayed graphically on a screen. This gives a very clear impression and the user can see quickly if the design is suitable and if necessary can modify the data files and so iterate towards an optimum solution. For precise evaluation in critical cases, results can also be presented as numerical values.

The natural lighting evaluation provided by the package gives a simple illustration of the way it works. To calculate daylight factors, the window and room dimensions and data on external obstructions are taken from the Geometry File and the reflectances of the relevant surfaces from the Thermal Properties File. The factors can then be displayed as values on a grid placed over a room plan as shown in *Figure 10.1*. From this output the designer can immediately see if some corners of the room will be excessively dark, or if permanent supplementary artificial lighting will be required.

The thermal analysis section of the package involves many more variables than the lighting section and so is rather more complicated to interact with. The user has a number of different analysis options depending on which factors he tries to hold constant, which can vary between fixed limits, and which can vary freely. At the simplest level, the user may specify that the internal air temperature be held constant. The program will use the data in the Climate File to find how the external air temperature will vary and from this can calculate the necessary plant capacity and the annual energy consumption. The internal air temperature can also be allowed to vary between specified limits and this gives an indication of the energy savings accruing from intermittent plant operation. The program can print out an operational strategy for the plant if required.

These variations would answer most of a designer's questions, but in general any factor can be fixed or allowed to float and different combinations can be useful in investigating particular aspects of the design. For example, in extending a building, the architect might be reluctant to scrap the existing heating plant as this would be very expensive, so he could fix the plant capacity and see how the internal temperature varied. If the performance was not hopelessly inadequate he might then choose to add more insulation or use smaller windows. Alterations to the Thermal Properties or Geometry File could then be made to check the adequacy of this. These alterations may be made interactively.

The output from the analysis can be graphical or textual. The terse textual form lists the magnitude and times of occurrence of the maximum, minimum and average values calculated, while the full textual form gives the values at specified time intervals for the entire period of interest. The graphical output gives a less precise but more vivid impression of the results. At the investigative stage the variation in all the factors involved would usually be plotted superimposed on one another. At a more detailed stage, one or two factors only might be isolated, the performance of the others having been decided. *Figure 10.2* shows a typical output in which the internal air temperature is held constant; the variation in external air temperature is displayed and the necessary plant output is shown as calculated.

The user is provided with a menu of the different thermal components on the screen which he can use to choose the factors to be displayed. The way the factors behave will quickly give insight into which ones are the most significant in the overall result for the specified design. Solar gains are incorporated into the integrated results for the thermal balance, and it is also possible to show which parts of the building are shaded from the sun at any time and on any day. Graphically, the results are shown as a shaded elevation, an example of which is given in *Figure 10.3*.

Condensation checks are another option associated with the thermal analysis section. Checks can be performed on surfaces and at interfaces. With

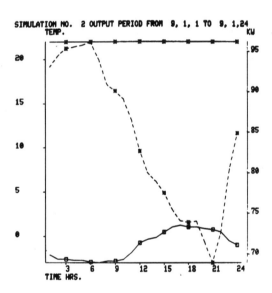

Figure 10.2 Plant capacity predicted by ESP (courtesy ABACUS)

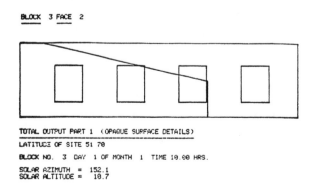

Figure 10.3 Sunlight reception predicted by ESP (courtesy ABACUS)

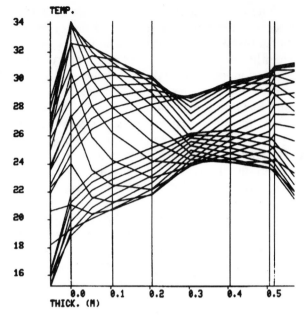

Figure 10.4 Fabric performance predicted by ESP (courtesy ABACUS)

modern methods of heating and new forms of construction, condensation can occur unexpectedly and should be checked for; but normally the calculations are too laborious to be undertaken in anything but a cursory manner. *Figure 10.4* shows the internal fabric performance of a multi-layered construction and the corresponding print of potential condensation risk.

The third area of analysis of the ESP package is concerned with acoustic evaluation. This is the least developed part of the package at present and the only analysis possible is the calculation of reverberation times in the rooms, from which their general suitability for speech or music can be checked.

CEDAR 3 — evaluation at the sketch design stage

CEDAR stands for Computer-Aided Environmental Design Analysis and Realisation. This was the name given to an integrated system using interactive graphics written by the UK Department of the Environment to analyse the performance of buildings constructed using the South-Eastern Architects Collaboration system (SEAC). The analyses available were mainly concerned with structural design and the billing of materials.

Evaluation of the experimental version of CEDAR was performed in 1973 and the system was judged satisfactory[126]. However, a fall in the SEAC building programme from £15m per year to about £8m per year meant that the potential for the system was much reduced. It was therefore decided to redevelop CEDAR for the Property Services Agency Method of Building which is a much more 'open' system than

SEAC. The new system, named CEDAR 3, is primarily concerned with environmental performance such as heating and daylighting, although it can also perform other important analyses including building cost estimation, predicting the running cost of major mechanical and electrical plant, lift selection, and some simple taking-off of quantities[127].

CEDAR 3, in contrast to the earlier work, is intended for use at an early stage of design to get the basic concepts right before too much work is done and the design hardens. To this end, the data is presented in outline rather than in detail and so does not take long to prepare or alter in order to investigate alternative arrangements. Unlike ESP, the building shape is defined interactively using a screen. In essence, the user dimensions a set of blocks which fit together to form the building. The blocks are restricted to orthogonal shapes and positioning. Once defined, the building can be assigned various properties at different levels of detail. This 'broad brush' approach cannot always exactly model a building, but it gives accurate enough results to allow the architect to check the feasibility of a scribbled design in a few hours, which may save weeks of abortive work or major compromises at a later stage.

The blocks are defined by first outlining the plan, then assigning the block a height and also a base level above the ground. Plan shapes can be laid out by typing the command 'DEFINE PERIMETER' (which may be abbreviated to 'DEF PER') followed by the x- and y-coordinates of one corner and then the lengths of each face of the block and the direction in which it runs. Directions are specified by the letters L, R, U and D, standing for Left, Right, Up and Down. This method of plan definition is in general the same as that used in CARBS. Input is also available using the cross-hairs cursor on the screen. The block is made three-dimensional by giving the 'DEFINE HEIGHT' command. It can then be positioned at its correct vertical location by the 'DEFINE BASELEVEL' command.

Any number of blocks may be defined, thereby outlining the form of the building. When the user is satisfied that he has a suitable arrangement he can issue a 'COMPLETE' command. This first checks that the arrangement conforms to CEDAR 3 rules, including the fact that all blocks touch at least one other block but do not interpenetrate. It then goes on to generate roofs for the blocks not covered by other blocks and generates the necessary external walls to form the shell of the building.

Elements of the building may be assigned attributes at several levels of detail. At the most general level, overall values such as the percentage of glazing present are assigned by means of a two-level menu. The upper level offers a choice of broad element categories such as roofs, internal partitions, and external envelope. Selecting a category with the screen cursor brings up a list of specific items with values assigned for each block, and selecting an item allows the assigned value to be changed. To assist fast evaluation, values exist for all items not explicitly set and these are often applicable. To perform more specific evaluations, it is necessary to define the blocks in greater detail. Various commands are therefore provided to divide up blocks into storeys, position internal walls, or define individual windows.

Having defined the building, the user has a range of outputs available. These include graphical representations of the building displayed on the screen which can be used for checking the correctness of the input data. Plans, sections and elevations can be produced as well as wire-line perspectives and axonometric projections. Other outputs are derived from the suite of applications programs included in the system. An important result is the annual energy consumption of the building which can then be used in calculating the annual running cost of plant and services. Another application program calculates the capital cost of construction using the Property Services Agency Early Cost Advice Method. The designer can quickly try different layouts using the MOVE command to rearrange blocks and so find a good compromise between running and capital costs. *Figure 10.5* shows how an architect using CEDAR 3 tried various designs over a period of three days during the pre-production trials[128] conducted in 1978.

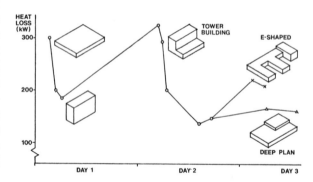

Figure 10.5 The variation of building performance during plan development (courtesy Property Services Agency)

The other important environmental analysis possible is the calculation of daylight levels in rooms, taking into account internal and external obstructions, internal reflectances, and the presence of rooflights. The results from this might lead to a change in the area of glazing and thus necessitate a recalculation of the running costs.

Considerable effort has gone into CEDAR 3 to achieve a robust production system that is free from errors, consistent and well documented. The investment at the time of writing is about 20 man-years and intensive development is still proceeding. Analyses that the team intend to add in the future include acoustic performance, solar heat gain and facade shadowing.

Each box in the following instructions represents a key to be pressed

Switch on calculator and printer
Feed card E/1A, printing upright, into the lower
slot on the right hand side of the calculator [CLR]
Feed in card E/1E printing inverted [CLR]
Feed in card E/1E printing upright [CLR]
Feed in card E/1A printing inverted

Key actions

[R/S] [R/S]
[1] [3] [5] [R/S]

[.] [3] [R/S]

[1] [3] [5] [R/S]

[.] [8] [R/S]

[9] [8] [.] [9] [R/S]

[.] [4] [R/S]

[0] [R/S]

[0] [R/S]

[3] [5] [R/S]

[5] [R/S]

[.] [5] [R/S]

[2] [.] [7] [5] [R/S]

Display blank during calculation

[R/S]
[2] [0] [R/S]

[1] [+/−] [R/S]
Display blank during calculation

[R/S]

Change sequence

[1] [0] [C]

[2] [.] [5] [R/S]

[A]

[B]

[R/S]

Print-out from PC100B (actual size)

```
AREA ROOF
          135.
    U ROOF
          0.3
AREA GRND FLOOR
          135.
    U GRND FLOOR
          0.8
AREA WALL 1
          98.9
    U WALL 1
          0.4
AREA WALL 2
          0.
    U WALL 2
          0.
AREA GLASS
          35.
    U GLASS
          5.
AIR  CHNGE
          0.5
H
          2.75
       3
G W/M °C
          1.14
DESGN INTL TEMP
          20.
DESGN EXTL TEMP
          -1.
DESGN HEAT LOSS   KW
          8.92
AVRGE HEAT LOSS W/°C
          424.


CHNGE
    U GLASS
          2.5
       3
G W/M °C
          0.91
DESGN HEAT LOSS   KW
          7.09
AVRGE HEAT LOSS W/°C
          337.
```

Figure 10.6 Typical output from an RIBA calculator program (courtesy RIBA Publications Ltd)

RIBA calculator programs

The availability of cheap programmable calculators has given the architect a powerful method for analysing many design problems. A good example of this is a package released in the UK in 1978 by RIBA Publications Ltd. It consists of a programmable calculator with printer and a set of programs stored on magnetic cards which perform simple environmental analyses[107,113]. The equipment was pictured in *Figure 3.28*; the calculator is a Texas Instruments model TI59 which rests in the much larger 'print cradle' that provides a permanent record.

The form of the input data is very general, even more so than that for CEDAR 3. The fabric data, for instance, consists of the total area of roof surface, the area of floor, the area of each wall in turn and the area of glazing, each figure being accompanied by its average U-value. Similarly, simple figures are given for ventilation rates and a program can then calculate the volumetric heat loss factor. Typical values for internal and external air temperatures can be given and the heat loss printed in kilowatts. *Figure 10.6* shows part of a typical calculation of this type. The results are of necessity rather approximate, but still provide a valuable guide in the fast analysis of the thermal performance of early sketch designs.

Having produced one set of results it is possible to change only one or two of the parameters to test their effect on the design. For example, in the illustration, the user altered the U-value of the glass to indicate a change from single glazing to double glazing. This sort of procedure allows the designer to test the viability of ideas in minutes.

Other programs exist to calculate gross energy consumption allowing for internal and solar gains and to calculate U-values for multi-layer constructions. Environmental analysis programs under development include those for condensation risk assessment, insulation gains, peak heat gain, and thermal inertia. RIBA Publications also intend to develop programs in other fields, including structural analysis. The current price of the package, including programs, is £389, a small sum compared to what can be saved in the running costs of even a single building.

11
Miscellaneous applications

The scope for computer programs in architecture

Architecture is a very wide subject, covering the arts, the sciences, the crafts and the integration of all these to produce the finished building. It is to be expected, then, that the range of computer programs of use to the architect is also very wide.

In theory, the more programs a user has to hand, the better; ideally, a computer solution would be available for every different problem that could conceivably be found in an architect's office. In practice, too many programs can be counter-productive in the same way as too many gadgets are in the kitchen. This is because a program, like a gadget, requires practice in its use before it can be used efficiently. If infrequent use is made of a program of any complexity, most users will require some time with the instruction manual to remember the necessary procedures, and even then will use the program in a hesitating and uncertain way. Most offices will find that the best solution is to have perhaps a dozen programs which will become well understood and used in a manner that takes advantage of their strengths and avoids their weaknesses. Even then, only three or four of these dozen programs will normally be used as much as once a week.

In this chapter brief details will be given of the more popular programs that do not fall conveniently into one of the categories already dicussed. For up-to-date and comprehensive lists of the programs available the reader is referred to Chapter 13 and to the Bibliography.

Design generation

As mentioned in Chapter 2, a design-aid program can be generative or analytic. A generative program produces a layout or schematic design using the information it is given on area relationships, while an analytic program is given a design and tests it using certain criteria. Examples of analytic design programs are those for simulation described in Chapter 9, in which movement within buildings is evaluated, and those for environmental analysis described in Chapter 10. There are obviously many other subjects

for which analysis may be performed and programs are available that, given a design, estimate the building cost, carry out structural analysis, size plumbing and drainage networks, and find electrical circuit loading.

The basis of virtually every generative design program is a matrix of the interactions between functional areas. Typically, the user will decide on a list of the rooms that will make up the building and then assign each pair of rooms a proximity value. Thus the value 5 might indicate that the rooms should be very close together, as with an operating theatre and the scrub-up room in a hospital; the value 0 that there is no connection between the rooms and so relative positioning is unimportant; and the value −5 that the rooms should be well separated, as with a kitchen and bathroom for instance. *Figure 11.1* shows a typical interaction matrix for a group of rooms.

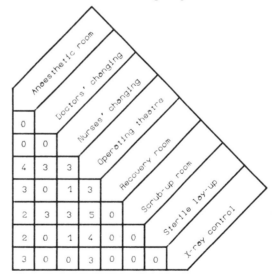

Figure 11.1 An interaction matrix

A less subjective way to generate an interaction matrix might be to study an existing building and find the cost of journeys between each pair of rooms. A program using this data could minimise circulation costs in the design, which might be an important factor. The drawbacks are that this sort of data is laborious to collect and that it does not allow for necessary separation between rooms. Separation might be required for hygienic reasons, to cut down noise interference, or even for purely psychological reasons. I was once involved in using a program to try to minimise the circulation in a hospital design and one of the results located the mortuary close to the geriatric ward as there was quite a lot of traffic between them. The architect felt, however, that the proximity might not be good for the patients' morale.

Given an interaction matrix of some kind, programs are available to generate a design at one of two levels. The first is a schematic design in which room symbols are laid out in a manner that corresponds to the optimum arrangement if the considerations of the building fabric are ignored. This form of output corresponds to a designer's early 'bubble diagrams' in which he scribbles different arrangements in order to clarify within his own mind the relationships involved. *Figure 11.2* shows a typical output produced

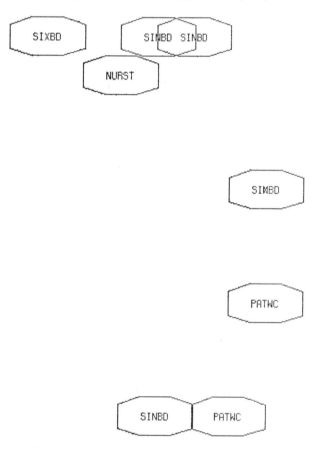

Figure 11.2 An output from the COMPROPLAN space-analysis program (courtesy the Percy Thomas Partnership)

by the COMPROPLAN program, part of the ARK/2 system. The second level of output takes the program a step further and uses the required room areas and some simple rules of building to produce an outline plan.

For either type of output, the first essential is to reduce the interaction matrix into a form that can be regarded as separation distances in two or three dimensions. This must require some distortion of the required proximities because, for example, a group of five rooms might need to be close together, while a sixth room needs to be close to one member of the

group but distant from another. In the 1960s many methods were devised to perform this transformation with as little distortion as possible. One popular technique was multi-dimensional scaling, in which the values in the interaction matrix are regarded as distances in *n*-dimensional space. One dimension is removed at a time with the distances being adjusted as little as possible to accommodate it, until finally the matrix represents an arrangement in two or three dimensions[140].

The association-graph technique involves drawing a diagram consisting of scattered points representing the rooms. A line is then drawn between the pair of rooms with the strongest interaction. A link is then drawn for the next strongest interaction, and so on. The location of the rooms on the diagram should be adjusted to prevent links cutting across earlier links, but if it is impossible to prevent crossings, the weaker link is ignored. The end result is that the rooms are forced into an arrangement taken to represent the optimum positioning[141].

Linear-programming methods require the user to assign a cost to each room being at each of a number of possible locations on a plan. This cost will typically be based on the amount of traffic to the room and the distance between the current point and the centre of the plan. The computer can then use the well-known linear-programming technique to find the arrangement that gives the lowest total cost[130].

Additive techniques position the room with the lowest overall interactions at the centre of the plan, then place adjacent to that room the room that is linked most strongly to it, then position the room most strongly linked to that pair, and so on. At each stage the next room added to the plan is the one that has the strongest links with the group already positioned and is located relative to the group so as to minimise circulation[149].

Permutation techniques start with a proposed layout and test all possible exchanges of position between every pair of rooms. The exchange that most decreases the total amount of circulation within the layout is then effected. The process is repeated until no further improvement can be made. This technique was extended to triads of rooms and to allow for some rooms to have fixed positions[131].

Cluster-analysis methods attempt to distinguish groups or 'clusters' of rooms that hang together strongly according to certain criteria[145]. There are many different criteria that can be used but a typical one is that every member of the cluster must link to every other member with at least a minimum strength. By relaxing the criteria, some of these groups will coalesce into larger groups until all activities are contained within one large group which represents the complete building. The results of a typical calculation applied to an architectural firm are shown diagrammatically in *Figure 11.3*. The partner's offices tend to cluster together because of

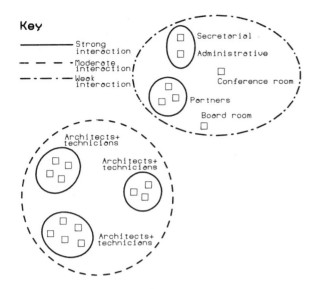

Key

—————— Strong interaction

— — — Moderate interaction

—·—·— Weak interaction

Secretarial

Administrative

Conference room

Partners

Board room

Architects+ technicians

Architects+ technicians

Architects+ technicians

Figure 11.3 A cluster analysis diagram

frequent and important discussions; the secretarial and administrative offices group together because of the large number of journeys within that cluster; and there are also three clusters of architects' and technicians' positions that represent separate design teams. The conference and board rooms do not cluster with each other or with other rooms at a high level. At a lower level of interaction, the design teams merge because of work sharing and similar needs; and at a lower level still, the partners, administrative staff and the conference and board rooms form a cluster.

These are some of the most popular techniques, although many others have been developed of greater or lesser validity.

To go on to produce a layout plan, a program needs to know the required area of each room. Simple rules can then be applied on the acceptable room proportions, on which rooms require an outside wall, or on structural limitations, and some sort of sketch plan can be drawn. The more elaborate programs of this type allow the user to specify several storeys and take into account the greater difficulty of vertical as opposed to horizontal communication. As well as trying to minimise circulation, many programs also attempt to optimise construction costs by reducing external wall lengths or avoiding awkward plan shapes.

Most layout-generation programs do not require or allow human intervention but produce results completely automatically. Programs that do allow some interaction have the advantage that the designer can override some of the program's decisions on the grounds of such non-quantifiable considerations as aesthetics, social conventions, and psychological factors. One program that allows for interaction has been produced at the Department of Architectural Science of the University of Sydney, Australia[137]. The producers of the program have gone to some lengths to make it acceptable to architects with no experience of computers. The program is extremely 'chatty' so as to give the impression of carrying on a dialogue with the user. It addresses the user by his or her Christian name in such terms as: 'Well, John, here's my design,' and encourages him frequently by commenting on the responses with words like: 'Good!', 'Great!' and 'Bonza!' More importantly, perhaps, it has the ability to extract the significant words from a sentence like: 'I want to add some rooms,' where most programs would require explicit commands. The program will respond to requests for help at any point and will list the options available to the user or explain in detail what input is required.

As input the user is expected to provide a list of room names and areas and a table of the interactions between the rooms. The program prompts for these by requests like: 'Please type in your room names.' As output the program will produce a plan on the teleprinter; a typical example is shown in *Figure 11.4*. The user can then select to modify interactions and change room areas. He can also specify which rooms have a window, and has some control over the positioning of rooms. After each set of changes the program types the lengths of the external and internal walls in the revised design and gives a cost factor

```
WELL WARREN HERE'S MY DESIGN ON YOUR INFORMATION


        +----+----+
        |LOUN LOUN|
        |         |
   +----+         +----+
   |LOUN LOUN LOUN LOUN|
   |                   |
   +                   +
   |LOUN LOUN LOUN LOUN|
   |                   |
   +----+              +
   |BD3 |LOUN LOUN LOUN|
   |    |              |
   +    +----+----+----+----+
   |BD3 |BD2 |BTHR|DNNG|KTCH|
   |    |    |    |    |    |
   +----+----+----+    +    +
   |BD2 |BD1  BD1 |DNNG|KTCH|
   |    |         |    |    |
   +----+----+----+----+----+


        ROOMDATA
        --------
ROOM      ROOM      ROOM AREA
NO        NAME      SQ FEET
   1 BED1            128.00
   2 BED2            128.00
   3 BED3            128.00
   4 LOUNGE          832.00
   5 DINING          128.00
   6 KITCHEN         128.00
   7 BATHROOM         64.00
TOTAL AREA          1536.00


THE FOLLOWING SYMBOLS WILL BE USED FOR FUTURE PRINTOUTS
   1 BED1      ⊔
   2 BED2      o
   3 BED3      ∘
   4 LOUNGE    ⊗
   5 DINING    φ
   6 KITCHEN   ∇
   7 BATHROOM  ∆


LENGTH OF PERIMETER          176.00   FEET
LENGTH OF INTERNAL WALLS     120.00   FEET
LENGTH OF MODULE               8.00   FEET
FIGURE OF MERIT (COST)       246.00


WELL WARREN, WHAT DO YOU WANT TO DO NOW?
CHANGE THE AREA OF THE LOUNGE
```

Figure 11.4 An output from a plan-generation program (courtesy University of Sydney Dept of Architectural Science)

which shows the losses in economic terms caused by the interventions.

Over the years many attempts have been made to write programs that will generate designs automatically and objectively, and in terms of the number of programs available this is one of the largest application areas. At present, however, there is very little interest in this sort of program among practising architects because it has been found that the designs produced are hopelessly naïve and inadequate. A certain amount of research is still going on but is almost entirely confined to universities and other educational establishments.

Design-generative programs have essentially failed because no matter how ingenious the mathematical techniques applied, the basis is that minimising communication is of great or overriding importance, and except in special circumstances like factory production lines or hospital operating theatres this is not a valid assumption. In most buildings, communications are not a problem and the architect will give much greater priority to an interesting or aesthetically pleasing layout and to other subjective factors that will very much concern the occupants but which cannot be expressed in an objective manner acceptable to the computer.

Communications have such a low priority, in fact, that some architects have deliberately designed office blocks and other buildings where the work tends to be sedentary so that the staff will have to walk further during the day and thus get more exercise. Similar policies have been followed in some scientific and research establishments to make the staff mix more and so encourage conversations that could lead to the exchange of valuable information.

Design costing

Of the various types of design-analysis program, simulation techniques and environmental analysis have been described in some detail. Most of the other types are too specialised to be of direct interest to the architect and do not have much effect on the basic concepts of the design. Programs to find the loading on electrical cable networks, for example, are valuable to the specialist consultant but whatever the results it is extremely unlikely that the building layout will need to be modified.

The main exceptions to this are programs that can estimate construction costs. If a designer can get some idea of the capital cost of a project at an early stage, alternatives can be tried that may be more economical or provide more facilities for the same cost. Checks can be made that the budget has not been exceeded and therefore work can be done right up to the cost limit without the risk of having to prune the design at some later stage.

The layout of housing estates is an area where this sort of program is especially valuable. The architect must provide as much living space as possible within a budget that is almost always constrained. Owing to the large number of factors involved, which include not only construction costs but also the provision of roads, drainage, electricity supply, and landscaping, such projects are difficult to cost and it is not easy to see which arrangements are the most economical or be sure that a design is not seriously over or under the cost limit. It was for these reasons that the Scottish Special Housing Association (SSHA) and the Department of the Environment commissioned a computer program that would perform a comprehensive cost evaluation and comparison of proposed housing layouts on given sites. The work was carried out by the Edinburgh Computer-Aided Architectural Design group (EdCAAD) at the Department of Architecture, Edinburgh University, and is currently being developed and extended by the SSHA[129,133,147].

The system on which the program is implemented has an interesting configuration and a high utilisation of computer machinery. The user works at a dual-screen graphics display. One screen typically might be used to hold the site plan at a small scale to give an overall reference, while the other shows a portion of the site at a large scale. Alternatively, one might display menus and messages to help the user to take action on a plan displayed on the other. The screen images are generated by a minicomputer which in turn is connected to a large time-shared computer. Picture processing is done by the local minicomputer which also handles all machine communications. The minicomputer provides the user with fast interactive facilities to generate the plan, while the time-shared computer performs the long calculations required by the evaluation programs.

Ideally, the user should also have a digitiser for convenient input of the basic site plan and initial layout, and a plotter to provide graphic output. The capital cost of all this is currently about £30 000, which is not unreasonable for a local authority or similar body that might spend several millions each year on housing projects.

The first step in investigating a layout is to input the site shape and topography, by placing a map of the site on the digitiser and inputting spot heights randomly. The program will then use these spot heights to interpolate the three-dimensional shape of the site within the computer's memory. At any subsequent time the user can ask for a contour map of any part of the site, at any scale and with any contour interval.

The user can now input the proposed layout. Roads can be defined by indicating points along their centre lines; the program will match the vertical alignment to the site shape. The user can then check the results to ensure that gradients are not too steep or the curves too sharp, and modify the plan or section if necessary. The banking and cutting necessary to construct the roads are automatically calculated, and the consequent earth movement will modify surrounding ground heights. Further finished site levels required for construction and landscaping can be input in a similar way to the specification of the original site levels.

The actual houses may then be positioned. This is simplified by the user's defining separately each different type of house that will be used; it is then only necessary to indicate their positions and orientations on the plan using the digitiser. The vertical position of each house is derived automatically from the site level at that point. Garage blocks and other buildings can also be located at this stage in a similar manner. The footpaths, fences, drainage lines and other site services are defined by indicating points along their lengths on the plan. Drainage involves both foul drainage from the houses and site drainage to remove surface water. The computer will calculate the depth at which the pipes must lie, using the minimum permissible depth and fall and the topography of the site. If necessary, the depths of other pipes in the network will be adjusted to accommodate the addition of a branch.

By these means, the complete sketch plan can be input very quickly; specification of the information, which is largely positional, is made straightforward by the use of the digitiser. The attached keyboard must also be used occasionally, e.g. for spot heights. *Figure 11.5* shows a typical layout as displayed on the screen.

Once a basic plan has been given to the computer, the user switches from the digitiser to the screens. Initially, one screen displays a menu from which

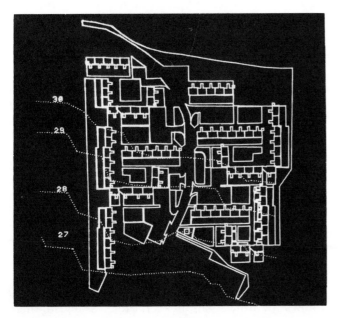

Figure 11.5 An output from the SSHA site evaluation program (courtesy Edinburgh Computer-Aided Architectural Design Group)

various options can be chosen. The option may be to make changes to some aspect of the design, such as shifting some houses or roads, or it may be to appraise the scheme by getting a breakdown of the costs and the materials involved. Housing changes may involve individual houses or entire blocks of conjoined houses; they can be added, removed or repositioned as required to investigate different layouts. Expanding the scale on one screen allows very accurate positioning to be achieved with ease.

Having made the alterations the user may wish to appraise the cost of the scheme. The simplest form of appraisal is a total cost broken down into five categories: superstructure, substructure, landscaping, drainage and roads. The user can also get a more detailed analysis of each of these categories. For example, housing costs can be listed by house and by block totals. Foundation costs are divided into such categories as the cost of trench excavation, the cost of hardcore, and of laying concrete strip. The drainage appraisal not only adds up and costs the lengths of piping but also takes for manholes at the branch points and for the cost of digging trenches to the correct depth. Similar breakdowns are possible for all the other aspects of the design, down to the cost of rotary tilling of the gardens before handover.

With these figures available, it becomes relatively easy for the architect to arrange the site to minimise the cost of the services and so have more money to allocate to providing housing.

Cut-and-fill calculation

Many programs exist that can help with certain specific problems faced by the architect. However, by their very nature they will be used infrequently, perhaps only once on each project or only on certain types of project, so mistakes will be made in use because of their unfamiliarity and also, being applied to individual problems, they are unlikely to make proportionately significant cost savings.

In certain circumstances, however, such programs can be valuable. A typical application is the optimisation of cut and fill: that is, reducing the expense of removing earth from some parts of the site and banking it on others to provide a level surface for construction. In most cases it would not be worthwhile using a program to calculate this because an accurate enough result could be obtained in an hour or so with the help of a pocket calculator; the use of a computer would take longer and not save very much money. However, if the site is very steep or there is bedrock near the surface, costs can rise dramatically and it might then be worth resorting to a computer.

The current costs of excavating earth are in the region of £1 per m³, but are very much higher if rock has to be removed. The costs of bringing in fill from outside the site are typically about £5 per m³. On a steep or uneven site, therefore, it may be worth trying the effect of moving the building a few metres to one side or the other to try to minimise costs.

The Design Office Consortium has developed a suite of six programs to help with the problems of site excavation. The original site levels and the proposed finished levels are input by means of a digitiser and a keyboard. The user can also give data from trial holes specifying the depth of topsoil and other strata. This information is given in generic terms; the user categorises the earth into 'soft' and 'firm' strata to give some idea of the difficulty of removal.

From this data the programs can produce various forms of output. The first program checks the data and prepares it for analysis by the other programs. The second program draws a plan on a screen showing the site boundaries and the positions of the buildings to be constructed while the third and fourth programs draw contour maps of the site with different degrees of smoothing. It is the fifth program that produces the most essential output as it calculates the amount of soil of various types to be removed and the amount of fill to be added. It also gives the ratio of cut to fill. The output can be broken down by different areas of the site if required so that building blocks can be considered individually. After considering this output, the user can try altering the data to investigate the effects of moving the building slightly or changing the base level, and so move towards a more optimal result.

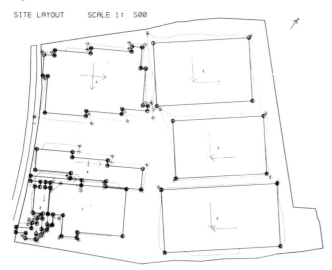

SITE LAYOUT   SCALE 1: 500

Figure 11.6 An output from the DOC cut-and-fill calculation program (courtesy Design Office Consortium)

The sixth program in the set draws the final site plan on the plotter showing the excavated regions, the required levels, banking and gradients. The contractor can use this output when preparing the site. *Figure 11.6* shows a typical example of such a plan.

Job costing

The average architect tends to feel that his responsibility is solely to produce the best designs possible

within his brief, but he is also part of an organisation that has to justify the work it does financially. If the office is in private practice it is essential that the fees received exceed the cost of the work done or the firm will go bankrupt. Even offices run by national or local government must take care not to use too many resources on a project as this will waste taxpayers' money or lead to an imbalance of effort put into different jobs. So there is a need to keep a continuous record of the time spent on each project and hence identify those that are running over budget or giving trouble.

Job-costing programs that tackle this sort of problem are widely available, but are often not suitable for professional organisations such as architects' or quantity surveyors' offices whose income comes from a large number of separate contracts with a relatively short life. This is in contrast to the more usual business situation where a manufacturer, say, has a certain number of outlets which do not often change. One program written specifically to handle the management problems encountered by architects, consulting engineers and quantity surveyors is called JCP (Job Costing Program), developed in the UK by Computer Consortium Services Ltd.

JCP takes details of the hours worked on each project from time sheets, and associates these with previously supplied information on each member of staff, including the skill category that each falls into and the rate their time is costed at. These figures can be used to find out how much has been spent on each job, and also what proportion of these costs can be assigned to the architects, what proportion to the draughtsmen and so on. Information can also be taken from expenses sheets, when supplied, and added to the total job cost. Against the outgoing figures the user can supply the amounts of the interim fees received. The financial position of the office on each job can therefore be continuously monitored.

The principal form of output available is the Main Job Costing Report. This summarises the situation for each job, giving the names of the staff that worked on it, the hours they spent, and the rate their time is costed at. It also gives the total costs on the job to date and can include expenses and the fees received to give the total financial picture. A typical Main Job Costing Report is shown in *Figure 11.7*.

Various sortings of the output are possible, but the most useful is probably to group together all the jobs that share a project leader so that they can be conveniently checked by the person responsible. This ensures that managers are presented with the minimum of paper necessary to convey the information they require. It is also possible to separate out the administrative tasks and non-fee-earning jobs. This allows the time spent on such things as accounting, training and internal meetings to be costed. Another useful form of output is the Time Sheet Check. This shows the total hours each member of staff has

```
A.D.VANCE AND PARTNERS,          J O B   C O S T I N G   P R O G R A M                    DEC  76
5 WINDMILL STREET,                                                                        PAGE  1
LONDON W1P 1HF.
                                          JOB COST SCHEDULE

***********************************************************************************************************
*JOB REF   JOB NAME     INDIVIDUAL STAFF COSTS*        MONTH TOTALS         *      TOTALS TO DATE        *            *
*                                                *                          *                            *   JOB SUMMARY   *
*           CAT  NAME     HOURS  RATE   COST *CAT HRS    COST   EXPENSES  *CAT  HRS    COST   EXPENSES *            *
***********************************************************************************************************
*121   GOODFOODS SUPERMARKET                    *                          *                            *            *
*                                               *                          *                            *            *
*          DRM MAINER J E  60.00 1.10  66.00*            CCS       1.25*DRM 155  156.00  CCS  1.25*BUDGET  1000  *
*              YOUNG F     75.00 1.20  90.00*DRM 135  156.00          *D/O  75  120.00          *PERCENT    90  *
*          D/O SNOW H      75.00 1.60 120.00*D/O  75  120.00          *ENG 287  526.00          *TOT COST 904.25*
*                                               *                          *AP   23  101.00          *            *
*                          ------  ------*    ---   ------    -------  ---- -------   --------*            *
*                          210.00 276.00*  210    276.00      1.25*    520   903.00      1.25*            *
*--------------------------------------------------------------------------------------------------------*
*127   EASTFORD- TENDER                         *                          *DRM  13   11.00          *TOT COST  79.00*
*                                               *                          *ENG  18   27.00          *            *
*                                               *                          *AP   10   41.00          *            *
*                                               *                          *     ---  -------         *            *
*                                               *                          *     41   79.00          *            *
*--------------------------------------------------------------------------------------------------------*
*12701  EASTFORD- PHYSICS BLOCK                 *                          *                            *            *
*                                               *                          *                            *            *
*          DRM JACKSON S   55.00 1.00  55.00*DRM  55   35.00          *DRM 507  558.00          *BUDGET  6000  *
*          ENG ACUFF R     34.00 3.75 127.50*ENG  34  127.50          *ENG 685 1108.50          *PERCENT    35  *
*          AP  ROBBINS     15.00 6.00  90.00*AP   15   90.00          *AP   92  459.00          *TOT COST 2125.50*
*                          ------  ------*    ---   ------            ---- -------           *            *
*                          84.00  252.50*   84    252.50             1284  2125.50          *            *
*--------------------------------------------------------------------------------------------------------*
*12702  EASTFORD- CHEMISTRY BLK                 *                          *                            *            *
*                                               *                          *                            *            *
*          ENG ACUFF R     50.00 3.75 187.50*ENG  50  187.50          *ENG  50  187.50          *BUDGET  8500  *
*          AP  ROBBINS     25.00 6.00 150.00*AP   25  150.00          *AP   25  150.00          *PERCENT    4  *
*                          ------  ------*    ---   ------            ----  -------          *TOT COST 337.50*
*                          75.00  337.50*   75    337.50              75    337.50          *            *
*                                               *                          *                            *            *
*                                               *                          *                            *            *
*                                               *                          *                            *            *
*                                               *                          *                            *            *
*                                               *                          *                            *            *
***********************************************************************************************************
```

Figure 11.7 An output from the CCS Job Costing Program (courtesy Computer Consortium Services Ltd)

worked, the holiday and sickness leave taken to date, and whether the hours worked are greater or less than the required number. The use of this output makes it much easier to observe and therefore administer individual performances.

Various other outputs can be produced that are of value on occasion. These include the Project Job List which provides a summary list of the current jobs in the office and how active they are, and the Expenses Report which totals the amount of expenses charged to each job and categorises them as required.

JCP reports are produced at times to suit the user, usually monthly from submitted time sheets, expenses, job and staff data. Managers or other controllers therefore receive all details concerning jobs under their control in time to make budgeting or staff allocation changes. At the end of each financial year it is possible to set job totals back to zero, and it is similarly possible to set staff holiday and sickness details back to zero at the end of the calendar year.

Word-processing machines

Programs like JCP can help with administration and accounting, which are two of the principal supporting services in the office. Another important service is clerical work. As the building process becomes more complex and more fragmented, architects are having to issue more production documentation and write more letters and memoranda to the various parties concerned. Aids such as dictating and photocopying machines have done a lot to help the clerical processes, and the use of computer scheduling can eliminate a lot of time-consuming and error-prone typing. Unfortunately, these aids are no longer keeping pace with the information explosion, and ever-more elaborate devices are needed to increase the productivity of the clerical staff.

In the last few years, a new sort of machine called a 'word processor' has been developed. In essence, this is a typewriter equipped with some form of storage for text and controlled by a microprocessor so that the text can be altered in parts or additions made as required and the revised version typed out[148]. This text-editing capability can increase productivity in a number of ways. At the simplest level, a letter can be typed into the storage system and from this a draft version typed onto paper. The author can then correct the draft; any alterations are made on the stored text and a fair copy is typed out. This is much quicker than correcting a letter on paper with erasing fluid, and gives a better result as there is no indication that amendments have been made; if words are inserted or removed, subsequent words on that line will automatically adjust themselves.

With manual methods, it is quite common for a secretary to retype a page completely if many errors are present, and retyping is of course essential if a line has been omitted or a sentence has to be added. This basic correction facility is also useful when producing drafts for discussion as agreed changes can be incorporated without major retyping.

Other advantages of word-processing machines arise from the possibility of being able to create standard letters or other text files which can be automatically retyped at any time with necessary changes. Thus standard letters to tenderers, local authorities, or applicants for employment, can be devised and output when required with different superscriptions and project names, if applicable. Similarly it is possible to store the addresses of organisations that are written to frequently and use these at the heads of letters and on envelopes or labels: this alone can save hours every month. This facility can be used at a higher level of complexity by storing standard paragraphs for specifications or Architect's Instructions and selecting them as required to make up the appropriate documents.

Many word-processing machines can use the microprocessor to perform more complex tasks that require some computation. One such task is searching for certain words or phrases; this facility could be used to find a paragraph number in a long document or to change, say, plastics finishes to wood finishes wherever they appear on a specification. Other tasks that require some processing are aligning columns of numbers on the last digit or on the decimal point, and the right justification of documents, i.e. altering word spacing to give an even right-hand margin as in this book, and hence improve the quality of presentation.

Some machines can change the position of lines within the stored text and so sort lines into alphabetical or numerical order. This is most useful for producing indexes, directories, catalogues and similar documents. It raises an interesting point, because it means that the word-processing machine can perform a certain amount of scheduling which previously required a computer and an elaborate program. For example, if a list of the equipment in various rooms is typed in, it can be corrected quickly and cheaply as the design progresses so that a high-quality document is always available, and it can also be sorted into the order of equipment descriptions so as to simplify totalling and rationalisation.

Many studies have been made on the increase in productivity made possible by word-processing machines, and the average figure seems to be between twice and three times the manual equivalent. The machines typically cost £4000–£5000 and so can pay for themselves within a year.

Word-processing machines can be divided into two types: stand-alone systems and shared-logic systems. Stand-alone systems are complete within themselves and each one has its own microprocessor, storage system and printing mechanism. A shared-logic system has a processing capability, storage unit and printer shared by a number of operators, each of whom has a keyboard and screen. Shared-logic systems can be more productive because it is economic to provide faster and larger storage systems and high-speed printers; despite this, a recent survey[139] showed that stand-alone systems have 99% of the market. The reason for this is possibly that if a shared-logic system breaks down, many operators are affected, which is not the case with stand-alone machines.

Shared-logic systems almost always have a screen on which information is displayed to the operator, but only 25% of stand-alone installations have this facility; the rest use the printer, so giving the same effect as with a conventional typewriter. This latter system has the advantage of familiarity for the ordinary typist, but most experts expect that the greater versatility of the screen as a display device will cause it to become much more popular in the future. *Figure 11.8* shows a popular stand-alone system that uses a screen.

Figure 11.8 A word-processing machine (courtesy IBM Ltd)

Various sorts of storage medium are in use at present. Magnetic cards are popular because they are convenient to handle and store. Their capacity is low, about 2–4 pages, but this is sufficient for the majority of letters. Magnetic cassettes can store about 40 pages of text, and this might be more convenient in an architect's office as it will allow most specifications and schedules to be held on a single storage unit, although it is rather more clumsy for letters. Floppy-disc units have the highest capacity at about 100 pages and are also the fastest, which is important if searches or sortings are to be made on long documents. They are, however, considerably more expensive than other media.

Most printers have typing speeds in the range 150 to 300 words (about a page) per minute. Higher speeds than these are convenient for drafts and specifications, but can rarely give results of correspondence quality.

12
The future

It is dangerous to prophesy on technological matters as they seem to have a disconcerting knack of getting their own back. History is littered with predictions that, with hindsight, seem ridiculously short-sighted; and these have come from even the most eminent men. Bertrand Russell, for instance, wrote in 1925 that 'physical science is approaching the stage where it will be complete and therefore uninteresting'. Lord Rutherford, probably the most important of the early workers in nuclear physics, often gave it as his opinion that atom splitting would never be put to any practical use. In 1956, the year before Sputnik 1 went into orbit, the UK's Astronomer Royal dismissed the idea of space travel as 'utter bilge'.

The track record is no better in the more specific field of predicting developments in computing. In 1948 the expert opinion was that one machine would suffice for all Britain's computational needs: today there are many thousand installations. In the 1950s, several authors pointed out that computers could never handle complex problems because the thermionic valves they would need for high performance would keep burning out at an impossible rate: even as they were writing, the first transistor computers were being marketed.

In more recent times, the blindness to the way things were going seems incredible in retrospect. I cannot find a single prediction in our own company's clippings files prior to 1970 that minicomputers would ever be important; everybody's view was that costs would drop by building larger and faster machines and that users would communicate with these by means of individual terminals. Just a few years later, minicomputers became, and remain, one of the most important sections of the market. The accepted view then became that eventually every office and household would have its own machine. Since then, the development of microprocessors has caused yet another revolution in expert opinion and it is thought that each individual will have control of a range of computing facilities, most of which will be dedicated to specific applications instead of being general purpose like conventional digital computers.

If the most eminent scientists and thinkers can get things so badly wrong, there is obviously little point in placing any reliance on predictions. It is better to make decisions on the basis of the situation as it exists at any given time and not try to anticipate developments in technology. About the only thing that can be said with confidence is that wherever things are going, they are going there fast. Hundreds of new products in the computing field are launched each month, many of them of great sophistication. The problem at present is that it is impossible to keep up with this rate in harnessing the power of these devices: we now have much more machinery than we know how to control.

Computing is probably the fastest-developing technology that has ever existed. The first fully electronic computer, named ENIAC, was built by the University of Pennsylvania in 1945. It contained 18 000 valves and occupied 90 m³ of space. It is now possible to buy for a very small sum a computer that can be held in the hand, but which is twenty times faster than ENIAC, contains the equivalent of over 250 000 separate circuit elements, and is also thousands of times more reliable and consumes less power than a light bulb. Some idea of the miniaturisation of complex circuits that is now possible is given by the picture of a microprocessor in *Figure 12.1*.

There is no reason to suppose that any sort of limit has been reached, and even more impressive comparisons will be possible in a few years' time, but the devices that now exist are already cheap enough and powerful enough to replace many comparatively crude electromagnetic controllers. This process has already begun, and many familiar machines that were previously controlled by a tangle of wiring, relays and clockwork can now be supervised by a small electronic package, with considerable gains in cost, reliability and effectiveness. These machines include: lifts, which can have much more sophisticated strategies to maximise efficiency under varying conditions; traffic lights, which can maintain optimum flow throughout the day; and household appliances such as washing machines, cookers and sewing machines which can offer a wide range of automatic programmes.

We have also seen the emergence of completely new machines which have not previously been economic to manufacture, but which with microprocessor control can be made cheap enough to capture a large market. These include personal computing devices like pocket calculators, digital watches,

Figure 12.1 A microprocessor chip (courtesy Ferranti Ltd)

word-processing machines, and entertainment devices that can play chess and other board games against a human opponent or control television games.

Many other machines will be made practicable or will be improved by the use of microprocessors. They include: car engines in which a microprocessor can control the petrol/air mixture to give the best economy or best performance much more accurately than a conventional carburettor; environmental controllers in buildings where increased economy can be achieved by switching off or reducing heating at certain times or in certain areas; telephones that can store and dial frequently used numbers; radios and televisions where continuous checking and adjusting of the tuning and volume can give better reception; and vending machines which can accept a variety of coins and give change if necessary. There are many such applications of microprocessors that spring to mind and many more that will only be 'obvious' with hindsight[150].

The existence of cheap control circuitry has started to have its effect on full-sized computers. Some of the most recent computers are of the 'array processor' type. This means that the central processing unit contains many microprocessors, each of which can be dealing with a separate part of the total problem.

Thus if the computer were playing chess, each microprocessor might be investigating a possible move. This concept of working in parallel as the human brain does, rather than just taking one thing at a time as computers have traditionally done, is a most important one. Parallel processing has been implemented before on a limited scale, but has always been very expensive. With cheap circuitry available it may become the preferred method of working owing to the greatly increased power of the machine.

In summary, it seems that in the next few years there will be a great proliferation of 'intelligent' machines that will be able to do a great deal more without human intervention than their present-day equivalents, if any. This increase in automation will reach into every part of our lives and will eventually require a radical reorganisation of working methods in almost every field. This reorganisation will be necessary because some of the tasks to be performed will be different and because the methods of carrying out tasks will also change. Almost everybody will be influenced by this change, but architects may be affected more than the other members of the building team because they are less familiar with the concepts involved and have lagged behind in technological development. It is not quite fair to say that the profession is still using methods that would be perfectly familiar to Sir Christopher Wren. There have been many improvements, especially in the field of communications with the introduction of dyeline machines and photocopiers, but architecture is still very labour-intensive.

The problems facing the architect can be identified, and it fairly safe to prophesy that there will be technological solutions to the worst of them. The precise nature of these solutions cannot be predicted because of the many possibilities that exist, some of which cannot even be guessed at; but, on the understanding that it is for entertainment rather than for information, some aspects of a possible scenario can be suggested.

Perhaps the most pressing problem in any office is the amount of draughting that has to be done. In the last analysis, every line in the design drawings must be individually drawn by hand, and must often be drawn several times over if changes are made or if plans are required at different scales or for different purposes. The inherent inefficiency of this necessitates a large draughting team with the attendant difficulties of communication so familiar to most architects nowadays.

Some form of computer-aided draughting will be introduced to solve this problem. Automatic copying of parts of similar drawings or repeated sections of the design can, even at the present stage of development, cut the manpower needed to a third or a quarter. Allowing for improvements in technology and programming, the performance ratio should quite soon become five or six to one, and on this basis the typical office in ten years' time will have several draughting workstations and most of the drawing will be done by the designers themselves rather than at one remove through technicians. Interactive systems will be used rather than non-interactive because of their higher performance and because their high overheads will become less important with the change in the relative costs of machinery and human labour.

Once such machines have been installed, it is natural and obvious to extend the programs to analyse the drawings and produce various supplementary results. Scheduling of equipment and fittings is an easy result to provide, and scheduling of materials is easy given a 2½- or three-dimensional system of computer-aided draughting. This latter result has the more important implications because it has not been the architect's responsibility in modern times, whereas he has been expected to produce lists of individual items like equipment, doors and windows, or at least to reference each one on the drawings. A number of installations can already automate over 50% of their bills of materials and there appears to be no reason why this should not reach 80%–90%.

Such a high degree of automation must put pressure on the current distribution of work among the design team. In Britain and the Commonwealth, quantity surveying is a separate profession and it seems possible that there will be attempts to renegotiate the present percentage fee. It should in any case mean a drastic reduction in the number of technicians who measure the quantities and an increase in the surveyors' role in advising architects on what materials should be used in construction. In other countries, where in most cases contractors measure quantities, there will be less need for reorganisation as far as the architect is concerned.

Automatic visualisation is another result that can be produced directly as a by-product of computer-aided draughting. Computer programs for perspectives are not widely used at present because of the labour of data collection, but once views are available without effort architects may come to use them as an important design aid and produce many perspectives so as to be able to 'walk around' and 'walk through' their buildings and check their appearance and arrangement.

Although such perspectives are adequate for the working designer they will probably be considered too unfinished for client presentation or publicity purposes. As tighter construction schedules make hand-finishing difficult, machines specific to visualisation will be used. These machines, which were described in Chapter 7 and are already available, can show full-colour views of buildings complete with shadows and if necessary can continuously change the viewpoint giving the effect of movement.

In principle, any result that depends for the bulk of its data on positional or dimensional information can be produced from a computer-aided draughting system. Environmental analysis, including heat loss, daylight factors and sunlight penetration can be performed given a relatively small amount of additional data such as U-values. Duct sizing and the routeing of services can be analysed or perhaps a network can be generated. Most such results are concerned with the detailed functioning of the building and will reduce the architect's dependence on the services engineers and consultants. Generally speaking, the use of computers will bring more of the design process under the architect's control and the continued erosion of his role by specialist contractors and consultants will be halted or even reversed.

Somewhat surprisingly, there is no sign at present that the use of computers will allow the architect to take over some of the tasks performed at present by the structural engineer. It might be thought that as all the data on column and wall dimensions and span lengths can be obtained automatically from a draughting system this would be merely a matter of evaluating the appropriate formulae, but in fact I know of no architectural practice that is attempting to take structural calculations beyond broad indications of feasibility. This may be because structural engineering is not such a rigid and formalised process as the architect tends to believe, but requires a lot of value judgements and the trading-off of some factors against others.

The use of interactive draughting systems will give the greatest increase in productivity, but there will still be a lot of scope for textual and numeric processing. The further development of minicomputers and microcomputers will bring extensive processing capability within the reach of even the smallest firms. Such general-purpose machines can be programmed to aid many of the architect's tasks, including job management by critical-path analysis and other means, basic design calculations, simulation studies of the way buildings will work in practice, and office accounting.

One of the most important areas for textual processing will be in the field of database retrieval. As buildings become more complex, more and more experience is being needed to design them. An office might need specialists in a dozen subjects, such as lifts, joinery, fire precautions, X-ray equipment, and laboratory servicing, to design a single building, because of the great amount of information that must be considered on all these matters. The specialists attempt to integrate their talents to produce a coherent design, but this is becoming more inefficient with time. It is here that a computer's ability to store and retrieve large quantities of information could ease the situation. Database techniques will allow relevant facts, existing solutions, recent innovations, research papers, technical articles and the names of firms that manufacture particular products to be handled quickly and conveniently.

It may be that each office will maintain its own database in the same way as they support libraries at present; but it is possible that the sheer volume and scope of the data will mean that specialist companies will offer the use of proprietary databases on various subjects. Attempts have been made before to provide such services using time-sharing bureaux, but they never became popular. A more promising approach may be to use one of the existing teletext facilities to distribute the information. Teletext is the transmission of data to domestic television sets, which therefore provide a cheap and versatile form of visual display terminal[153]. The transmission can be by broadcast or through a telephone link to the set. In the UK, the British Broadcasting Corporation has provided a broadcast service known as 'Ceefax' and the Independent Broadcasting Authority one called 'Oracle' since 1974. The Post Office has developed a wired teletext method generically known as 'Viewdata' and initiated a commercial service called 'Prestel' in 1979. All such systems require some modifications to a standard television receiver before it can display teletext, and all have the same basic format for a screenful of information: up to 960 characters can be shown, arranged as 24 lines of 40 characters. Simple graphics facilities are also available, and any of seven fully-saturated colours may be used.

Commercial organisations can pay for screens to be added to the services, and currently such things as entertainment and restaurant guides, railway timetables, an encyclopaedia, scientific articles, stock market prices, a news service and many others are available. Prestel currently provides over 150 000 screens of information, and this figure is expected to at least double. The broadcast teletext services cannot provide more than about 800 screens because of bandwidth limitations, so they are inherently smaller than a wired service where different information can be sent on each line.

In 1979, an organisation named Contel launched a pilot information service for the construction industry using Prestel. Currently, the information offered includes technical references, cost information on building types and materials, guides to design criteria, and news items. The intention is to expand this in scope and content. These developments in databases will make possible a shift away from the current emphasis on personal experience, which cannot usually encompass the intricacies of many solutions, to the awareness of broad alternative strategies, leaving the details to be filled in by database references.

A few years ago all applications were being fitted into general-purpose digital computers with varying success, but now there is a tendency for machines to be built for specific purposes. Draughting systems, visualisation machines and calculators are examples of special-purpose machines, and more will be developed in the future. Machines for database handling and for simulation are two possibilities that spring to mind, as both of these applications involve types of processing that would benefit from dedicated circuitry.

Word-processing machines are a type of special-purpose computer that is already in widespread use, although not as yet in architects' offices. They will become more necessary as the need to coordinate and communicate with the many participants in the construction process increases, and as the volume of production documentation to be prepared becomes greater. The overwhelming amount of paperwork is a problem that frustrates many designers at present, as they have to spend so much time composing and checking it. The increased use of standard letters and the possibility of making up specifications by editing those produced for other jobs or by selecting from a library of standard paragraphs will reduce this load to some extent, although of course the main benefit is that the quicker issue of documentation will speed up the design process.

The pace of design is increasing so fast that in the future, even if letters and documentation can be produced in a fraction of the time presently needed, the day or two required for postal delivery may begin to seem unacceptable. An obvious solution is to use the telephone more, but an architect very often needs to convey information using drawings, which cannot be described verbally, or using specifications and schedules, which are normally too lengthy to dictate. A machine that allows the architect to make more use of the telephone is the facsimile copier; this device is attached to a telephone and can scan a page and output a copy on a matching device on the receiving instrument. The cost of transmission is far higher than that of postage and a maximum paper size of A4 is usually imposed, but this method could become the preferred means of dispatching urgent material.

Taking the principle of electronic copying a step further, it is possible to bypass human intervention completely by having the computers belonging to the various participants in the construction process pass information between themselves. In principle, both textual data and drawings can be sent from one computer to another over the public telephone network, and many commercial organisations, especially banks, are already doing this on a large scale. Obviously this step will have to wait until computers are much more widespread in the construction industry, and it is also necessary that standard interfaces be agreed so that the different trades and different computers can communicate. A start has been made on this[151] and eventually it may be possible for architects and consultants to work on the same drawings more or less simultaneously and not have to rely on periodic issues to exchange information or to coordinate the work.

Another aspect of this sort of development is that even the architect's office itself could be fragmented. Each architect could work at home on his own computer and send the work down the telephone line to a colleague's machine or to a central office machine. Meetings and discussions could take place by telephone. This method of working could become popular as staff could live where they liked without wasting time and money in commuting. Female architects might also like working from home when they have young children to care for, instead of their valuable training being lost to the profession for years, as at present. By the turn of the century, we might see a typical large practice having only a small and centrally located office for coordination and occasional conferences.

As reliance on machines increases, there will be concern that they be made as reliable as possible. With the use of solid-state electronics, the processing parts of the system are already very reliable: it is the peripheral devices that, being largely mechanical, are liable to breakdowns. Magnetic discs are perhaps the worst offenders; spinning at high rates and having very close tolerances they are expensive to build and need constant maintenance and repair. They are, however, an essential part of almost every computer installation.

Because of these problems, there is considerable interest in alternative forms of mass storage that can supplement or replace magnetic discs. One of the most promising developments to date is 'magnetic bubble' storage. The principle of magnetic bubble techniques is that in certain substances it is possible to introduce regions of reverse magnetisation which can be moved about within the material by electric charges. A storage device can therefore be built which consists of a fine grid of wires laid over a plate of material with this property. Each square of the grid may or may not contain a region or 'bubble' of reverse magnetisation and, by varying the charge on the wires, bubbles can be moved from one square to the next. Data can be put into the medium coded as the presence or absence of bubbles, and when required the information in the appropriate squares can be shifted under a reading head.

As magnetic-bubble storage does not need any moving parts, it is extremely reliable and in most circumstances is a lot faster than mechanical storage systems, although it is still not as fast as the computer's own memory. The Intel Corporation recently launched a magnetic-bubble storage element that can hold about 62 000 numbers and sells for around £1000. This is still several times more expensive than magnetic disc storage, but the price gap will narrow very quickly.

Printers and plotters are other widely used peripheral devices that are largely mechanical in operation. The reliability problems with these machines are not so acute because they do not move at the extremely high rates of disc drives and do not require the same precision. Despite this, they still need frequent maintenance, are noisy and have to be supervised. Plotters especially should be supervised in operation to ensure that a pen has not dried up. The development of electrostatic printers and plotters represents a significant development over the older types. In these machines, ink particles are put onto the paper by the use of magnetic fields; thus the print head or pen cartridge, which are the parts that move at the highest speed, are eliminated. This gives greater reliability, greater speed and reduced noise level. On the debit side, the quality of result is not as good as that obtained with an impact printer or a pen plotter, and electrostatic devices are more expensive. However, as time goes on, the output quality can be expected to improve and the increased speed and lower level of supervision required will make these machines a popular alternative.

On the input side of the system, there will be a search for mechanisms that can collect data for the computer more quickly and efficiently. This is not a question of the speed of transferring data from media such as cards or tape, because this is already very high, certainly higher than most architectural problems would require. The bottleneck at present is that the actual typing in of data or instructions at a keyboard and the pinpointing of coordinates on a digitiser are very slow compared to the speed of all the other parts of the system.

At one time it was thought that optical character recognition machines would help to solve this problem. These devices can accept a page of typing and read it by recognising the shape of the characters as a human does. There is much less interest in this form of input nowadays, even though the use of microprocessors has made the machines much cheaper to build. The reason for this is that it has been recognised that because they were only capable of reading typed or printed characters, and most often only certain styles of typeface, it is cheaper and more efficient to type the data onto media suitable for direct computer input and to output it later on the printer if a copy on paper is required.

Quite recently, ScanData Corporation, who specialise in optical character recognition devices, have developed a machine that can accept hand printing. This data has to be prepared on special forms to give consistent positioning of characters, but can then be input without further processing. As most data is written out by hand before it is typed, and then has to be checked by the originator, the use of these machines can greatly speed up data preparation.

Another advanced method of data input is voice data entry. A number of manufacturers have devised machines that can recognise a limited set of words and phrases and transmit them to a computer. This method of input allows the user to have both hands free and give his instructions to the computer verbally[155]. An application of this method of input might be when using an interactive draughting system. The user could have a light pen in one hand, follow a sketch drawing with the other, and speak to the computer in order to call up predefined elements, change the scale and so on. Voice data entry is already widely used in cartography, where accurate use of a digitiser requires the use of both hands. Voice data entry also has the advantages that it is a quicker and more natural method of working than the use of a keyboard for architects and draughtsmen, who are seldom good typists.

The firm of EMI Threshold Limited has recently launched a range of voice data entry devices based on the Threshold 500 microprocessor. The various models are able to hold from 32 words or short phrases up to several hundred. Each user has to 'train' the machine to recognise his voice by speaking each word several times before starting work: the result of this session can then be stored on a cassette for future re-use. This procedure allows the machine to deal with the dialects and accents of a range of users. A basic 32-word model costs about £5500 at present, which is several times more expensive than a light pen, but again the price can be expected to drop as the cost of the circuitry does.

It can be seen that the use of microprocessors and cheap control circuitry is not only improving the performance of computers, but is also being used to make the peripheral devices themselves more powerful. This trend is being repeated over the entire field and already many terminals can verify the accuracy and consistency of data before they pass it to the computer; plotters can store standard shapes and lettering styles within themselves so as to reduce the amount of data to be transmitted; and printers can arrange information passed to them in a required page layout.

The final development would of course be a machine that could rival the power of the human brain, just as machines have for centuries rivalled or surpassed the power of the human body. This is not in the near future, but it is perhaps closer than most people realise. The human brain is estimated to contain ten thousand million nerve cells, or neurons[156], while the largest commercially available integrated circuit contains about a hundred thousand elements in a very small package. Thus in these terms a not unusually large machine could have the same complexity as the brain. However, the problem is not that simple, for two reasons. The first is that each neuron does a certain amount of simple processing and so cannot be considered the equivalent of a single transistor or diode. The second is that the neurons are connected in parallel, with millions of pathways being active at once, whereas conventional computer design follows a single line of processing. Thus there must be a large increase in the number of elements per circuit and there must be a radical redesign of circuit functioning before a reasonable model of the brain can be produced. Against this, however, must be set the fact that the brain works by the chemical propagation of impulses while a digital computer works by electricity, and the difference in speed is three million to one.

If computing goes on developing as it has been doing in the last thirty years, the future is one of fast and accelerating change. It seems inevitable that architects will be caught up in this flood, bu whether they find the prospect exhilerating or terrifying, and whether they cope at all, no doubt depends on individual resistance to culture shock.

13
Sources of information

Only a few years ago, the architect who decided to make use of computers was very much on his own. Every application was a pioneering one, and there were only a handful of workers in any field. Today, the situation has completely changed; many architects are using computers and the main application areas are well established. There is now a wide pool of experience for the newcomer to draw on and a number of organisations and many publications that may be of use to him.

The most important organisation, as far as the British architect is concerned, is undoubtedly the **Design Office Consortium**. This was formed in 1971 with the objective of encouraging the use of computer techniques in the building industry. The membership includes representatives of all the participants in the building process, but architects form the largest single contingent. Virtually every practice that makes use of computers is a member of the Consortium; it thus forms an unrivalled body of expertise.

The Consortium will advise on all aspects of computing and can offer a consultancy service to any firm that wants to get started and needs advice. Files are kept on the programs and machinery available that are likely to be of interest to architects and visits can usually be arranged to working offices to see how they operate in practice. For established members, the Consortium publishes a quarterly newsletter describing the latest developments and organises visits to look at interesting applications and discuss them with their users.

As well as acting as an information distribution service, the Consortium also carries out research and evaluation projects. Programs are evaluated at various levels, the highest being where all programs of a certain type are used and compared on a live or realistic project. The times taken and the computer costs incurred are tabulated with the equivalent manual time. The reports on these detailed evaluations are invaluable for any prospective user.

The cost of membership varies with the size of the office and the grade of membership, but at the time of writing full membership for an office employing 11–50 staff costs £120 per year. The Consortium receives about half its income from outside contracts and is also supported by the Department of the Environment. The address for all enquiries is: The General Manager, Design Office Consortium, Guildhall Place, Cambridge CB2 3QQ.

The **National Computing Centre** is another body that exists to help computer users. The Centre was founded in 1966 with the object of promoting the wider and more effective use of computers throughout the UK. Being a national body, it is far bigger than the Design Office Consortium but much less specific as it has to concern itself with the entire range of computing activities. Its size allows it to maintain comprehensive files on programs and machines and one of its most important functions is to provide an information service. Most of the more straightforward inquiries are free to members but a small charge is made if more complex or detailed searches are required.

As well as supplying information, the Centre can also provide an advisory service for intending computers users. The aid that is available includes short feasibility studies, specification of tenders and assistance in selection and getting started.

The Centre is involved with publishing works of interest to all those concerned with computing, from popular works for the layman on subjects such as privacy of information to technical studies for the student or professional programmer.

The Centre provides computer training at appreciation level for managers and in analysis and programming for the practitioner. The training is available as courses, either public or in-house, or as material which is suitable for colleges or self-instruction. Seminars on computing topics are also organised.

On a level of less direct benefit to the user, the Centre is concerned with establishing and encouraging the use of standards and cooperating and co-ordinating with other bodies that are influenced by the use of computers.

There are three classes of membership, but most architectural practices will fall into Class B. Membership of this class costs £110 a year at present. The Centre is additionally financed by the Government and also receives some income from programs which it has developed itself. There are five offices around the country, but the Head Office to which enquiries can be made in the first instance is at the following address: The National Computing Centre Ltd, Oxford Road, Manchester M1 7ED.

Computing has its own professional body, the **British Computer Society**, which is roughly equivalent to architecture's RIBA. The Society aims to raise standards in all aspects of the design and the use of computers, and within that role also functions as a learned society. The membership of the Society is high, about 24 000 at the time of writing, although there is some resistance in the computing world to the idea of computing being a profession at all.

Advantages in membership include the possibility of joining some of the many special-interest groups functioning under the Society's aegis, including a computer-aided design group. There is also a comprehensive library, and members receive free the *Computer Journal*, which is a learned publication, and the *Computer Bulletin* which is less technical and contains Society news and articles of general interest.

Being a professional Society, it cannot be joined directly, except as a student. Full membership requires studying for the examinations or acquiring enough experience in computing to obtain exemption. Enquiries should be addressed to: The Secretary, The British Computer Society, 13 Mansfield Street, London W1M 0BP.

The above organisations are of course independent bodies and can be relied upon for disinterested advice; however, specific manufacturers and bureaux can also be valuable sources of information. As they are in business, they will try to meet a potential user more than halfway; given a problem expressed in non-technical terms they will attempt to see if their products could be useful and will often allocate programmers to writing demonstration programs or give free runs on test data. If moving from one manufacturer or bureau to another, there will quite often be an offer of conversion of at least some of the programs written on the other machine. Free advice is obtainable from most bureaux on writing or correcting programs. Training courses in the use of machines or specific programs are also commonly available, either free or for nominal sums. A list of manufacturers or of local computer bureaux can be obtained from the Design Office Consortium or the National Computing Centre or through the advertisements in the technical press.

Programs useful to architects can now be obtained from many sources, but one body that exists solely to produce this kind of program is the **Computer-Aided Design Centre**, several of whose products have been described in this book. The Centre was set up in 1969 by the Ministry of Technology with the intention of its becoming the primary national centre for the development and application of computer-aided design techniques in industry. It is currently financed by its commercial activities and by the Department of Trade and Industry.

The Centre has a large staff and a great deal of machinery and has produced a large number of programs covering many aspects of design, including architectural design. These programs are available at reasonable costs or can be used on a royalty basis on one of the Centre's computers. The Centre has a large amount of expertise in writing computer-aided design systems and will accept commissions to produce special-purpose programs. Enquiries relating to architectural programs can be addressed to: The Marketing Department, Computer-Aided Design Centre, Madingley Road, Cambridge CB3 0HB.

Many books have been published on all aspects of computing, but as the science of computing is developing so fast on all fronts, these books tend to go out of date very quickly, and few have a practical life longer than five years. The Bibliography includes books that give more detail on various application areas and those that describe the work in progress at various sites and so outline the current fields of development. The Bibliography also includes reference works that list programs currently available. These include lists of the programs for specific applications, such as producing perspectives, and general lists that try to include every existing program that might be of interest to the architect.

If use is made of computers, most offices will want to subscribe to periodicals in order to keep abreast of the latest developments. Most of the periodicals published are of a general nature and are intended to have a broad appeal to all computer users; but there are a few that are aimed specifically at the growing number of architectural practices that use computers in their work.

The general-interest periodicals can be helpful in a number of ways. They publish details of new machinery coming onto the market and some of these items will be of interest to any small installation. A new model of terminal, for instance, could boost productivity or increase reliability. New programs with reasonably wide application are examined and some of these, such as those for database management, could well be profitably used by architects. Advice and hints on techniques are regularly printed, and again these can be of interest to anyone running a small computer installation. Much of the value of periodicals comes from the large number of advertisements that most of them carry. These include promotions for machinery and for programs and technical details are often given. A study of these will give the prospective user an idea of the range of products available and their average price and performance.

The two main weekly periodicals of general interest in the UK are *Computer Weekly* and *Computing*. These two publications have a lot in common; both have the general format of newspapers and both print roughly the same mixture of news, special articles and features on subjects of interest. Both papers are free to people using computers or otherwise connected with the trade. The addresses are: *Computer Weekly*, IPC Electrical-Electronic Press Ltd, Dorset House, Stamford Street, London SE1 9LU; *Computing*, 76 Dean Street, London W1A 1BU.

As well as the weekly papers, there are magazines of general interest, mostly American, that appear at longer intervals. The same comments apply to these as to the weeklies, but because of their nature they concentrate more on articles and features and less on day-to-day news.

Of the periodicals of special interest to the architect, the *Bulletin of Computer-Aided Architectural Design* is perhaps the most important. It is published quarterly and currently costs £5.00 for a year's subscription. The *Bulletin* is completely devoted to the use of computers in architecture and so all articles and news are of direct relevance. Orders should be sent to: Bulletin of Computer-Aided Architectural Design, Architecture and Building Aids Computer Unit, University of Strathclyde, Department of Architecture, 131 Rottenrow, Glasgow G4 0NG.

Two other journals of interest are *Design Studies* and *Computer-Aided Design*, both of which are published by IPC Science and Technology Press Ltd. *Design Studies* is concerned with the theory and the study of design techniques and methodology in a range of fields, including architecture, town planning, industrial design and environmental psychology. Not all articles published, therefore, are relevant to the working architect and not all of these are concerned with the use of computers. However, a good proportion of them will be of interest. The journal is a quarterly and the current annual subscription is £40.00. *Computer-Aided Design* is a journal devoted to the application of computers to design problems. Again, a wide field is covered and only occasional papers are printed on architectural matters. The journal is published six times a year and the current subscription is £27.00 a year.

Both *Design Studies* and *Computer-Aided Design* are very professional and well produced and can be obtained from: IPC Science and Technology Press Ltd, Westbury House, Bury Street, Guildford, Surrey GU2 5AW.

Glossary

The attempt has been made to avoid abbreviations and technical terms in this book, but if the reader decides to become involved with computers he will find that the whole subject is hedged about with jargon and strange acronyms. This section is intended to explain the most common terms and concepts that will be encountered.

Algol (Algorithmic language) One of the first of the modern generation of *high-level languages*. It is popular in Europe principally for scientific applications.

Analogue computer A computer that uses a continuously varying quantity to represent numbers within itself. In practice, electrical voltage is usually chosen.

APL (A Programming Language) A *high-level language* that makes extensive use of mathematical notation. It is very powerful and compact, but needs more skill to use than most other languages.

Assembly language A computer language that is very close to the basic instruction set of the machine. It is thus efficient in use, but difficult for humans to understand.

Backing store See *mass memory*.

BASIC (Beginner's All-purpose Symbolic Instruction Code) A *high-level language* very suitable for small programs or for introducing the concepts of programming.

Batch processing A system in which the user submits his problem to the computer and later receives the results. To be contrasted with *interactive processing* in which the user may intervene during the execution of the program.

Baud A measure of transmission speeds. For most applications, 100 baud is approximately equal to 10 characters per second.

Binary Having two possible states. Very appropriate to electronic circuitry as a current may be flowing or not flowing.

Bit (binary digit) The basic unit of information in a *digital computer*. A number of bits may be taken in conjunction to represent a numerical value or a *character*.

Bootstrapping A process in which the first few lines of a program read in the rest. Normally used initially to start up a machine by loading the *operating system*.

Bubble memory A form of *mass memory* in which information is stored by the arrangement of small magnetised regions held within a suitable medium.

Bug A fault in a computer program, or, occasionally, in the machinery. Hence **debugging**: the process of removing bugs.

Byte See *character*.

CAAD Abbreviation of Computer-Aided Architectural Design.

CAD Abbreviation of Computer-Aided Design.

Card A popular means of representing data using holes in a stiff paper card. Cards can normally hold 80 *characters* of information, although there are other sizes.

Cartridge disc One of the forms of *disc storage*.

Central Processing Unit (CPU) The part of the computer system that carries out the calculations and coordinates all the other parts.

Character A single symbol such as a letter of the alphabet. It is represented within the computer by a number of *bits* grouped together. Either six or eight bits are almost always used; if eight, the group is sometimes called a **byte**.

COBOL (Common Business Orientated Language) The most commonly used *high-level language*. It is orientated towards commercial applications.

Compiler A computer program that transforms a program written in a *high-level language* into elementary machine instructions.

Core storage In modern usage, equivalent to *main memory*.

Database A structured set of information which can be interrogated and updated by the computer.

DBMS Abbreviation of Database Management System.

Debugging See *bug*.

Digitiser, pencil follower or **tablet** A data-input device looking like a drawing board, which will generate coordinates when touched with a special pen. These can be sent directly to the computer or stored for later input.

Digital computer A computer that holds and manipulates numbers in an exact form; normally as assemblies of *bits*.

Disc storage A form of *mass memory* in which information is held as magnetised spots on the surface of a disc. The physical arrangement may take several forms: a **disc pack** is a number of discs on a common spindle; a **cartridge disc** is a disc about the size of a long-playing record and permanently enclosed in a rigid case; a **floppy disc** is about the size of a 45 rpm record, is flexible, and is permanently enclosed in a cardboard sleeve.

Down A computer is said to be 'down' when it is out of action.

Floating point number A number that can have a fractional part. Such numbers need more circuitry to handle them than *integers* and many *minicomputers* do not provide this circuitry, so floating-point calculations must be done by program.

Floppy disc One of the forms of *disc storage*.

Fortran (Formula Translation Language) One of the earliest and most widely understood *high-level languages*. It is favoured for general purpose use, but especially in scientific and engineering applications.

GPSS (General Purpose Simulation System) A *high-level language* for modelling activity systems.

Hard copy Output printed on paper, as distinct from that appearing on a screen or within some storage system.

Hardware Computer machinery.

High-level language A computer language that makes concessions to the programmer and is thus easier to use. It requires a *compiler* to convert it into a form the machine can understand.

Integer A number that cannot have a fractional part.

Integrated circuit (IC) An electronic circuit a few millimetres square constructed on a single wafer of silicon and embedded in plastic for protection and to support the outside connectors. **Large Scale Integration (LSI)** describes such a circuit containing roughly the equivalent of a few thousand elements. **Very Large Scale Integration (VLSI)** describes such a circuit that may contain the equivalent of as many as 100 000 elements. It is the development of this technology that has caused the fall in computer prices.

Interactive processing A system in which the computer and the user carry on a dialogue. This is more flexible and more powerful than *batch processing* as the user can guide the course of the calculations or amend the data; it is, however, more expensive. Interactive processing is often implemented as *time-sharing*.

I/O Abbreviation of Input/Output. These processes are regarded separately from the process of calculation because they are relatively so much slower.

Job Control Language (JCL) The language by which the user controls the progress of a problem to be solved by *batch processing* methods. The instructions specify which files contain data, which output devices the results should go to and so on.

The Job Control Language works by sending requests to the *operating system*.

Joystick An interactive data input device that can be used for identifying points on a *visual display unit*.

K The symbol for the number 1024 (2^{10}). Computers find it easier to work in such units as they are a power of two and so can be conveniently expressed in *binary* form. Many quantities are measured in units of K, but among the most common are *main memory* size and the storage capability of various *mass memory* devices.

Light pen An interactive data input device that can select lines or points drawn on a *refresh display*.

Line-printer A device for the speedy printing of results. Typical speeds are in the region of 1000 lines per minute.

Load and go A system in which a program that has been processed by a *compiler* is put into the computer and immediately used to solve the problem.

LSI See *integrated circuit*.

Machine independence A program is machine-independent if it will run on with little or no change on any machine. In theory, *high-level languages* confer this benefit.

Magnetic tape A form of *mass memory* in which information is held as magnetised spots on the surface of a tape. It is cheaper but slower than *disc storage* to which it is the principal alternative form of bulk storage on most machines.

Main memory The memory of the computer itself. It is faster to reference, but more expensive and more limited than the various forms of *mass memory*.

Mass memory or **backing store** The storage capability a computer has in addition to its *main memory*. Most installations use *disc storage* and *magnetic tape*.

Microcomputer A computer based on a *microprocessor*. It is fitted with some form of *main memory* and possibly *peripherals*.

Microprocessor A complete *central processing unit* constructed on a single *integrated circuit*. It can be used in many complex control applications.

Microsecond (μs) A millionth of a second.

Millisecond (ms) A thousandth of a second.

Minicomputer Now a rather ill-defined term, but broadly a physically small, rugged and cheap computer with comparatively limited capabilities.

Modem (Modulator/Demodulator) A device that converts electronic signals from a computer or a *terminal* into acoustic signals for transmission by telephone and vice versa.

MTBF (Mean Time Between Failures) The average time a device will operate between breakdowns. The most common measure of reliability.

Multiprogramming The running of several independent jobs at once within a computer. This makes best use of the machine because one job can be performing calculations while the others are performing the much slower input and output operations.

Nanosecond (ns)   A thousand-millionth of a second. Most *central processing unit* activities are measured in this unit.

Off-line   An activity that does not involve the computer at the time of taking place, but did at some earlier time, or will at some later time. Examples are the computer producing a *magnetic tape* that will later be used to control an independent device, such as a *plotter*; and the punching of *cards* for later input to the computer.

On-line   An activity that directly involves the computer. *Interactive processing* is an on-line activity.

Operating system   The program or programs that control the activities of the computer. It responds to requests from the *job control language* amongst other things.

Optical Character Recognition (OCR)   A method of inputting data in which the visual form of the characters is used to convey information, instead of holes in *cards*, or magnetised spots on tape. Often, only a standard typeface is acceptable.

Paper tape   A means of representing data by holes in a strip of paper tape. The tape is nowadays usually 25mm wide with 8 possible positions for the holes across its width.

Pencil follower   See *digitiser*.

Peripheral device or peripheral   A machine that is connected to the computer and is normally used to input data or to output results.

PL/1 (Programming Language 1)   A *high-level language* intended to be usable in both commercial and scientific areas. It has very many features and therefore takes some time to learn thoroughly. It is gaining popularity, however.

Plotter   An output device that produces line drawings from computer instructions. The output is normally on paper, but occasionally on microfilm. The most popular type of plotter is the **drum plotter** in which the paper runs over a revolving drum and lines are drawn by combining the motions of the drum and the pen. The **flatbed plotter** is more accurate but more expensive. With this type, the paper lies on a flat surface and the pen alone moves.

Plug compatible   Describes a device that will connect directly to a specified computer without modifications.

Programmable calculator   A hand-held simple computer based on a *microprocessor*.

Raster display   A type of *visual display unit* where the image is made up of many dots, and each possible dot position is associated with a location in a *main memory* block. By changing the information in memory it is therefore possible to change the image.

Real time   Actual elapsed time. A computer is operating in real-time mode, for example, if it is controlling traffic.

Refresh display   A type of *visual display unit* in which a computer repeatedly redraws the image, at least 16 times per second. Continuous changing of the image is therefore possible.

ROM (Read Only Memory)   A type of *main memory* which permanently contains certain programs or data. It supplements memory that can change the information it holds.

Software   Computer programs.

Spooling   An acronym for Simultaneous Peripheral Operation On-Line. The ability that some computers possess to perform input or output via *peripheral devices* whilst at the same time leaving the *central processing unit* free to perform calculations.

Storage tube   A type of *visual display unit* in which the image is stored on the inside face of the screen. Additions are possible, but erasures require complete redrawing of the image.

Subroutine or **subprogram**   A block of computer instructions that carry out some process that is repeatedly required. Reference can be made to this block whenever this process has to be carried out; thus duplication within a computer program is avoided.

Tablet   See *digitiser*.

Teleprinter   A typewriter-like device used to communicate with a computer. A form of *terminal*.

Terminal   A device used to communicate with a computer. Most often, it will be a *teleprinter* or a *visual display unit*.

Time sharing   A process in which the computer takes advantage of the comparatively slow response time of humans and of the slow speed of *terminals*, by switching its attention between many users. Ideally, each user has the impression that he has the sole use of the computer.

Virtual memory   A system in which the computer uses its *mass memory* as an extension of its *main memory*. It makes possible very large and complex programs, but can often be very inefficient owing to the greater retrieval times of mass memory.

Visual Display Unit (VDU)   A device resembling a television receiver, but usually equipped with a keyboard. Some units can only handle alphanumeric information, while others can support graphical work as well. The device is often used as a *terminal*. The two most common forms of visual display unit are *refresh displays* and *storage tubes*.

VLSI   See *integrated circuit*.

Word   A number of *bits* grouped together to represent a numerical value or a group of *characters*. The most common form of organisation is to have 4 characters, each of 8 bits, thus giving a 32-bit word.

Word-processing machine   A device used for manipulating text files such as those used in correspondence. Usually controlled by a *minicomputer* or a *microprocessor*.

Bibliography

Chapter 1   Past and present

1 Alexander, C., *Notes on the Synthesis of Form*, Harvard University Press (1964)
2 Alexander, C., 'From a set of forces to a form', *Interior Design*, (Oct 1967), pp 36–61
3 'DHSS launches yet another hospital system and drops Harness', *Architects' Journal*, (Sep 1975), pp 449–450
4 Davis, C., 'The Harness system', *Hospital Engineering*, (Jan 1974), pp 3–11
5 Jones, J.C., 'A method of systematic design', *Conf. on Design Methods*, Pergamon, London (1963)
6 Ministry of Health, *Hospital Building Notes* (35 parts), HMSO, London (1961–1973)
7 Ministry of Health, *Hospital Design Notes* (5 parts), HMSO, London (1964–1968)
8 Newman, W.M., 'An experimental program for architectural design', *Computer Journal*, (May 1966), pp 21–26
9 Radford, R., 'The "Harness" whole hospital planning concept', *Hospital Building and Engineering*, (Sep 1971), pp 24–29
10 Ray-Jones, A., 'Computer developments in West Sussex', *Architects' Journal*, (Feb 1968), pp 421–426; pp 489–498
11 Sutherland, I.E., 'SKETCHPAD: a man-machine graphical communication system', *AFIPS Conference Proc.*, Detroit (1963), pp 329–346

Chapter 2   Using computers

12 Auger, B., *The Architect and the Computer*, Pall Mall, London (1972)
13 Campion, D., *Computers in Architectural Design*, Elsevier, London (1968)
14 Campion, D. and Reynolds, T., 'Computers in architecture in the UK', *DMG-DRS Journal*, (Oct 1974), pp 182–199
15 Carter, J., 'Computers and the Architect' (4 articles) *Architects' Journal*, (3 Oct 1973) pp 813–819; (10 Oct 1973) pp 865–868; (24 Oct 1973) pp 1003–1011; (31 Oct 1973) pp 1053–1059
16 Cooley, M.J.E., *Computer-Aided Design — its Nature and Implications*, AUEW (TASS), Richmond (1972)

17 Cooley, M.J.E., 'Contributions to discussion', *Computer-Aided Draughting Systems Conf. Proc.*, IPC Science and Technology Press, Guildford (1973), pp 91–93
18 Cooley, M.J.E., 'Are you going to jump for a computer?', *Building Design*, (May 1978), p 25
19 Cross, N., *The Automated Architect*, Pion, London (1977)
20 Gero, J. (Ed.), *Computer Applications in Architecture*, Applied Science Publishers, London (1977)
21 Guttridge, B. and Wainwright, J.R. *Computers in Architectural Design*, Crosby Lockwood Staples, London (1973)
22 Mitchell, W.J., *Computer Aided Architectural Design*, Petrocelli Charter, New York (1977)
23 Negroponte, N. (Ed.), *Computer Aids to Design and Architecture*, Petrocelli Charter, New York (1976)
24 'The RIBA Annual Report 1975', *RIBA Journal*, (May 1976), pp 195–210
25 Stanton, P., *Pugin*, Thames and Hudson, London (1972)

Chapter 3   Office organisation

26 Checksfield, A.E., 'The elements of success in a computer installation', *Eurocomp Conf. Proc.*, Online Ltd, London (1974), pp 427–438
27 George, M., 'Living with a terminal', *Computing*, (Oct 1973), pp 14–15
28 Hewitt, M., 'How you can give that new arrival the best start in life', *Computing*, (Aug 1977), pp 12–13
29 Hollingdale, S.H. and Tootill, G.C., *Electronic Computers*, Pelican (1965)
30 Lansdown, J., 'Microprocessors and the architect', *RIBA Journal*, (Sep 1979), pp 416–417
31 Newman, W.M. and Sproull, R.F., *Principles of Interactive Computer Graphics*, 2nd edn, McGraw-Hill, New York (1979)
32 Paterson, J., 'Micro-computers: a revolution for architects', *RIBA Journal*, (Feb 1978), pp 63–64
33 Tyler, T., *Electronic Versus Paper Media*, SBS Publishing, San Jose, California (1978)
34 Vélez-Jahn, G., 'Microcomputers and building elevations', *PArC 79 Conf. Proc.*, AMK GmbH, Berlin (1979), pp 93–103

35 Walker, B.S., *Introduction to Computer Engineering*, University of London Press (1967)
36 Wilkes, M.V., *Time-Sharing Computer Systems*, Macdonald, London (1968)

Chapter 4   Choosing programs

37 Alcock, D., *Illustrating Basic*, Cambridge University Press (1977)
38 Dorn, P.H., 'Programs are not books', *Datamation*, (Nov 1977), pp 231–233
39 Freed, R.N., 'Copyrighting programs is unwise', *Datamation*, (Nov 1977), pp 227–231
40 Hutton, G. and Rostron, M., *Computer Programs for the Building Industry*, Architectural Press, London (1979)
41 Kelman, A., 'British software is a prey to poachers', *Computing*, (Aug 1979), p 13
42 Lee, K., *Computer Programs in Environmental Design* (3 vols), Environmental Design Research Centre, Boston, Mass. (1973)
43 Sherrington, H., 'What is an application package?', *Eurocomp Conf. Proc.*, Online Ltd, London, (1974), pp 265–274

Chapter 5   Using databases

44 Burgess, D. and Leather, G., 'Information scheduling by computer', *RIBA Journal*, (Jan 1968), pp 36–38
45 Campion, D., 'The application of an on-line database package in an architectural design environment', *Eurocomp Conf. Proc.*, Online Ltd, London (1974), pp 305–320
46 Fairhead, J. and Campion, D., 'Room data scheduling', *DoE Construction*, (Mar 1977), pp 32–33
47 Gero, J.S., 'Specifications by computer', *Architectural Science Review*, (Mar 1976). pp 10–13
48 Gordon, A., 'The architect and coding', *Build International*, (Dec 1968), pp 43–48
49 Hutton, G. and Rostron, M., 'Classification, coding and indexing', *Building*, (Oct 1968), pp 93–96
50 Judd, D.R., *Use of Files*, Macdonald, London (1975)
51 Kewney, G., 'Databases need intermediaries', *Computing*, (Jan 1978), p 2
52 Martin, J., *Principles of Data-Base Management*, Prentice-Hall, Englewood Cliffs, N.J. (1976)
53 MRI Systems Corp., *System 2000 Reference Manual*, MRI, Austin, Texas (1973)
54 Paice, C.D., *Information Retrieval and the Computer*, Macdonald, London (1977)
55 Paterson, J., *Information Methods for Design and Construction*, John Wiley and Sons, New York (1977)
56 Peck, P.L., 'What top management should do to achieve secure and private systems', *Eurocomp Conf. Proc.*, Online Ltd, London (1974), pp 795–811
57 Pettit, G., *Computer-Aided Specifications*, Leeds Polytechnic, Research Project (Mar 1976)
58 Snow, C. and O'Sullivan, P., 'Building information retrieval in France', *Building*, (Aug 1973), pp 65–66
59 Whitton, D., 'A working model of a computer-based information retrieval system', *Building*, (Dec 1969), pp 53–56

Chapter 6   Computer-aided draughting

60 Bijl, A., Renshaw, A. and Barnard, D., 'Computer graphics in design', *Construction Research and Development Journal*, (Jan 1971), pp 205–215
61 *MEDALS*, Computer-Aided Design Centre, Cambridge (1975)
62 Cropper, A.G. and Evans, S.J.W., 'Ergonomics and computers', *Computer Bulletin*, (July 1968), pp 94–98
63 Davison, J.A., 'RUCAPS: cost-effective draughting for the building industry', *CAD 78 Conf. Proc.*, IPC Science and Technology Press, Guildford (1978), pp 654–677
64 Dunn, N., *CARBS — User Introduction Manual*, Clwyd County Council (1974)
65 Earl, W.K. and Goff, J.D., 'Comparison of two data entry methods', *Percep. and Mot. Skills*, (1965), pp 369–384
66 Hoskins, E.M., *Computer-Aided Building: A Study of Current Trends*, ARC Ltd, Cambridge (1973)
67 Hoskins, E.M. and Jacobsberg, J.R., *Drawing Systems Survey Report*, ARC Ltd, Cambridge (1976)
68 Hughes, P.G., 'The incorporation of an ARK/2 computer-aided design system into an architectural practice in England', *PArC 79 Conf. Proc.*, AMK GmbH, Berlin (1979), pp 145–152
69 Purcell, P., 'Computer graphics in system building', *Industrialised Building Systems and Components* (Mar 1970), pp 51–52
70 Reynolds, R.A., 'A comparison of graphical information handling techniques in architectural practice', *CAD 78 Conf. Proc.*, IPC Science and Technology Press, Guildford (1978), pp 62–74
71 Richens, P., *The OXSYS System*, ARC Ltd, Cambridge (1976)
72 Richens, P., 'The OXSYS system for the design of buildings', *CAD 78 Conf. Proc.*, IPC Science and Technology Press, Guildford (1978), pp 633–645
73 Stewart, C.D. and Lee, K., 'Can a 54-year-old architectural practice find romance and happiness with an interactive computer system?', *Progressive Architecture*, (July 1971), pp 64–73
74 Watt, B.J. and Powell, B.M., *An Introduction to the PTP Computer-Aided Design Centre*, Percy Thomas Partnership (1977)

Chapter 7   Visualisation

75 Beacon, G.R. and Boreham, P.G., 'DIY CAAD with the architectural modeller's tool kit', *PArC 79 Conf. Proc.*, AMK GmbH, Berlin (1979), pp 593–599.

76 Bensasson, S., *Computer Programs for Building Perspectives*, DOC Ltd, Cambridge (1977)

77 *THINGS*, Computer-Aided Design Centre, Cambridge (1975)

78 Campion, D. and Robey, K.G., 'Perspective drawing by computer', *The Architectural Review*, (Nov 1965), pp 380–386

79 Lyons, J.W. and Stokes, S.T., 'Visualisation techniques', *DoE Construction*, (Sep 1976), pp 23–26

80 Pyne, R., 'Artistic package with an eye for detail', *Computing*, (June 1977), p 10

81 Thornton, R.W., 'Interactive modelling in three dimensions through two-dimensional windows', *CAD 78 Conf. Proc.*, IPC Science and Technology Press, Guildford (1978), pp 204–208

Chapter 8   Job management

82 Battersby, A., *Network Analysis for Planning and Scheduling*, Macmillan, London (1970)

83 Bennett, F.L., *Critical Path Precedence Networks*, Van Nostrand-Reinhold, New York (1970)

84 Campion, D., 'Computer-aided job planning', *Building*, (Apr 1969), pp 163–172

85 Campion, D., 'Job planning by computer — the pros and cons', *Building*, (Aug 1969), pp 99–100

86 Drover, D.R., 'COMPACT — computer planning and control techniques', *Construction Research and Development Journal*, (Apr 1971), pp 29–34

87 Goleman, H.A., 'Network planning: management tool for architects', *Architectural Record*, (Feb 1967), pp 93–94; (Mar 1967), pp 93–94

88 Jeanes, R.E. and Britten, J.R., 'Network diagrams — some notes on alternative presentations', *Building*, (June 1966), pp 102–106

89 Stafforth, C. and Wolton, H. (Eds), *Programs for Network Analysis*, National Computing Centre (1974)

90 Winsor, R., 'An alternative to critical path', *Architects' Journal*, (Aug 1975), pp 425–428

Chapter 9   Simulation techniques

91 *Movement in Buildings Simulator*, ARC Ltd, Cambridge (1973)

92 Campion, D.G., 'Design simulation by computer', *Architectural Review*, (Dec 1966), pp 460–464

93 Doidge, C.W., *University Space Utilization* (Doctoral thesis), University College, London (1969)

94 Fleming, J., *LIFT-A1: A Computer Simulation of the Design of Lift Installations in Buildings*, ABACUS, Glasgow (1973)

95 Forwood, B.S. and Gero, J.S., 'Computer simulated lift design — analysis for office buildings', *Architectural Science Review*, (June 1971), pp 41–48

96 Gordon, G., *System Simulation*, Prentice-Hall, Englewood Cliffs, N.J. (1978)

97 Hendren, P.A., *A System for Dynamic Simulation using Computer Graphics*, Oklahoma State University (1967)

98 *General Purpose Simulation System V: User's Manual*, IBM Corp., New York (1977)

99 Jackson, C., 'Analytical techniques: simulation case study', *Architects' Journal*, (Mar 1970), pp 585–591

100 Laing, L.W.W., 'AIR-Q — a flexible computer simulation model for airport terminal building design', *DMG-DRS Journal*, (June 1975), pp 288–293

101 Marmot, A. and Gero, J.S., 'Modelling elevator lobbies', *Building Science*, Vol. 9, No. 4 (1974), pp 277–288

102 Maver, T.W., *TRAFIK: A Program Package for the Study of Circulation in Buildings*, ABACUS, Glasgow (1970)

103 Moroney, M.J., *Facts From Figures*, Pelican (1951)

104 Reynolds, R.A., *Comparison of Six Simulation Systems* (Internal report), Cusdin Burden and Howitt, London (1972)

105 Schriber, T., *A GPSS Primer*, Ulrich's Books (1972)

Chapter 10   Environmental analysis

106 Bensasson, S. and Burgess, K., *Computer Programs for Daylighting in Buildings*, DOC Ltd, Cambridge (1978)

107 Bolland, S., 'RIBA calculator programs', *RIBA Journal*, (Sep 1978), pp 365–366

108 Burgess, K.S., *Computer Programs for Energy in Buildings*, DOC Ltd, Cambridge (1979)

109 Campion, D., 'Computer-aided acoustical analysis', *Building*, (May 1970), pp 111–116

110 *CIBS Guide, Section A1 — Environmental Criteria for Design*, Chartered Institution of Building Services, London (1978)

111 Clarke, J., *ESP — A Program Package Dealing with Environmental Systems Performance*, ABACUS, Glasgow (1976)

112 Clarke, J.A., 'A design-orientated thermal simulation model', *CAD 78 Conf. Proc.*, IPC Science and Technology Press, Guildford (1978), pp 121–129

113 'Helping Builders "Save It"', *Computing*, (Nov 1978), p 20

114 Department of the Environment, *The Building (First Amendment) Regulations*, HMSO, London (1978)

115 Forwood, B.S., *A Selective Bibliography of Computer-Aided Design and Analysis of Building Environment and Service Systems*, University of Sydney (1973)

116 Gronhoug, A.C., *Computer Terminal Programs to Aid Economic Selection of Fuel for Heating Systems*, Dept. of the Environment (1977)

117 *IES Code: Recommendations for Lighting Building Interiors*, Illuminating Engineering Society, London (1968)

118 *Proceedings: Symposium on Computers in Practice for Building Services Engineers*, Institute of Heating and Ventilating Engineers, London (1976)

119 'The use of computers in lighting', *Light and Lighting*, (June 1971), pp 172–173

120 *The Environmental Evaluation of Buildings* (working papers 15, 27 and 28), Centre for Land Use and Built Form Studies, Cambridge (1970)

121 Nevrala, D.J., Robbie, J.V. and Fitzgerald, D., *A Comparison of Five Digital Computer Programs for Calculating Maximum Air-Conditioning Loads*, Lab. Report 62, Heating and Ventilating Research Assoc., UK (1970)

122 Owens, P.G. and Barnett, M., 'A computer program to calculate air-conditioning loads', *Building Services Engineering*, (Nov 1976), pp 151–165

123 Parsons, J., 'Computer-aided design in action', *Construction Research and Development Journal*, (Apr 1971), pp 58–66

124 Powell, J.A., 'Use of simple methodology in the compilation of a computerised acoustic design package for architects and builders', *Bulletin of Computer-Aided Architectural Design*, (July 1973), pp 8–14

125 Smith, P.J., 'Graphical shadow computation in building complexes using an integrated energy analysis program', *CAD 78 Conf. Proc.*, IPC Science and Technology Press, Guildford (1978), pp 84–96

126 Thompson, B.G.J. and Hughes, J., 'An experimental investigation of the performance of a computer-aided building design system', *IFIP Congress 74*, Stockholm, Sweden (1974), pp 773–777

127 Thompson, B.G.J. and Webster, G.J., 'Progress with CEDAR 3: a computer-aided design system for the sketch plan stage', *CAD 78 Conf. Proc.*, IPC Science and Technology Press, Guildford (1978), pp 678–692

128 Thompson, B.G.J., Lera, S., Beeston, D. and Coldwell, R., 'Application of CEDAR 3: Case studies', *PArC 79 Conf. Proc.*, AMK GmbH Berlin (1979), pp 321–333

131 Armour, G.C. and Buffa, E.S., 'A heuristic algorithm and simulation approach to relative location of facilities', *Management Science*, (Feb 1963), p 294

132 Barnett, I., 'Computerized cost estimating', *Architectural Record* (Mar 1967)

133 Bijl, A. and Shawcross, G., 'Housing site layout system', *Computer Aided Design*, (June 1975), pp 2–10

134 'Job costing and budgeting for architects', *Building* (Feb 1971), pp 124–125

135 Burberry, P., 'Analytical techniques: layout', *Architects' Journal*, (Feb 1970), pp 521–524

136 Clarke, G. and Griffin, P., 'Office costing for architects', *Building*, (Feb 1967), pp 88–90

137 Gero, J.S., Julian, W. and Holmes, W.N., *The Development of a System for Heuristic Optimization of Topological Layouts Using High Level Interaction*, University of Sydney (1973)

138 Goodsman, R., 'Managing architects' offices', *DoE Construction*, (Dec 1976), pp 30–31

139 *Word Processing Market Opportunities in the UK*, IDC Europa, London (1978)

140 Kruskal, J.B., 'Nonmetric multidimensional scaling: a numerical approach', *Psychometrika* (June 1964), pp 1–27

141 Levin, P.H., 'The use of graphs to decide the optimum layout of buildings', *Architects' Journal* (Oct 1964), pp 809–815

142 *Traffic in Buildings* (Working papers 17–20), Centre for Land Use and Built Form Studies, Cambridge (1970)

143 Maver, T.W., 'PACE 1: Computer-aided building appraisal', *Architects' Journal*, (July 1971), pp 207–214

144 Mosley, L., 'A rational design theory for planning buildings based on the analysis and solution of circulation problems', *Architects' Journal*, (Sep 1963), pp 525–537

145 Needham, R.M., 'Application of the theory of clumps', *Mechanical Translation*, Vol. 8 (1965)

146 Noble, J. and Turner, J., 'Evaluating housing layouts by computer', *Architects' Journal*, (Feb 1971), pp 315–318

147 Tatham, L., 'A better plan to build upon', *Computing*, (July 1975), pp 11–12

148 Thornton, C., 'Words are cheap', *Computer Management*, (July/Aug 1979), pp 35–43

149 Whitehead, B. and Eldars, M.Z., 'An approach to the optimum layout of single-storey buildings', *Architects' Journal*, (June 1964), pp 1373–1380

Chapter 11 Miscellaneous applications

129 *SSHA System*, ARC Ltd, Cambridge (1975)

130 Archer, L.B., 'Computers in building: planning accommodation for hospitals and the transportation problem', *Architects' Journal*, (July 1963), pp 139–142

Chapter 12 The future

150 Barron, I., 'The microcomputer's part in your future', *Computing*, (Mar 1975), pp 14–15

151 *The Effective Use of Computers Within the Building*

Industries of the European Community, CIAD Consortium, Brussels (1979)

152 Cross, N., 'Impact of computers on the architectural design process', *Architects' Journal*, (Mar 1972), pp 623–628

153 Enticknop, N., 'The allure of the silver screen', *Computer Management*, (July/Aug 1979), pp 6–14

154 George, F.H. (Ed.), *The Robots are Coming*, National Computing Centre, Manchester (1974)

155 Naylor, C., 'In the beginning was the word', *Computer Management*, (Mar 1979), pp 8–13

156 Von Neumann, J., *The Computer and the Brain*, Yale University Press (1958)

Index

ABACUS, 110, 115, 137
Acoustic analysis, 11, 15, 63, 115, 117, 118
Activity-orientated diagram, 93
Activity relationship table, 98–99
Additive techniques, 122
Aesthetic considerations, 7, 80, 82, 91, 124
Air-conditioning, 15, 114
AIR-Q, 110
Alexander, C, 1
Algol, 40, 43, 104, 138
Analogue computer, 34, 138
APL, 43, 44, 138
Applied Research of Cambridge, 77, 78, 83, 111
Arc generator, 68
Archer, L.B., 1
Architect's Instructions, 5, 10, 128
ARK/2, 66, 76–77, 122
Array processor, 130
Arrow diagram, 93–94
Artificial intelligence, 134
Artificial lighting analysis, 14, 15, 63, 113
Assembly language, 25, 43, 44, 138
Associated Union of Engineering Workers, 8
Association graph, 122
Astronomer Royal, 129
Audit trail, 46–47
AUTOPROD, 90
Axonometric projection, 90, 118

Backup procedure, 25, 48
Barbour Index, 10
Bar chart, 42, 95, 96, 98
Basic, 44, 138
Batch processing, 17–20, 25, 69, 138
BBC, 132
BDS, 77–78, 113
Benson Electronics, 32
Bill of quantities, 1, 2, 6, 16, 63, 74, 77, 131
BoCAAD, 137
Bootstrapping, 25, 138
British Computer Society, 136
Bubble diagram, 77, 122
Bubble memory, 133, 138
Buckminster Fuller, 80
Bug, 138
Building Regulations, 2, 33, 112
Building Services Research and Information Assoc., 112
Bureaux services, 18, 19, 39, 132, 136
Burster, 19
Buying machinery, 35
Buying programs, 44

Calcomp, 32
Calculator, pocket, 3, 32, 125, 129, 132

Calculator, programmable, 32–33, 120, 140
CAPRICODE, 15, 95
CARBS, 73–74, 113, 118
Card punching machine, 19
Card reading machine, 19, 48
Cards, punched, 17, 18, 19, 27, 48, 133, 138
CARDS, 54–56
Cartridge disc, 26, 139
Catalogues, 49–51
CEDAR, 3, 117–118
Ceefax, 132
Central processing unit, 24, 138
Check digit, 50
Chip (*see* Microprocessor)
Chartered Institution of Building Services, 112
Circulation analysis, 11, 15, 102, 111, 123, 124
CLASP, 7
Cluster analysis, 122–123
Clwyd County Council, 73, 74
COBOL, 40, 43, 44, 138
Codes, 49–50, 59, 66, 75, 77, 78, 79, 98, 100
Colour display, 29, 82, 131, 132
Communications port, 27
Compiler, 40, 43, 138
Composite activity, 94–95
COMPROPLAN, 122
COMPROSPACE, 76
COMPROVIEW, 77
Computer-Aided Design, 137
Computer-Aided Design Centre, 4, 71, 72, 86, 90, 136
Computer-Aided Design Centre visualisation programs, 86–90
Computer Bulletin, 136
Computer Consortium Services, 126
Computer Journal, 136
Computer Weekly, 136–137
Computing, 136–137
Condensation risk analysis, 15, 33, 117, 120
Conferences, 2, 39
Costing of designs, 6, 15, 124–125
Costing of jobs, 6, 8, 15, 27, 126–127
Contel, 132
Contractor, 1, 16, 59, 92
Conversion of programs, 40–41
Cooley, M.J., 8
Copyright on programs, 44
Cost effectiveness, 4, 12, 27, 41, 46, 69, 72, 74, 83, 105, 128, 131
Critical activity, 92, 93, 98
Critical path, the, 93

Critical path network, 8, 93–95, 98
Critical path techniques, 8, 15, 34, 39, 77, 92–100, 131
Cumulative distribution, 109
Cursor, 29, 30, 75, 76, 118
Cut and fill, 15, 34, 125–126

DAISY, 74–76, 78
Database principles, 43–44, 45–51, 138
Database use, 10–11, 34, 40, 51–58, 63, 131–132
Data preparation, 37, 41, 48, 49–51, 69–70, 83, 84–86, 98–100, 102–104, 105–106, 112–113, 115–116, 118, 124–125, 133–134
Date listing, 98
Daylight analysis, 2, 11, 14, 15, 33, 39, 63, 113, 116, 118, 131
Debugging, 42–43, 138
Decentralisation of offices, 132–133
Decision Graphics, 76
Deleaver, 19
Demonstrations, 41–42
Dept. of Health and Social Security, 2, 3, 15, 95
Dept. of Housing and Urban Development, 4
Dept. of the Environment, 112, 117
Design analysis, 11–12, 101, 121, 124
Design costing, 6, 15, 124–125
Design generation, 1, 2, 3, 11, 121–124
Design Office Consortium, 39, 83, 86, 126, 135, 136
Design Studies, 137
Detail design, 6, 15–16, 33, 46, 51, 62
Digital Equipment Corp, 25
Digitiser, 30, 65, 66–67, 76, 78–79, 86, 124, 125, 126, 134, 138
Disc storage, 20, 24, 25, 26, 48, 91, 133, 138–139
    cartridge, 26, 139
    floppy, 26, 128, 139
    pack, 20, 139
Distribution
    cumulative, 109
    negatively-skewed, 104
    Normal, 106
    positively-skewed, 104
    Poisson, 106
Documentation of programs, 4, 38, 39, 40, 41
Drainage network design, 14, 121, 125
Draughting by computer, 3, 12–13, 16, 42, 59–79, 130–131
    interactive, 1, 2, 12, 27–32, 63–64, 65–69, 74–79, 131
    non-interactive, 27, 63–64, 69–74, 131

147

Drawbacks of computers, 2–3, 7–8, 10, 12–13, 24–25, 28, 34, 69, 83–84
Drum plotter, 31, 140
Dummy activity, 93–94
DYNAGRAPHIC, 78

EdCAAD, 124
Editing databases, 10, 11, 46, 47, 48, 53–55, 56–57, 116
Editing drawings, 12, 28–29, 62, 63, 64, 65, 66, 69, 76
Editing text, 53–54, 128
Elastic band lines, 67, 75
Electrostatic printer/plotter, 32, 133
Elevations, 34, 64
EMI Threshold, 134
Energy crisis, 112
Engineering design, 1, 12
ENIAC, 129
Environmental analysis, 1, 2, 6, 8, 14, 15, 27, 33, 34, 63, 64, 69, 74, 78, 112–120, 121, 131
Environmental consultant, 6
Environmental control, 5, 24, 27, 130
Ergonomics, 29–30, 66
ESP, 115–117
Evans and Sutherland, 82
Event-orientated diagram, 93–94

Facsimile copier, 132
Factories Act, 112
Feasibility study, 76, 117, 135
Feedback, 6–7, 15, 30
Films, 36, 42
Fire control, 102, 106, 114
Fixed-structure database, 45–46, 53, 54–56, 58
Flatbed plotter, 31, 140
Flicker, 28, 76
Float time, 93, 95, 96, 98
Floppy disc, 26, 128, 139
Fortran, 40, 43, 44, 85, 90, 104, 139
Fragmentation of design team, 5, 6, 131
Function key, 29, 30, 65, 66, 75, 76

Gantt chart (see Bar chart)
Glare factor, 14, 33, 113
GMW Computers, 78, 90
Gollins, Melvin, Ward Partnership, 78
GPSS, 106–110, 139
Graphic techniques (see Draughting; Visualisation)
Graphic languages, 40, 63–65, 69–70, 71–74, 85–90
GREYSCALES, 86, 90
Grosch's Law, 17
Grosch's Second Law, 18
Guides to programs, 39, 135, 136
GINO, 72

Half-tone image, 82, 84, 86, 90, 91, 131
Hard copy, 21, 31, 139
HARNESS, 2, 3
Head crash, 26
Hewlett-Packard, 21
Hidden-line removal, 81–82, 89–90
HIDDEN LINES, 86, 89–90
High-level language, 3, 24, 25, 34, 38, 40, 43, 44, 85, 139
Hitch, Col. F.A.N., 90
Hospital Building Notes, 2

Hospital design, 2, 3, 10, 95, 110, 111, 114, 121, 122
Hospital Design Notes, 2
Housing estate layout, 14, 124–125
Human brain, 134

IBM, 18, 25
ICL, 18
Illuminating Engineering Society, 113
Imlac International, 78
Imperial College, London, 1
Independent Broadcasting Authority, 132
Independent float, 93
Industrialised building, 2, 7, 74, 77, 117
Information handling by computer, 10–11, 34, 40, 51–58, 63, 131–132
Input media, 17, 18, 19, 20, 21, 22–23, 27, 48, 69, 133–134
Integrated circuit, 32, 139
Intel Corp., 133
Interaction matrix, 1, 121, 122
Interaction, principles of, 17–18, 20–23, 42, 139
Interactive design generation, 123–124
Interactive draughting, 1, 2, 12–13, 21–22, 27–32, 63–64, 65–69, 74–79, 131, 133–134
Interactive environmental analysis, 116, 118, 119
Interactive simulation, 105
Interactive visualisation, 86, 90–91
Interface conventions, 74, 132
Interior design, 6, 53, 115
Interior perspectives, 64–65, 78, 80, 82, 90, 91, 131
Internet (UK), 99
Interpenetration of solids, 85, 90, 118
Interrogation of databases, 6, 10–11, 15, 46, 47, 53, 54–55, 57, 58, 131–132
Inverted schedules, 47, 55

JCP, 126–127
Job costing, 6, 8, 15, 126–127
Job management, 8, 15, 34, 39, 77, 92–100, 131
Jones, J.C., 1
Joystick, 30, 67, 75, 76, 139

King's College chapel, 83
KWIC indexing, 51

Lancashire County Council, 80
Landscape architect, 6
Lasdun, Sir Denys, 83
Laser plotter, 32
Laser-Scan, 32
Layout generation, 1, 2, 3, 11, 121–124
Law of Errors, 27, 35
Leeds Polytechnic, 90–91
Legislation, 2, 112
Lift control, 129
Lift design analysis, 15, 102, 110, 118
Lighting analysis
　artificial, 14, 15, 63, 113
　natural, 2, 11, 14, 15, 33, 39, 63, 113, 116, 118, 131
Light pen, 29–30, 67, 134, 139
Linear programming, 122
Line-printer, 19, 21, 27, 49, 139
Loughborough University of Technology, 99

Lower-case, 21, 27

Magnetic bubble storage, 133, 138
Magnetic disc (see Disc storage)
Magnetic tape, 18, 20, 48, 139
Magnetic tape cassette, 23, 128, 134
Mainframe computer, 23, 32
Maintenance of programs, 42–43, 44
Management consultant, 6
Matrix, interaction, 1, 121, 122
MEDALS, 71–72, 87
Memory, computer, 19–20, 24, 25, 28, 29, 32, 34, 41, 83–84, 139
Menu, 66, 76, 78, 79, 90, 91, 118
MIBS, 111
Microcomputer, 17, 32–34, 131, 139
Microfiche, 49
Microfilm, 32, 49
Microprocessor, 32, 34, 82, 127, 128, 129–130, 134, 139
Minicomputer, 3, 17, 23–27, 32, 40, 73, 86, 90, 91, 105, 124, 129, 131, 139
MIT, 1
Modem, 22
MOM, 76
Mongolian horde approach, 43
MRI Systems Corp., 56
Multi-dimensional scaling, 122
M & BDL, 73, 74

National Building Specification, 10
National Computing Centre, 135–136
National Research Development Corp., 77
National Theatre, 83
Negatively-skewed distribution, 104
Network, critical path, 8, 93–95, 98
Network, simulation, 102, 104, 107
Newman, W., 1
Noise transmission, 15, 115
Non-interactive draughting, 27, 63–64, 69–74, 131
Normal distribution, 106
Norwegian Computing Centre, 99

Offices, Shops and Railway Premises Act, 112
Off-line, 22, 140
On-line, 140
Operator, computer, 18, 35–36, 69, 86, 110
Optical Character Recognition (OCR), 133, 140
OPTIMA, 99
Oracle, 132
Outline design, 15, 32–33, 52, 62, 114, 118
Overlaying, 12, 59–60, 69, 75
Oxford Method of Building system, 77
Oxford Regional Health Authority, 77
OXSYS, 77

Package programs, 38–39, 40, 110–111
Paper tape, 18, 23, 133, 140
Pencil follower (see Digitiser)
Percy Thomas Partnership, 76
Peripheral devices (see Disc storage; Plotter; Printer)
Periodicals, 36, 136–137
Permutation technique, 122
Perry, Dean and Stewart, 76
Personal computing, 32–34, 129–130

Perspectives, 13, 41, 42, 64–65, 74, 77, 78, 80–86, 89–91, 118, 131, 136
Physical storage media (*see* Paper tape; Punched cards)
Pipe network analysis, 1, 14, 63, 69, 121, 125
PL/1, 43, 44, 140
Plotter, 2, 18, 31–32, 60, 65, 70, 76, 78, 98, 126, 133, 134, 140
  drum, 31, 140
  electrostatic, 32, 133
  flatbed, 31, 140
  laser, 32
Pocket calculator, 3, 32, 125, 129, 132
Poisson distribution, 106
Positional indicating device (*see* Digitiser; Joystick; Light pen)
Positively-skewed distribution, 104
Post Office, 132
Post Office Tower, 8
Precedence diagram, 93
Prestel, 132
Print cradle, 33, 120
Printer, 19, 21, 27, 28, 33, 49, 96, 128, 133, 134
Privacy, 48–49
Product data, 10, 46, 51, 132
Production documentation, 2, 3, 5, 6, 10–11, 15, 16, 26, 47, 63, 127
Programmable calculator, 32–33, 120, 140
Property Services Agency, 4, 117, 118
Projection, axonometric, 90, 118
Pugin, 6
Purpose-written programs, 38
Punched cards, 17, 18, 19, 27, 48, 133, 138

Quality of life, 8, 28, 69
Quantity surveyor, 1, 6, 10, 16, 63, 95, 100, 131
Queues, 102, 105, 107, 108, 109–110

Raster screen, 29, 140
Rationalisation exercise, 7, 11, 16, 47
Redundancy in visualisation, 85, 88, 90
Refresh screen, 28, 29, 67–68, 76, 78, 140
Reliability, 17, 26, 133
Repetition techniques, 5, 7, 12, 59, 80, 128, 130
Resource assignment table, 99–100
Resource schedule table, 99–100
Resource scheduling, 95–96, 99–100
Reverberation time, 33, 115, 117
RIBA, 10, 136
RIBA calculator programs, 120
RIBA Plan of work, 15, 95, 98
RIBA Publications Ltd., 120
RIBA Scale of Fees, 5
Room briefing schedule, 15, 37, 51–52, 53
Root node, 45
RUCAPS, 78–79
Russell, Bertrand, 129
Rutherford, Lord, 129

ScanData Corp., 133
Scheduling, 10, 16, 27, 34, 37, 39, 42, 46, 47, 48, 49, 55, 58, 63, 69, 74, 131
SCOLA, 2, 3
Scottish Special Housing Association, 124

Screen, 1, 2, 21, 27, 28, 29, 30, 60, 63, 65, 66–69, 75–79, 82, 84, 90–91, 104, 116, 118, 124–125, 128, 132
  raster, 29, 140
  refresh, 28, 29, 67–68, 76, 78, 140
  slave, 65
  storage, 28, 67–68, 77, 90, 140
  storage/refresh, 28–29, 76
SEAC, 117–118
Security, 48–49
Selling ahead, 42
Services engineer, 1, 6, 14, 59, 112, 131
Services engineering, 1, 13–15
Shadowing analysis, 34, 80, 91, 114, 117, 131
Shared-logic system, 27–28, 78, 124, 128
SIMULA, 104
Simulation, 11–12, 15, 16, 34, 39, 101–111, 131, 132
Simulation packages, 110–111
Sketch design, 15, 62, 115–116, 120, 125
SKETCHPAD, 1, 12
Slave screen, 65
Solar gain, 14, 15, 114, 117, 120
South-East Regional Hospital Board, 10
Specifications, 10, 53–54, 128, 132
Speed of processing, 3, 10, 17, 23–25, 32, 34, 77, 78, 91, 105, 129–130
Spooling, 32, 140
Standard graphic element, 1, 12, 28, 59, 64, 66–69, 71–72, 74–79, 134
Stereoscopic visualisation, 90
Storage of results, 39, 49
Storage screen, 28, 67–68, 77, 90, 140
Storage/refresh screen, 28–29, 76
Structural engineer, 1, 6, 59, 131
Structural engineering, 1, 2, 33, 69, 74, 77, 117, 120, 121, 134
Subjective assessment, 1, 7, 80, 82, 84, 91, 121, 122, 124
Sunlight analysis, 14, 15, 34, 80, 91, 114, 117, 120, 131
Supplementary results with draughting systems, 27, 63, 69, 70, 72, 74, 76–79, 131
Sutherland, I.E., 1, 3, 12, 70
System building, 2, 7, 74, 77, 117
Systems analyst, 36
System 2000, 56–58

Tablet (*see* Digitiser)
Technical literature, 10, 36, 39, 41, 112, 131, 132, 136–137
Tektronix, 28–29, 74, 76
Teleprinter, 15, 20, 21, 23, 26, 34, 77, 112, 123, 140
Teletext, 132
Tendering, 5, 16, 128
Terminal, 17–18, 20–23, 26, 35, 69, 78, 112, 129, 134, 140
  teleprinter, 15, 20, 21, 23, 26, 34, 77, 112, 123, 140
  visual display unit, 21–22, 34, 140
Terminal chamber, 23
Texas Instruments, 21, 120
Thermal analysis, 1, 2, 6, 14–15, 33, 63, 64, 112, 113–114, 116–117, 118, 120, 131
THINGS, 86–89, 90
3-dimensional draughting systems, 64, 73, 113, 131

Time-sharing, 17–18, 20–23, 27, 65, 77, 124, 132, 140
Training, 17, 18, 25, 44, 78
Transformation of graphic elements, 67–68, 72, 75, 76, 78, 79
Transformation of solids, 88–89
2-dimensional draughting system, 64–65, 69, 70, 71–72, 73, 74–77
2½-dimensional draughting system, 64–65, 66, 69, 70, 73–74, 77–79, 131

University research, 4, 44, 124
University of Edinburgh, 124
University of Manchester, 35
University of Pennsylvania, 129
University of Sydney, 123
User's manual, 41, 44, 56

Variables
  continuous, 103–104
  discontinuous, 104
Variable-structure database, 46, 53, 56–58
Viewdata, 132
Virtual storage, 25, 140
Visual display unit, 21–23, 34, 140
Visualisation, 13, 41, 42, 64–65, 74, 77, 78, 80–91, 118, 131, 136
  data preparation, 82–83, 84–89
  in colour, 82, 131
  machines, 82, 131
Voice data entry, 133–134

West Sussex County Council, 2, 3
Whiz-kid barrier, 36
Wire-line perspectives, 81, 118
Word processing machine, 127–128, 130, 132, 140
Work scheduling, 27
Working details, 7, 62
Wren, Sir Christopher, 130